THE SEARCH FOR A METHODOLOGY
OF SOCIAL SCIENCE

BOSTON STUDIES IN THE PHILOSOPHY OF SCIENCE

EDITED BY ROBERT S. COHEN AND MARX W. WARTOFSKY

VOLUME 92

STEPHEN P. TURNER

Department of Sociology, University of South Florida

THE SEARCH FOR A METHODOLOGY OF SOCIAL SCIENCE

*Durkheim, Weber, and
the Nineteenth-Century Problem of
Cause, Probability, and Action*

D. REIDEL PUBLISHING COMPANY

A MEMBER OF THE KLUWER ACADEMIC PUBLISHERS GROUP

DORDRECHT / BOSTON / LANCASTER / TOKYO

Library of Congress Cataloging in Publication Data

Turner, Stephen P., 1951–
  The search for a methodology of social science.

  (Boston studies in the philosophy of science; vol. 92)
  Bibliography: p.
  Includes index.
  1. Social sciences—Methodology—History. I. Title. II. **Series: Boston studies**
in the philosophy of science; vol. 92.
Q174.B67   vol. 92   001′.01 s   85–19620
[H61]
ISBN 90-277-2067-3

Published by D. Reidel Publishing Company,
P.O. Box 17, 3300 AA Dordrecht, Holland.

Sold and distributed in the U.S.A. and Canada
by Kluwer Academic Publishers,
190 Old Derby Street, Hingham, MA 02043, U.S.A.

In all other countries, sold and distributed
by Kluwer Academic Publishers Group,
P.O. Box 322, 3300 AH Dordrecht, Holland.

Printed in The Netherlands

for Summer

TABLE OF CONTENTS

PART II / DURKHEIM AS A METHODOLOGIST

PART III / WEBER ON ACTION

EDITORIAL PREFACE

Stephen Turner has explored the origins of social science in this pioneering study of two nineteenth century themes: the search for laws of human social behavior, and the accumulation and analysis of the facts of such behavior through statistical inquiry. The disputes were vigorously argued; they were over questions of method, criteria of explanation, interpretations of probability, understandings of causation as such and of historical causation in particular, and time and again over the ways of using a natural science model.

From his careful elucidation of John Stuart Mill's proposals for the methodology of the social sciences on to his original analysis of the methodological claims and practices of Émile Durkheim and Max Weber, Turner has beautifully traced the conflict between statistical sociology and a science of factual description on the one side, and causal laws and a science of nomological explanation on the other. We see the works of Comte and Quetelet, the critical observations of Herschel, Buckle, Venn and Whewell, and the tough scepticism of Pearson, all of these as essential to the works of the classical founders of sociology. With Durkheim's essay on *Suicide* and Weber's monograph on *The Protestant Ethic,* Turner provides both philosophical analysis to demonstrate the continuing puzzles over cause and probability and also a perceptive and wry account of just how the puzzles of our late twentieth century are of a piece with theirs. The terms are still familiar: reasons vs. causes, and reasons as causes, as factors in individual behavior and social processes; inexorability of rates of occurrence in populations vs. individual variations and free choice; imputed rationality and individual responsibility; characteristic beliefs in values as causal factors in individual and social behavior.

Turner's investigation is no doubt sympathetic to scientific understanding in history and sociology, but there is some gloom by the end of his story. As he looks at the tasks Weber set, "the interpretation of subjective meaning, rationalizations, and the stylized forms of commonsense explanations he called ideal-typical", he concludes that the apparatus of statistical analysis could not give warrant to any among the "enormous set of conceivable descriptive concepts" (p. 226). Indeed he goes further to point out that whatever attribution of reasons and motives has been satisfactory in social explanation (and the variety is large) will not be supported by empirical statistics, and in fact only "carry some cognitive weight which is independent of the statistical evidence for the (explanatory) model". And so Professor Turner will have us ask today (as much as in a critique of Durkheim and Weber and Pearson), "whether there is a path of 'ascent' from common sense and statistical results to a more precise and higher level of theory". Perhaps the statistical road to explanatory law-like social science is illusory? At any rate, caution and modesty are still entirely appropriate.

December 1985   ROBERT S. COHEN
                         Center for Philosophy and History of Science
                         Boston University

                         MARX W. WARTOFSKY
                         Dept. of Philosophy
                         Baruch College, CUNY

PREFACE

The writings of Durkheim and Weber have canonical status in sociology, and their place in this canon sometimes obscures their place in the historical stream of the development of problems. Perhaps this is especially true in the case of the methodological texts, where the precursors and sources of their writings are to be found in the traditions of disciplines other than the discipline for which the texts were meant to serve as a foundation.

The aim of this book is to show how the dispute over cause, law, and probability developed during the nineteenth century and to locate Durkheim's and Weber's arguments in this stream of discourse. The roots of the later writings, and therefore their deeper connections and the connections between these writings and such figures as Pearson, cannot be fully grasped without this history. Part of this book covers well-traveled ground. Mill, and to a lesser extent Whewell and Comte, all of whom are essential to this story, are familiar to the twentieth-century reader, and I will present them in a compressed fashion, designed to capture the skeletal form of their relevant methodological arguments, and the atmosphere in which they wrote. The discussions of Durkheim and Weber cover ground that is also well traveled, and here again I will assume an elementary familiarity with the issues that arise in connection with their methodological works. The peculiar boundaries between these regions of familiarity and unfamiliarity are not merely incidental to the book. Bits and pieces of the story of the dispute are extremely well known. Other parts of the story are shrouded. So the book is necessarily an attempt to relate the familiar to the unfamiliar. In doing this, the familiar is usually transformed – and in the case of some of Durkheim's and Weber's most familiar statements and themes – substantially transformed.

To the extent that this conversation has continued since the time of Durkheim and Weber, it has lost the coherence it had. Changes in statistical practice, in particular, have pushed the relations between philosophical models of scientific explanation and the everyday methods of the social sciences into its own kind of darkness. The newer forms of these issues are for the most part beyond the scope of this book, as is the more general problem of the logic of what I have called here 'statistical commentary', or practical statistical interpretation. This is not to suggest that the broader history of practices of statistical interpretation is not relevant to this text, nor that it is unimportant. Indeed, that history, were it to be written, would teach us a great deal about the history of science as well as social science, and perhaps, in the end, transform our understanding of scientific practice.

English translations of many of the more famous French and German texts discussed in the book are widely available. Some of them, such as Martineau's version of the *Cours* and the translation of Quetelet's *Sur l'homme*, were prepared with a degree of participation and the authorization of the authors. In general, I have quoted available translations, and selected, where necessary, the best translation, among translated books, short translations given in articles, and the like. In several cases, where none of these were adequate, it was usually because of ambiguities in the original texts, so I have paraphrased, sometimes quoting the original. In the sections on Durkheim and Weber, I have provided parallel citations to the original French or German.

One of the motivations that seems to have eluded sociologists of science is the good fellowship one finds in scholarly work, and which I have certainly found and enjoyed in the course of working both on Weber and on Durkheim. The suggestions, advice, help, and encouragement of many people have touched this book, among them Robert Eden, Bob Strikwerda, Whitney Pope, Robert Alun Jones, Guy Oakes, Stjepan Mestrović, Larry Scaff, Larry Laudan, and of course Regis Factor, my frequent collaborator.

The book was helped along by many others as well. My wife, Summer, deserves more than the dedication. Without her efforts at keeping all the loose ends from degenerating into confetti, the book would never have been completed. The President's Council of the University of South Florida supported the completion of the book with a timely grant.

Portions of the text have appeared elsewhere, although they appear here in much-altered form. Material has been drawn from 'Weber on Action', *American Sociological Review* (1983) **48**:506–519; 'Durkheim as a Methodologist', Part I: 'Realism, Teleology and Action', *Philosophy of the Social Sciences* (1983) **13**:425–450; 'Durkheim as a Methodologist', Part II: 'Collective Forces, Causation, and Probability', *Philosophy of the Social Sciences* (1984) **14**:51–71; reproduced here by kind permission of I. C. Jarvie, Managing Editor; 'Objective Possibility and Adequate Causation in Weber's Methodological Writings', *The Sociological Review* (1981) **29**:5–28; copyright 1981; S. P. Turner and R. A. Factor; reproduced here by kind permission of Regis A. Factor; and 'Explaining Capitalism: Weber on and against Marx', a chapter in R. Antonio and R. Glassman, eds., *A Weber-Marx Dialogue*, University Presses of Kansas (1985).

Passages from Volumes VII and VIII of the collected works of John Stuart Mill, *A System of Logic: Ratiocinative and Inductive*, edited by J. M. Robson, Books I–III (© University of Toronto Press, 1973, world rights except for British Commonwealth countries other than Canada and © Routledge and Kegan Paul, 1973, remaining British Commonwealth Rights) and Books IV–VI and appendices (© University of Toronto Press, 1974, world rights except for British Commonwealth countries other than Canada, and © Routledge and Kegan Paul, 1974, remaining British Commonwealth rights), are quoted by permission of University of Toronto Press and Routledge and Kegan Paul. The quotation from the L. L. Bernard papers is by the kind permission of Jessie Bernard and the University of Chicago Library.

PART I

THE EARLIER CONVERSATION

CHAPTER ONE

TWO GENERATIONS

The early 1870s mark a division in the history of social science methodology. On one side of this line is the body of methodological thinking that arose in the dialogue among Comte, Mill, Buckle, and Quetelet and with their critics. Comte and Buckle had died in the fifties. Mill died in 1873. By the time of Mill's death, *A System of Logic* had "attained an authority in England that was positively papal" (Collini *et al.*, 1983, p.130), and the views of the four major figures in the earlier conversation had attained considerable public notice, not to say, in the cases of Comte and Buckle, notoriety. Each had acquired disciples who were to prove their loyalty again and again during the next forty years, by giving unstinting and often highly sophisticated defenses of their masters. And each of these writers was to have influence on the earliest graduate students of sociology in the United States, particularly in the first decades of the twentieth century.

From all this one might have expected that discourse on methods would have proceeded continuously, through the critical revision of the views of these writers, or through the exploitation of the very interesting differences between them and their critics and adversaries. This was *not* what happened. In the 1870s there was an irruption of great complexity, in part a matter of a shift in the center of intellectual life and science, in part a reaction against the authority of these writers – Jevons, e.g., created a sensation with the violence of his attacks on Mill's "papal" *Logic* (Passmore, 1967, p.133). The conversation about the possibility and possible character of a social science shifted decisively, pushing the disciples of Buckle, Quetelet, and Comte to the fringes, and replacing the Millian form of the project of social science with Spencerianism and comparative history.

Durkheim and Weber were schoolchildren in the early 1870s, so for them Comte and Mill were remote figures, separated by the central events of nineteenth-century European history. In these years the Commune seized power in Paris, the last major revolutionary outburst of the century, and the Franco-Prussian war led to the unification of Germany. Theirs was a world where 1848 had become myth, and the political ideas of the earlier generation had come to seem naive and flawed. The 'forty-eighters' were admired, but the nostalgia was mixed: the sense of the naivete of the political ideals of the revolutionary year was tempered by the realization that no better ideals had replaced them.

The debts of the classical sociologists, Durkheim and Weber, to the generation of Comte, Mill, Buckle, and Quetelet (of which Spencer was a junior member), were enormous. Durkheim relied heavily on distinctions and substantive ideas found in Spencer and Comte, on turns of language that originated with these writers, and to a considerable extent on the *Problemlage* they devised. The language of solidarity used by Durkheim in the *Division of Labor in Society* draws on these predecessors. The usages 'mechanical' and 'organic' were discussed by Mill in his 1861 essay, 'Considerations on Representative Government', where he identified the two analogies with opposed kinds of 'political reasoners', and treated them as clichés (Mill, 1910, pp.175-76). Comte's anxiety over egoism and the disintegrative effects of progress is thematically central to Durkheim. The Durkheimian notion that suicide rates are proof of the determinate character of social occurrences is found in Quetelet, and the methodological argument to the effect that these statistical regularities reflect discoverable laws was central for Buckle.

Weber's first methodological writings were published a decade after Durkheim's, and he continued to revise his opinions on such central issues as cause in the next decade. He was thus farther removed from the earlier conversation. But the large theme of Weber's historical sociology – rationalization – is a subtle, darker reformulation of the teleological intellectualism of the earlier conversation, and his account of the place of Protestantism in the rise of modern rationality echoes a theme of Buckle's. Weber's methodological foci – especially individualism, the use of rational reconstruction, the implications of the idea of atomic description – were also more reminiscent of the concerns of Mill than of his peers.

When Durkheim and Weber returned to the problems of cause, law, and probability, they faced novel objections, under very different circumstances, and as part of very different conversations. They responded to the central arguments of the generation after Mill, Comte, Quetelet, and Buckle. Dominant opinion in the middle generation repudiated the earlier conversation; yet this middle generation was the first generation to have a coherent past to repudiate. In this negative sense, the writings of Buckle, Comte, Spencer, Quetelet, and Mill constituted the distinctly *methodological* tradition of the social sciences: we are shown this tradition by the attacks made upon it.

Durkheim's and Weber's return to the issues of causality, law, and probability represented a revival and adaptation. The heritage was manifestly in need of revision, and appeared to many of their contemporaries to be discredited or passé. Yet this heritage was more than simply one overgrown path among many. Even as the social sciences of the day failed repeatedly to live up to their promises, the basic intuition of the earlier writers that the human realm could not be exempt from the workings of causality continued to be strengthened by the successes of natural science, by the rapid increase in systematic factual information about social life, and by the secularization of social description.

Durkheim and Weber were thus the inheritors of the vague but powerful ideas about the causal character of human life which were the consensual basis of the earlier conversation, of the impressive methodological armamentaria left by the earlier writers, and of the legacy of failure in execution they also left. In a sense, Durkheim and Weber were 'successors', who could pick up the tools they had inherited and continue to refine and perfect their application. But in another sense they were not: the tools, impressive as they seemed, could not be made to work. So in this sense they were analogues rather than successors, persons who were faced with related problems but who could not rely on the achievements of those who had gone before them; they could at best selectively appropriate the usable remains of their failed efforts. And this is how they saw themselves.

CHAPTER TWO

BEYOND THE ENLIGHTENMENT: COMTE AND THE NEW PROBLEM OF SOCIAL SCIENCE

THE ORIGINS OF THE EARLIER CONVERSATION

A. Elley Finch's *On the Inductive Philosophy, Including a Parallel between Lord Bacon and A. Comte as Philosophers: A Discourse Delivered Before the Sunday Lecture Society, Nov. 26, 1871*(1872) provides us with a glimpse of the methodological world of the earlier conversation. The lecture shows the coherence of the conversation, as well as its optimism. The natural sciences represented more than a model for social science: they were also coparticipants in the struggle between theism and science. Much of the distinctive flavor of methodological writing in this period is given by the omnipresence of this struggle, which took the form of the epistemological question of the relations between "the several methods which the mind has pursued in its search after truth," methods which Finch, following Comte, called "the Theological, the Metaphysical, and the Scientific" (Finch, 1872, p. 2). Finch mentioned James Herschel, William Whewell, and a good many other physicists and writers on the history of astronomy, physics, and electromagnetism, and ran their views together with those of Comte and Bacon – a useful reminder that the writers were part of the same movement of thought as Comte, Mill, and Quetelet and that what this movement of thought represented was problematic – even odious – to conventional public opinion.[1] The movement of thought was a community of discourse as well. They discussed one another's views on astronomical and physical subjects. They shared roughly the same ideas of which sorts of social science had been successful. Finch's examples are representative: political economy, the 'psychology' of Locke and James Mill, and the emerging statistical literature, including the commentaries on the Census and such descriptive works as Mayhew's *London Labour and London Poor*, correspond to a collection of communities of discourse which also overlap. The despair over the possibility of the social sciences, which is part of the backdrop to the methodological writings of Weber and Durkheim, had not yet set in. Finch pointed only to successes. He noted that Malthus's "arguments were pronounced by Archbishop Whately to be as unanswerable as the Elements of Euclid" (1872, p. 33), and treated them as "an almost perfect instance of the Inductive Method." The method of statistics, described as "the grand inductive weapon of sanitary science" (1872, p. 32), was enlisted in the struggle with religion. "The theological theory of disease," Finch said, is "becoming gradually stamped out by statistics" (1872, p. 32). The sense that all these enterprises shared a common front against theology was reciprocated: Conte's *Cours* and Mill's *Principles of Political Economy* were placed on the *Index librorum prohibitorum* by the Catholic Church.

Finch's talk was 'public', and the writing he reported and commented on was also, to a large extent, public. We can occasionally glimpse the image these writers had of this audience in their texts. When Harriet Martineau introduced her translation and abridgement of Comte's *System*, she expressed the hope that it would appeal "to the largest number of intelligent readers" (Martineau, 1858, p. 4), observing that

while the researches of the scientific world are presented as mere accretions to a heterogeneous mass of facts, there can be no hope of a scientific progress which shall satisfy and benefit those large classes of students whose business it is, not to explore, but to receive (1858, p. 5).

She went on to note that "the growth of a scientific taste among the working classes of this country is one of the most striking of the signs of the times" (1858, p. 5). The urge to reform through education was shared with the other members of this generation. Quetelet wrote a popular tract on elementary statistics, and eagerly supported a cheap edition of his most famous work for the English public. Comte gave classes in astronomy to workers. The peculiar conjuncture of the lack of professional boundaries (the sense of professional distinctiveness, so characteristic of later writings, is largely absent in these writings), the vague but omnipresent force of the problem of science and religion, the immediacy of the aim of the education of the working-class, the struggle with theism, and the quickening success of the movement for reform made for an atmosphere congenial to grand methodological syntheses, as well as to the less grand attempts at reconciliation and explication made by writers such as Finch. In both the grand and the less grand attempts, one can see the extent to which the intellectual developments of the preceding half-century made for a broad sense of the intellectual pregnancy of the time, and the methodological writings reflected the salience of these large questions. The elements of these syntheses and reconciliations ultimately conflicted. But at the time, the conflicts were less visible than the commonalities.

BACON AS PRESENCE

The very idea of a social science puts science, and particularly the cognitive practices and 'methods' of science, in a distinctive light. Indeed, it would not be too much to say that the possibility of the extension to the social realm of scientific methodology, and particularly the concept of scientific law, is the source of many of the constitutive questions of modern philosophy of science, for the abridgement of practice which the philosopher undertakes in making this extension is particularly abstract and general.

When Finch compared Comte and Bacon, he was comparing two living presences – Bacon as the protagonist of the modern conception of the sciences, Comte as the progenitor of a threatening account of the implications for man of the continuing intellectual successes of science. Mill and Comte, for whom the possibility of social science was the defining problem, were compelled to revise the classical writings on the character and the classification of the sciences, particularly Bacon's *Novum Organum* and the writings of the *philosophes*, such as Condorcet and the Encyclopedists.

Bacon's 'influence' in this period is the subject of a great many empty historians' commonplaces, some of which had a contemporary origin. What is unquestionably true is that Bacon served as a convenient talking-point for a wide range of abstract problems. Bacon himself disappeared in the talk: he became the object of many obscurely motivated passions, and, as Mill complained, the subject of much slovenly interpretation. Many of these commonplaces are familiar. Lecky accused Baconian philosophy of "exercising a decidedly prejudicial influence on the English intellect, by producing an excessive distaste for the higher generalisations, and for all speculations that do not lead directly to practical results" (1866, p. 443), a claim that has been repeated endlessly to the present day. But the image of Bacon was not as clear as this commonplace suggests. Finch read Bacon as an empiricist and inductivist, but he also described the very different early Comte as "the one who has most considerably extended and verified the application of the inductive method" (1872, p. 23). Kuno Fischer's classic text, which interpreted Bacon to several generations of Continental students and had as its aim locating Bacon in "the theatre of modern philosophy" (Fischer, 1857, p. ix), came to a different conclusion.

Fischer treated contemporary philosophy as "a field of battle" between realism and idealism, and remarked that, since Kant's attempt at the unification of the two tendencies, "there has not been a philosopher of importance, who has not desired to be at once a realist and an idealist"

(1857, p. x). Subsequent German Idealism, he conceded, had not done very well at this task of uniting 'tendencies'. Bacon was his paradigmatic 'realist'. This interpretation fastens on a deep Baconian theme which cannot be reduced to inductivism or empiricism. For an audience of idealists, Bacon preached a kind of skepticism about ideas, which he held against the standard of a real law-governed order of the world beneath and beyond the world of common sense, and of raw experience. Rather than deny experience, Bacon asked the question

How does experience become natural science? For at first it is nothing but a perception of single facts, a collecting together of manifold instances, an enumeration of the things perceived, and their properties; and the experience of common minds scarcely ever rises above this ordinary level. By what means, then, does ordinary experience become scientific (and thus, consequently, inventive) experience? (Fischer, 1857, p. 66).

Fischer said that Bacon posed this question negatively in the first book of the *Novum Organum*, and solved it in the second. The negative answer is the theory of *idola*, the positive answer is a methodological doctrine about access to reality. Both answers were repeated, updated, and used by virtually all of the figures who wrote on the methodological problems of social science in the nineteenth century.

Bacon quoted the saying of Jesus, "'Except ye become as little children, ye shall not enter into the kingdom of Heaven'," which he explained in this way:

The idols of every kind ... must be abjured and renounced with a firm and solemn resolution, and the understanding must be wholly freed and cleared from them, that the access to the kingdom of man, which is founded in science, may be same as that to the kingdom of Heaven, where no entrance is possible, save by assuming the character of children (quoted in Fischer, 1857, pp. 76–77).

As Fischer saw, Bacon's 'inductivism' was always subordinated to this image of reality hidden by *idola*. His scepticism about ideas resonated strongly with Continental philosophy: it made him its bad conscience, the 'tendency' that was impossible either to assimilate conclusively or defeat. When 'empiricist' writers, such as Mill, took over Bacon's reasoning about the method of induction – as in Mill's presentation of the Canons of Induction – the realism in which Bacon embedded his reasoning was dropped. For Bacon, the ultimate aim of the methods is to assay the correctness of representation. The role of negative instances was to show that a supposed law is "no better than an idol" (Fischer, 1857, p. 102).

One consequence of this, which does not fit well with inductivism, is that there is an asymmetry in the 'power' of instances. The root of the problem is universality, which, as Bacon acknowledged, "is never to be completely attained by the way of experience, but can only be approached. By the method of induction, the negative instances can never be drained to the lees" (Fischer, 1857, p. 120). No 'method' can overcome this limitation on the power of induction. "Tables and co-ordinations of instances" (which are characteristic both of Bacon's methods and Mill's Canons) are, Bacon said, not enough to enable our understanding to "form axioms" (Fischer, 1857, p. 100). Bacon's response to this was a theory of the differential *weight* of instances. His premise was that in science we are required, as a matter of practical necessity, to reduce "the many cases to a few, so that a few will serve ... in the place of many" (Fischer, 1857, p. 121). Those instances which must be granted the greatest differential weight Bacon called 'prerogative instances'. Fischer characterized these as "*pregnant* instances from which much may be inferred by an accelerated induction, by a rapid separation of the contingent from the necessary" (1857, p. 125, emphasis in original), in which we are shown, almost at a single glance, "the true difference (*vera differentia*), the operative nature, the law of the phenomenon" (1857, p. 122). This doctrine, in its various guises, marched through the nineteenth century in a course parallel to inductivism.

PREVISION, HYPOTHESIS, AND INDUCTION

The obscure promise that Bacon's realism held out to the social sciences was the possibility of the systematic repudiation, replacement, and correction of our present beliefs about human kind and society. This deeply rooted theme can be glimpsed in Bacon's sixteenth-century disputes with the defenders of the common law tradition. The Enlightenment, which perfected the application of the tools of criticism to the social realm, explicitly asked questions that Bacon had only suggested. At the same time, advanced opinion had refined the problem of extending the concept of law to the social realm. The level that this had reached by the end of the Enlightenment is shown in a query of Condorcet's, posthumously published in 1795:

If man can predict, almost with certainty, those appearances of which he understands the laws; if, even when the laws are unknown to him, experience of the past enables him to foresee, with considerable probability, future appearances; why should we suppose it a chimerical undertaking to delineate, with some degree of truth, the picture of the future destiny of mankind from the results of its history? (Condorcet, 1971, p. 193).

Asking the question in this way was an improvement over Montesquieu, whose notions of the laws of nature went back to the idea that "to have a perfect knowledge of these laws, we must consider man before the establishment of society: the laws received in such a state would be those of nature" (Montesquieu, 1949, p. 3). The teleological notion of natural man, and the related notions of free development and intervention, are rarely buried very deeply, even in the middle of the nineteenth century. Like Kant, whose essay on Universal History was published three years later, Condorcet was not free from a kind of teleological historicism. His sketch of universal history held "that the human race will be meliorated by new discoveries in the sciences and the arts," and "by farther progress in the principles of conduct, and in moral practice; and lastly, by the real improvement of our faculties, moral, intellectual and physical" (1971, p. 194). 'Intellectual improvement' was to be the answer to the problem of universal history that the conversation of the early nineteenth century was to revolve around and improve upon.

Comte's law of the three stages – his version of this answer – was given in the opening pages of the *Cours de philosophie positive* (1858, 1975a, originally published 1830–42):

The law is this: – that each of our leading conceptions – each branch of our knowledge – passes successively through three different theoretical conditions: the Theological, or fictitious; the Metaphysical, or abstract; and the Scientific, or positive. In other words, the human mind, by its nature, employs in its progress three methods of philosophizing, the character of which is essentially different, and even radically opposed: viz., the theological method, the metaphysical, and the positive. Hence arise three philosophies, or general systems of conceptions on the aggregate of phenomena, each of which excludes the others. The first is the necessary point of departure of the human understanding; and the third is its fixed and definite state (Comte, 1858, pp. 25–26).

The extent to which this is a departure from past doctrines is easily overstated. Comte reads like an Encyclopedist; he shared both an audience and the concerns of the Encyclopedists, who were close to him in time, and – the failures of the Revolution notwithstanding – continued to provide the main intellectual resources for progressive French intellectuals of the post-Napoleonic period. The sociological ideas of Comte were often simply taken over from Saint-Simon, who shared these antecedents.

The difference between Saint-Simon and his one-time secretary Comte is in the extent to which they aimed at constructing a systematic methodological account of their social theories. The shadow of Bacon falls here. Bacon and the Encyclopedists are the first philosophers mentioned in Comte's *Cours*, and the list of antecedents he claimed suggests that he wished to be read as attempting a marriage of the tradition of scientific reasoning represented by Bacon and Hume with the vision of progressive

human institutional and intellectual development presented by the Encyclopedists, especially Condorcet and d'Alembert, both of whom are
repeatedly mentioned in the *Cours*. In his later *System* (1875, originally
published 1851–56), the controversial work in which Comte propounded
the religion of humanity, Bacon lost favor. The Positivist library of the
1850s recommended the reading of 'The Discourse on Method of
Descartes, preceded by Bacon's Novum Organon, and followed by
Diderot's 'Interpretation of Nature' (Comte, 1975b, p. 480). Bacon
manages but a week in Comte's 'Positivist Calendar' of Saints in the religion
of Humanity – during the *month* devoted to Descartes. And Comte stated
some reservations about rewarding Bacon with as much as a week. As he
explained, the calendar represents historical luck as much as sheer merit:
"Of the six thinkers ranked under Bacon [i.e., who had their 'Saint's days'
in Bacon's week, among them Hobbes and Pascal], three were in my
judgment his superiors, but their superiority lacked the opportunity to
evidence itself by their giving as great an impulse as Bacon gave to intellectual progress" (Comte, 1975b, p. 470).

The demotion reflects more than a change in taste. Although he assimilated a great deal of the tradition of inductivism and empiricism, Comte's
distinctive contribution as a methodologist of science was in his systematic
substitution of *different* problems for the problems of these traditions. For
Comte, the problem of science was not the epistemological question of the
basis of science, a question which, for his audience, was motivated primarily by the dispute of science with theology, but the new problem of the
character of a fully developed, 'positive' science. To be sure, this question
subsumes other, more traditional problems, including the problem of religion, but it also puts them in a different, and in a sense more soluble, form.
Epistemology by this time had begun its long obsession with skepticism.
Comte's new problem was one that held the promise that the lessons of the
history of science could serve as a guide for questions of method, and
enable the separation of questions of method from questions of epistemology. The step that distinguishes Comte is that he did not, as his predecessors and contemporaries did, make the distinction between science and
nonscience in epistemological terms – of the certainty, infallibility, or
'empirical' origin of scientific ideas (Laudan, 1981, p. 142). Science, Comte
said, is not merely a compilation of facts. "The unfailing test which distinguishes real *science* from vain *erudition*" is "prevision" (translated in
Laudan, 1981, p. 142, emphasis in original). Condorcet had reasoned that
the analogy between history and the sciences lay in the possibility of

predicting appearances from previous appearances – something that can be done with accuracy when the laws of the appearances are understood. Prediction, however, is a cognitive value which potentially conflicts with others, and Comte, unlike Condorcet, dealt with the conflicts that soon arose by turning against inductivism. The moment was ripe for this. Archbishop Whately notwithstanding, few of the leading ideas of contemporary science could be said to be 'almost perfect examples' of induction. So Comte's evasion of the epistemological problem of inductive 'grounding' enabled him to address these new developments in ways his epistemology-centered contemporaries could not.

'Fictions', such as the atomic hypothesis, embody the conflict between prediction and induction. In contrast to inductivists, Comte accepted the 'scientific' character of predictive hypotheses of 'ratiocinative' origin, and held that "their scientific value depends entirely on their conformity ... with the phenomena"(translated in Laudan, 1981, p. 146). His reasoning is illustrative of his 'historical' method. Hypotheses that "relate simply to the laws of phenomena," such as are used in astronomy, have this role in inquiry: "A fact is obscure; or a law is unknown: we proceed to form an hypothesis, in agreement, as far as possible, with the whole of the data we are in possession of; and the science, thus left free to develop itself, always ends by disclosing new observable consequences, tending to confirm or invalidate, indisputably, the primitive supposition" (Comte, 1858, p. 200–1). This class of hypothesis, he said, is "very small." Those in the larger class, which "aim at determining the general agents to which different kinds of natural effects may be referred," do not fulfill the condition of admitting "of a positive and inevitable verification at some future time" (Comte, 1858, p. 200).[2] These nevertheless have a historical place. Their origin is "connected with that inquisition into the essence of things which always characterizes the infancy of the human mind." Hence they are part of the unavoidable process of transition from the metaphysical to the positive stage. A number of contemporary sciences, including 'thermology' and the study of light and electricity, which still used notions of 'fluids' (Comte, 1858, p. 203–4), were, according to Comte, in this position. 'Social philosophy' is also in this state. Given the state of development of these sciences, reliance on these fictions is historically necessary. They represent an unavoidable stage. The psychological temptation to endow the fictions with existence is protected against by the recognition of their historical filiation to theological problems of substance. Comte treated the atomic hypothesis as a "logical artifice" (translated in Laudan, 1981, p. 155), and this suggests a picture of the successive disappearance of the substantial elements of fictions: the characteristics of the metaphysical stage gradually disappear from our scientific concepts until only their logical shell remains.[3]

The 'grounding' for this kind of reasoning about hypotheses is historical, and this leaves us with the question of the relation between this reasoning and the epistemological problem of refining and securing 'sensations', which continued to be the starting point of methodology, in large part, for Mill. Comte did not mount an extensive negative argument against this tradition, but isolated comments which add up to the repudiation of much of the tradition are to be found throughout his works. A number of points are made against empiricist accounts of the nature of observation. Comte noted that there is no absolute separation between observation and reasoning, and that observation, at least the sorts of observations that are useful to science, are dependent on theory for connecting observations to one another, for remembering them, and so forth: without some relevant theoretical ideas, "for the most part we could not even perceive" facts (translated in Laudan, 1981, p. 146).

Statements such as this do not put Comte in the camp of William Whewell, for whom "There is a mask of theory over the whole face of nature," much less in the camp of Kant. But there is a deeper basis for the comments, in Comte's implicit rejection of the Baconian notion of the ascent from common sense. Bacon made some suggestive remarks in the *Novum Organum* having to do with the history of knowledge, and one saying, "Truth is the daughter of time" was often quoted by his successors. It appears, for example, on the title page of Fischer's book (1857). Bacon never acted upon his insight that knowledge has a history, and if we compare the Baconian problem of the relation of common sense to scientific knowledge, we can see why. Comte's law of the three stages has the effect of reformulating the notion of common sense by giving it a history, a history beginning not in the workaday world, but in the shadowy world of primitive imaginings. The world of the primitive is, of course, neither a purely empirical world nor a mundane 'commonsense' world, but itself a 'theoretical' world. The history of the development of our scientific ideas is the history of the *transformation* of their ideas to ours.

THE CLASSIFICATION OF THE SCIENCES

The themes of hypothesis and prediction, the revision of common sense, and the problem of fictions run through the writings of nineteenth-century social science methodology. They rarely appear in explicit forms. To discover Comte's views on hypothesis, one must dig them out. In contrast to his immediate predecessors, such as Condorcet or Saint-Simon, he *had* views on these subjects – but he lacked rhetorical structures in which they could be effectively expressed. This leaves us with a large problem of interpretive reconstruction, particularly in the face of questions about the status of the law of the three stages. The thematic task of the application or elaboration of the law of the three stages was both critical and 'empirical': empirical to the extent that it was an account of history, critical where the task was the analysis of various forms of thought in terms of the extent to which they are 'positive' or 'theologico-metaphysical', an interpretive task dictated by the fact that "there is no science which, having attained the positive stage, does not bear marks of having passed through the others" (Comte, 1858, p. 26).[4] The rhetorical form the discussion takes is the elaboration of a classification of the sciences. This is a highly traditional form: a whole series of classifications had been produced in the preceding centuries, and the problems were well defined.

Comte's stated motive for attempting a new classification was that prior classifications had failed because they attempted to locate, in the same scheme, types of knowledge that are radically contrary, an error that resulted, Comte thought, from the failure to recognize the successive stages of the development of knowledge (Comte, 1858, p. 39). Theology was indeed the stumbling block for Bacon and d'Alembert, whose schemes were, as Darnton has recently pointed out, implicit demotions of theology, demotions which they did not dare make explicit (Darnton, 1984, pp. 197–206). Comte, living in a different political world, was free to organize knowledge in a quite different way. The scheme he chose solved the problem by demoting theology to the lowest rung of intellectual development.

Comte rejected the use of the *a priori* methods of classification which had failed in the past, and applied the positive method itself to the problem – to let "the real affinities and natural connections presented by objects ... determine their order" (Comte, 1858, p. 39). The rule of organization he settled on involved the dependence of the study of a given scientific subject on the laws of a 'preceding' subject. Two rules of dependence – the dependence of the more complex on the more simple and the less general on the more general (Comte, 1858, p. 44) – define the table. Comte argued that these two principles, as they applied to the five fundamental sciences, "Astronomy, Physics, Chemistry, Physiology, and finally Social Physics," defined an order that was in fact in essential conformity with history (Comte, 1858, p. 46).

The axis of his classification schemes divides the sciences into two halves, the organic and inorganic. The inorganic is subdivided into celestial physics, or astronomy (which is further subdivided into geometrical and mechanical branches, the former less 'complex' than the latter) and terrestrial physics (which is subdivided into mechanical [physics] and chemical, again in order of increasing complexity and dependence). In the organic half, which is concerned with 'vital phenomena' and therefore less 'general' than the preceding sciences, the scale of increasing complexity and successive dependence continues, with the subdivision occurring between 'organic physics' or physiology, which is concerned with the individual, and social physics. Comte was careful not to let the division into organic and inorganic be taken as any sort of 'vitalism'. The organic phenomena "include all the qualities belonging to" the inorganic, "with a special order added," namely, "organization." "We have not," he added, "to investigate the nature of either, for the positive philosophy does not inquire into natures" (Comte, 1858, p. 44).

For present-day readers, the problem of the classifications of the sciences lends an antique air to the *Cours*, for the problem is associated for us not only with the nineteenth century but with the artistic depictions of the tree of knowledge of earlier centuries. Mill and Spencer, however, wrote at length on problems of classification, and the genre continued through Karl Pearson's refutation and replacement of Spencer's classification (1937). Classification was a framework within which these writers could address one another's views. For Comte's predecessors, the framework provided a means for addressing not only questions of the place of theological reason and revelation, but also the general question of the relations between the arts, or bodies of practical knowledge, and various kinds of speculation, natural philosophy, and literature. The 'arts' Comte left out of his classification; he had much to say on the subject of the historical relations between practical knowledge and science (e.g. Comte, 1974, pp. 113–141; cf. 1858, pp. 303–4), but he did not attempt to build these considerations into his classification.

In contrast to previous classifiers, Comte's concern was with science only, and only parts of science. He divided science into two types, abstract and concrete: abstract sciences concerned with the laws governing phenomena, concrete sciences concerned with particular classes of beings, such as zoology and botany. He ignored the 'concrete' or descriptive sciences, save when they bore on questions of the abstract sciences. In devising organizing principles, he considered only the theoretical sciences, and his account of the successive development of one science out of another is an account of the successive development of theoretical sciences. However, Comte did not distinguish very clearly between considerations of theoretical form and considerations of the properties of the facts the theories were about. This meant that the scheme was fundamentally a classification with respect to theoretical form and the logical relations between theories in different branches of science; 'complexity' and 'generality', and for that matter the distinction between sciences involving 'organization', are characteristics of theories. So his classification was a solution to a new, and limited, problem.

Comte's conclusion from his classification, that social physics was the study of a phenomenon of great complexity, meant that its closest affinities with respect to theoretical form would be to biology, the science closest in complexity and which shares the principle of organization. The idea of society as organic in character is not original with Comte: this and the idea that the science of society would be a kind of 'social physiology' was the central doctrine of Comte's early mentor, Saint-Simon. But Saint-Simon had never given a methodological argument for this belief, nor had he given the detailed account of the logical properties of biology which Comte was to give.

COMPLEXITY AND TELEOLOGY

The analogy to biology was the source of as many problems as it resolved, for the organism was an intellectual battleground throughout the nineteenth century. Comte's position in this battle was clear. "For almost a century," he said, "the best minds have agreed that physics should be excused from penetrating the mystery of weight, and content itself with revealing the laws by which it works; but that does not prevent sound physiology from being daily reproached with teaching nothing on the inner essence of life, of feeling, and of thought" (Comte, 1974, p. 112; cf. 1858, p. 304). Comments like this made his name anathematic to scientists such as Pasteur, who wished to retain some remnants of the vitalist tradition. Antivitalist scientists caught up in these disputes, even such notable figures as Claude Bernard, tended to temper their deterministic, materialistic views by making concessions to public opinion which they considered to be scientifically meaningless. Comte was an intellectual predecessor who could be conveniently thrown to these wolves.[5] Comte's reputation suffered from this dissociation, and his views were often distorted in the process of dissociation, as well as by the confusing quasi-teleological variations on the concept of the organism which were introduced in the wake of Darwinism.

Comte began his discussion of biology by dismissing "the so-called independence of general laws attributed to living bodies, and still loudly proclaimed at the beginning of this century by the great Bichat himself," a doctrine which Comte, with a singular lack of prevision, said "is no longer openly maintained except by metaphysicians" (Comte, 1974, p. 111; cf. 1858, p. 304). Comte knew that this did not mean that the "tug of war" between scientific and metaphysical conceptions of biology was over. He saw that it "can only cease when the character of biological science is examined in the light of the highest positive philosophy, whose rule alone will ensure that the study of living bodies follows unhesitatingly the path marked out for it by its true nature" (Comte, 1974, p. 112; cf. 1858, p. 305). The "extreme complexity" of organic phenomena, however, makes the task of examining biology in the light of the more advanced sciences difficult (Comte, 1974, p. 112; cf. 1858, p. 305).

Complexity is also one of the reasons why metaphysical notions are so difficult to root out in biology.

> The spirit of biological science would certainly lead us to believe that the very fact that such and such an organ is part of a living being means that it contributes in a definite, though perhaps as yet unknown, manner to the acts that make up the existence of that being: which amounts to there being no organ without a function, any more than function without an organ. Since the development of the exact correlation between ideas of organization and ideas of life constitutes the typical aim of all biological research, such an attitude is eminently appropriate and indeed indispensable. But it must be admitted that this tendency to regard every organ as necessarily exercising a certain action degenerates very frequently into blind, antiscientific admiration of the actual mode in which the various vital phenomena are produced (Comte, 1974, pp. 121–22; cf. 1858, p. 332).

Comte regarded this attitude as ultimately theological in inspiration; his Positivist 'historical' claim was that the "principle of conditions of existence" (Comte, 1974, p. 122; cf. 1858, p. 332) has replaced the "dogma of final causes" in much the same way as chemistry had replaced "the primitive idea of the creation and destruction of matter" with "the idea of decomposition and recomposition" (Comte, 1974, p. 121; cf. 1858, p. 331). The fact of complexity meant that biology can never "attain a perfection comparable to that of the more simple and general parts of natural philosophy" (Comte, 1858, p. 302), but this did not change the basic character of biological inquiry, which retained "the usual end of obtaining a rational prevision; the subject here being the mode of action of a given animal organism, placed in determinate circumstances; or, reciprocally, the animal arrangement that may be induced by any given act of animality" (Comte, 1858, p. 370).

Comte's antiteleological *intentions* could not be clearer. The extent to which he lived up to them, however, is open to question, most visibly in connection with the concepts of parts and wholes. As Lucien Levy–Bruhl, writing at the end of the century, suggested, Comte "does not himself reject [the principle of final causes] as entirely as he at first seems to do" (Levy–Bruhl, 1903, p. 88). He did not contest, Levy–Bruhl suggested, the Kantian principle of "internal finality," which Levy–Bruhl glossed as the "reciprocal causality" which "appears in living beings, where the whole and the parts are reciprocally end and means" (Levy–Bruhl, 1903, p. 88). Levy–Bruhl quoted a remark of Comte's to the effect that "we shall cease defining a living being by the collection of its organs, as if these could exist isolated.... In biology the general notion of the being, always precedes that of any of its parts whatever" (quoted in Levy–Bruhl, 1903, p. 88). Comte's word for this state of organized being is 'consensus', and it is this term, Levy–Bruhl claimed, that is equivalent to Kant's internal finality.

In retrospect, this is a conclusion that stems from a failure of historical perspective on the part of Levy–Bruhl. A good many of Comte's usages, such as harmony, equilibrium, and consensus, were deliberately chosen because at the time he wrote they were *non*teleological. In the course of the bitter dispute between materialists and vitalists which took up much of the rest of the century and raged most fiercely in France, teleologists appropriated these terms, or gave them teleological interpretations, and determinists responded by abandoning them – the most effective way of avoiding the *tu quoque* arguments which by the end of the century had been refined to a high level of dialectical subtlety by the defenders of teleology. Comte, writing before most of these discussions, used a wider range of terms, and used them more freely than did 'determinists' of a later period.

Considerations of historical context do not, however, entirely dispose of the issues here. Comte was concerned to avoid reductionist arguments that made organisms simply into machines. He regarded such writings as Descartes's foray into mechanistic biology as premature. But he did not attempt to give any sort of argument for the usage 'organism' itself, or to inquire into its ontological status. The reasons for this apparent neglect are to be found in his theory of the historical progression of concepts: he accepted that the task of positive science in the face of pregiven concepts is to take concepts found in the earlier theological or metaphysical stages and transform them into nomic concepts. In the case of the organism, he suggested that a great deal is pregiven, especially by the 'art' of medicine. Comte pointed to the historical fact that "it is in virtue of the growing needs of practical medicine ... that physiology began to detach itself from the common trunk of primitive philosophy, and to form itself more and more in accordance with positive ideas" (Comte, 1974, p. 114; cf. 1858, p. 305), a process he saw himself as continuing. The historical character of his methodological argument, in short, allowed him to avoid the sorts of arguments that made the organism into some sort of externally defined object, an enterprise which he would have labeled 'metaphysical'. He made the same sort of move in the context of sociology.

FUNCTION AND RECIPROCITY

In biology, this 'historical' argument gave him several important results. The pregiven practice of medical 'interventions' allowed him to take over the concept of an organism and to formulate a preliminary definition of the domain of biology in terms of organisms that have various features (such as imperfection, variability, pathology, 'modifiability', and the like). It also supported his conclusion that experimental and comparative methods are the pre-eminent methods appropriate to biological science. In refining the definition of the problem domain of biology, he considered various definitions of life, and proposed a modified form of Blainville's characterization of life in terms of respiration, "the double interior motion, general and continuous, of composition and decomposition" (Comte, 1858, p. 306) – itself a resolutely nonteleological conception. Comte conceded that this definition might be better expressed, and he glossed it by making explicit what he took to be implied in the definition, the relation between the organism and a "medium to minister to the absorption and exhalation" (Comte, 1858, p. 306).[6]

From this definition of life as a relation of reciprocal action between organism and environment, he argued, it

immediately follows that the great problem of positive biology consists in establishing, in the most general and simple manner, a scientific harmony between these two inseparable powers of the vital conflict, and the act that constitutes that conflict: in a word, in connecting, in both a general and special manner, the double idea of organ and medium with that of function (Comte, 1858, p. 307).

'Function' is given a sense only in the context of these relations of 'reciprocity'.

The idea of function is, in fact, as double as the other; and, if we were treating of the natural history of vital beings, we must expressly consider it so: for, by the law of the equivalence of action and reaction, the organism must act on the medium as much as the medium on the organism. In treating of the human being, and especially in the social state, it would be necessary to use the term *function* in this larger sense: but at present there will be little inconvenience in adopting it in its ordinary sense, signifying organic acts, independently of their exterior consequences (Comte, 1858, p. 307, emphasis in original).

'Function,' then, is *defined* in terms of reciprocal actions between organ and medium, which is, again, a determinedly nonteleological definition, the nonteleological character of which Comte underlined by using sentence constructions that make it clear that he was equating 'function' with 'action', and 'organ' with 'agent', and treating the point of view that begins with the organ and inquires into the 'actions' it performs as nomologically equivalent to the point of view that inquires into the actions *caused* by an agent (cf. Comte, 1858, p. 368). The substitutions were consciously directed at the problem of 'final causes'. Comte consistently reconstrued 'teleological' explanations in terms of 'law' and 'rational prevision'. Moreover, he was eager to extend these substitutions to applications in the social realm (Comte, 1858, p. 489).

The distinctive starting point of biology, the concept of the organism, itself appeared to demand a teleological understanding. Comte treated this as only a matter of appearance: starting with the act and starting with the agent are *logically* interchangable starting points; historically, the starting point of physiology is with anatomy, the agent, and organs. If we consider, as Comte did, the *history* of the study of organisms, and treat the problem of developing biology as a science as a problem of replacing metaphysical notions with 'positive' concepts, Comte's attitude toward biological teleology becomes clear. Organisms are complex, organized objects, with a distinctive prescientific 'metaphysical' tradition surrounding them. There need be no special argument for treating organisms as a distinctive kind of object: they are pregiven as distinctive, although the treatment is based on metaphysical and theological notions. The positive attitude toward these concepts is that they are part of the emancipation of biology from theology, and therefore are of importance only as transitional devices. Their fate is to be replaced by positive concepts. The best answer to the teleologists is not to philosophize against them, but to perform the replacement. And to do this is not a matter of dialectics, but of the advance of scientific theory. Comte saw a way that biological science may be reasonably expected to develop in the direction of replacing the principle of final causes by the concept of conditions of existence, and his 'definition' of life does no more than point out this path.

In spite of Comte's care in explaining particular teleological usages 'positivistically,' a number of usages that seem retrospectively to be 'teleological' remain. A few of these usages are important in the later literature and require discussion. Comte used 'equilibrium' in a variety of contexts, but primarily in connection with purely physical phenomena, such as electricity (Comte, 1858, p. 245), atmospheres, and liquids (Comte, 1858, p. 206). He expressed his admiration for Lagrange's theory of equilibria (Comte, 1858, p. 803). The idea of an organism's equilibrium in relation to its environment seems to be a later usage. It is relevant to note that while Levy-Bruhl explained Comte's views of the relation between organism and 'milieu' in terms of equilibrium (Levy–Bruhl, 1903, p. 89), this was not the way Comte expressed them. He used the word 'equilibrium' in connection with biology only to make the contrast between the numerical mechanical laws of equilibria that are relevant to the motions of all bodies and the nonnumerical formulations appropriate to biology (Comte, 1858, p. 326). In discussing phrenology he spoke of the equilibrium of the faculties as a key to understanding the ego (Comte, 1858, p. 380), but treated this equilibrium nonteleologically, as when he remarked that habit "may be scientifically attached to the law of inertia, as geometers understand it in the positive theory of motion and equilibrium" (Comte, 1858, p. 379).

Other usages are more ambiguous. 'Harmony' was used in a number of contexts relating to the maintenance of life, as in his explanation of the principle that is the replacement of the "dogma of final causes" in biology (Comte, 1858, p. 331), the principle of the conditions of existence:

The philosophical principle of the conditions of existence is in fact simply the direct conception of the necessary harmony of the statical and the dynamical analyses of the subject proposed. This principle is eminently adapted to the science of biology, which is continually engaged in establishing a harmony between the means and the end; and nowhere else, therefore, is seen in such perfection, that double analysis, statical and dynamical, which is found everywhere (Comte, 1858, p. 332).

The 'harmony' here is analytical or heuristic – harmony between analyses, or as Comte said, a matter of "philosophical co-ordination" (Comte, 1858, p. 333). Comte conceded that there is a difficulty here, and commented that in

statical biology [i.e. anatomy and taxonomy] ... it even appears as if, in regard to them, we were involved in a vicious circle: for if, on the one hand, the rational classification of living beings requires the antecedent knowledge of their organization, it is certain, on the other hand, that anatomy itself, like physiology, can not be studied, in regard to all organisms, without an antecedent formation of the biological hierarchy (Comte, 1858, p. 333).

Comte suggested that we simply accept the dependence of statics on dynamics, "placing the theory of organization before that of classification"

(Comte, 1858, p. 333). The achievement of harmony, in this context, becomes a test of our conceptions.

The philosophical character of this test is obscure, in part because of Comte's tendency to run together questions of theoretical form and questions of the properties of the subject-matter. He claimed that

The whole system of biological science is derived, as we have seen, from one great philosophical conception; the necessary correspondence between the ideas of organization and those of life. There can not be a more perfect fundamental unity of subject than this; and it is unnecessary to insist upon the almost indefinite variety of its modifications, – statical and dynamical (Comte, 1858, p. 314).

He took this to be the 'basis' of the comparative method in biology. His thought was that there is some "basis of structure and composition" common to all the possible forms of organization we call life, and something common in their physiology: the comparative method studies the variation of the secondary aspects of these common features. This again is a kind of conceptual premise, and Comte himself suggested that it derives from "the definition of life" (Comte, 1858, p. 314).

If the fundamentally nonteleological character of the concept of life can be taken as established, all of these biological usages may be interpreted nonteleologically.[7] Bichat's definition of life is in terms of the "harmony between the living being" and the environment (Comte, 1858, p. 304), and Comte used Blainville to revise this definition. The revision, as we have seen, treats life as a nonteleological reciprocity involving "the two correlative conditions of a determinate organism and a suitable medium" (Comte, 1858, p. 306). Comte then spoke of this definition as being "confirmed" (Comte, 1858, p. 307), by which he seems to have meant 'underwritten by the discovery of the laws which govern these conditional relations'.

EXTENDING THE BIOLOGICAL MODEL

"The most fundamental dogma of the whole of positive philosophy, that is to say, the subjection of all real phenomena to invariable laws, only results with certainty from an immense induction, without really being deducible from any notion whatever." Comte wrote this in an 1851 letter (translated in Levy–Bruhl, 1903, pp. 84–85), but the peculiarity of this half-historical, half-analytical argument from the history of thought to the methodology and substance of sociology was apparent to Comte before this. In a chapter in the *Cours*, on 'Fundamental Characteristics of the Positive Method in the Study of Social Phenomena', which appears as part of Book VI, 'Social Physics', he proceeded, characteristically, by presenting a historical discussion of the place of methodology in science.

In every science conceptions relating to method are by their nature inseparable from those relating to doctrine.... If up till now we have avoided the vain and sterile separation of method from doctrine with regard to the least complex of phenomena, it could not be otherwise when the greater complexity of the subject and its present non-positive state actually dictate this course (Comte, 1974, p. 137; cf. 1858, p. 451).

The present state of social science exhibits features that mark it as an occupant of the theologico-metaphysical stage – a preponderance of imagination over observation, the "exclusive search for absolute ideas," and so forth. As with biology, we can see which concepts are more 'positive' than others by analogizing from the history of sciences closer to the positive stage.

The analysis of biology, of which Comte had established the relevance through his classification of the sciences, suggested the general range of theoretical and methodological problems and solutions that a positive science of society would involve. Thus Comte's procedure was to make analogies, not between society and organisms – a pastime of many later thinkers – but between the conceptual devices and methods appropriate to the two sciences. This involved him in some 'substantive' comparisons between society and organisms, but the comparisons are modest. The path here had of course been marked by Saint-Simon, who employed many of the same social images and historical diagnoses as Comte. Comte did not *argue* that society is an organism. He was aware that any such argument would be no better than the "vain ontological speculations" he denounced in other contexts (Comte, 1858, p. 326). We can, however, begin with the wealth of social concepts from the theological and metaphysical stages and revise them. Nor are we limited to *a priori* revisions. From the experiences of history, especially recent French history, we can identify difficulties in these metaphysical conceptions which point us in the direction of 'positive' concepts.

Accordingly Comte gave a critical revision of preceding social concepts. The contemporary social problem was conventionally characterized in France as the reconciliation of order and progress, and the chief lesson of recent history was, as Comte expressed it, the fact of the difficulty of the 'modification' of social institutions. Comte's use of the term 'modification' was meant to point to a comparison between medical men and statesmen, both of whom share the difficulty of intervention in a complex set of relations that are only partially responsive to their actions, in spite of their apparent 'power'. The Revolution, of course, appeared to Comte as the great example of the recalcitrance of social institutions to political reform, and the difficulty of successfully introducing the most 'rational' of social novelties. This recalcitrance was not his theme alone, but was central to the message of Catholic critics of the Revolution, such as de Maistre. Comte firmly located these thinkers, adherents of the self-proclaimed party of 'order', in the 'theological' stage. Liberalism, which he described as the party of 'progress', he located in the metaphysical stage.

Thus the question of the 'modifiability' of social institutions was both a question of immediate political significance and a question whose scientific time had come – a point made by Comte in his prefatory discussion of the "opportuneness and necessity of this new science" of sociology (Comte, 1858, pp. 399–450). The details of Comte's discussions of substantive social issues, labeled by Comte himself as premature and written in a polemical style that differs in tone from the rest of the *Cours*, need not concern us here. Inasmuch as positivism is in the business of substituting concepts, the methodological feature of interest here is the *form* of the substitutions Comte suggested, and the considerations he took to govern the substitutions. It is the similarity of the problem-structures of physiological statics and dynamics and social statics and dynamics that is the basis of Comte's detailed argument on the extension of the fundamental concepts of science to society. 'Rational prevision' remains the goal of science in this context as well.

The positive form of the 'theological' concept of 'order' is the 'statical' concept of a consensus of reciprocities.

No association whatever, even of the smallest number of individuals, and for the most temporary objects, can subsist without a certain degree of reciprocal confidence, intellectual and moral, among its members, each one of whom has incessantly to act upon views which he must admit on the faith of some one else (Comte, 1858, p. 410).

Association requires trust, and trust in shared beliefs. Trust is a kind of 'reciprocal action', so the substitution is nonteleological and 'ideational.' The ideational aspect points toward the 'dynamical' problem of the progress of ideas, of which the law of the three stages, governing the invariant successsion of types of ideas, purports to provide an account. The concerns of liberalism, which Comte labeled as 'metaphysical', are similarly transformed: the atomic, disenfamilied individual of liberalism and of political economy was rejected by Comte as a metaphysical abstraction.[8] The unit which Comte took to be 'natural' is the family, and in support of this he pointed to the evidence of the biological study of animal sociality.

The fact of reciprocal action and reaction means that there is what Comte called "spontaneous harmony" between the parts, and the parts and the whole, of the social system considered, so to say, as a natural object

(Comte, 1858, p. 459). This harmony is not established by intervention (Comte, 1858, p. 461), but by the various laws governing actions and reactions, laws to which political interventions are of course also subject. The "master thought" of social physics is this "radical consensus" of the social system, 'radical' because it is a consensus lying beneath the superficial consensus of opinion and beneath social conflict. This 'radical consensus' obtains at the moment of revolution itself. As Comte explained this 'master thought', it is simply the notion of "universal social interconnection" governed by law (Comte, 1858, p. 461). The thought itself has methodological implications. To study a body of facts governed by law in this way, we need to follow the 'organic' procedure of starting with the whole. We cannot follow the inorganic sciences' rule of proceeding

from the simple to the compound. . ... the reverse method is necessary in the study of Man and of Society; Man and Society as a whole being better known to us, and more accessible subjects of study, than the parts which constitute them (Comte, 1858, p. 463).

The laws relating the parts of the system are laws of co-existence; the laws relating to change are laws of invariant succession. The so-called 'problem of order' between egoistic individuals did not arise directly for Comte: when he spoke of 'harmony' he had in mind the conceptual problem of the relation of statics and dynamics. This does not directly correspond to the problem of social harmony, or for that matter, 'functional integration', though it is indirectly related to both by virtue of the fact that for Comte the simultaneous achievement of order and progress in the present depended on a particular kind of intellectual development, namely the development of a postmetaphysical, post-theological synthesis of social ideas. Since positivism is, by virtue of the law of the three stages, ordained to provide these ideas, the achievement of a conceptual grasp of the relation between statics and dynamics is part and parcel of orderly social progress (Comte, 1858, p. 457).

The categories of statics and dynamics are a conceptual device, so the problem of relating statics and dynamics is a conceptual problem: statics and dynamics are two aspects of the same theory, rather than two distinct provinces of inquiry. 'Statics' is defined in social physics much as it is in biology. It is the study of the laws of action and reaction of the parts of the social system, and the relation of the parts to the whole. Comte said little else in justification of this notion of 'the whole', and seemed content to give a prudential justification for its use. His rationale here depends on a point that he has already established under the heading of the insufficiency of political action: that the various elements of society (whatever 'elements' may turn out to mean – Comte doesn't say), tied as they are in causal relations of action and reaction, cannot be usefully studied apart from one another.

THE 'HISTORICAL METHOD'

The nomic structure of sociology thus resembles that of biology. But this does not imply that the methods of sociology will resemble those of biology. Early in the *Cours*, Comte remarked on the independence of considerations of method in the narrow sense (which he called procedure – the choice between observation and experiment, for example) from the positive method itself: "the Positive Method must be constantly modified in a uniform manner in the range of the same fundamental science, and will undergo modifications, different and more and more compound, in passing from one science to another. . . .. Though the Method is always the same, its procedure is varied" (1858, p. 48). The extension of the method of science to the social realm demands this abstraction, which serves as a bridge to the narrower questions of method or procedure in particular sciences.

The step of defining 'procedures' for sociology is curiously abbreviated in the *Cours*, perhaps because the circularity of his analyses, and in particular of his interpretive reconstructions of the history of the sciences, would have been glaringly obvious had he explained them. However, when Comte made comments on procedure, they separated him from the empirical and statistical social scientists we are to encounter around Quetelet. Comte cautioned that "all the resources of the anterior sciences . . . would be almost useless, and even deceptive, without the addition of the historical method, properly so called, which investigates, not by comparison, but by gradual filiation" (1858, p. 816).

Filiation, the historical method which Comte claimed was the distinctive method of sociology, is explained in various ways in the *Cours*. The 'method' admittedly yields only previsions which "can hardly become very precise" (1858, p. 496), and owes a great deal to *a priori* reasoning (1858, p. 816) and hypothesis. But in social science, he said,

there is more need than anywhere else of theories which shall scientifically connect the facts that are happening with those that have happened: and the more we reflect, the more distinctly we shall see that in proportion as known facts are mutually connected we shall be better able, not only to estimate, but to perceive, those which are yet unexplored (1858, p. 475).

The threat of circularity and of substituting apriorism for science is conceded: "I am not blind to the vast difficulty which this requisition imposes on the institution of positive sociology – obliging us to create at once, so to speak, observations and laws, on account of their indispensable connection, placing us in a sort of vicious circle" (1858, p. 475). But the 'requisition' is not avoidable.

Comte was content with the claim that this 'method' was workable and an advance. His example of the successful application of the method, Lagrange's "exposition of the filiation of the chief conceptions of the human mind in regard to rational mechanics, from the origin of the science to our own time," found in the prefatory chapters of the sections of the 'Analytical Mechanics' (1858, p. 496), is as far away from the speculative history of writers such as Condorcet as possible – but at the same time very far from the historiography of the historical profession as it was to emerge in the next century.

The historical method is obviously also far removed from the statistical method, and Comte's remarks on statistics define him in relation to much of what was to follow. While the probability theorists are granted a high rank in such places as the Positivist calendar of Saints, their forays into sociology are treated as a "gross illusion" of "excusable origin" (1858, p. 492). Comte remarked that "The most perfect methods may, however, be rendered deceptive by misuse: and this we must bear in mind. We have seen that mathematical analysis itself may betray us into substituting signs for ideas, and that it conceals inanity of conception under an imposing verbiage" (1858, pp. 483–84). His verdict on the applications of the methods is harsh.

It is impossible to conceive of a more irrational conception than that which takes for its basis or for its operative method a supposed mathematical theory, in which, signs being taken for ideas, we subject numerical probability to calculation, which amounts to the same thing as offering our own ignorance as the natural measure of the degree of probability of our various opinions (1858, p. 493).

This is vague, but it suggests a theme that was to be taken up by others: that accepting statistical results as, so to say, a stopping point for inquiry is to accept ignorance. The same point is made, with similar vagueness, in his book on biology, where he denounced the

alleged application of what is called statistics to medicine, from which some scientists expect miracles, and which nevertheless could only lead to a profound and outright deterioration of the medical art, henceforth reduced to blind enumerations. Such a method, if we may call it by this name, would really be nothing but sheer empiricism, disguised under a vain mathematical appearance (translated in Virtanen, 1960, p. 60).

With this comment, Comte took up a polar position, against the statistical social science that was developing at the time, and for a social science that was highly theoretical in character.

CHAPTER THREE

MILL AND 'THE ASCENT TO CAUSES'

Mill had a famous and complex relationship with Comte. As Comte entered his later, 'religious', phase, Mill's admiration cooled, as the oft-told story goes, and he worked at distancing himself from Positivism. Nevertheless, their opinions often overlapped, and appeal to the one often meant assent to the views of the other – a point obscured in the later nineteenth century by European nationalism. Germans roundly denounced 'French Positivism', but not infrequently took over much the same reasoning in Millian form. Durkheim, who loyally held that Comte was the largest source of his methodological inspiration and was portrayed by his French associates as "a real heir" of Comte (Levy-Bruhl, 1903, p. 359), devoted more of the *Rules* to issues that arise in connection with Mill than to those that arise with Comte. In a sense, Mill's *A System of Logic* was a completion of Comte's project, for although Comtean formulations were often sufficiently precise to deal with certain topics, particularly the sciences' "usual end of obtaining a rational prevision" (Comte, 1858, p. 370), they were vague with respect to others, particularly those pertaining to the logic of experimental reasoning.

CAUSES, CONDITIONS, AND INDUCTION

Comte's mode of procedure in the *Cours* permitted him to bypass many traditional questions about causality by dismissing them as theological or metaphysical. In contrast, Mill considered it his obligation to meet all comers – in no one is the ethic of responsible controversy so ingrained (Bain, 1882, pp. 74, 76 *et passim*)– and in the course of doing this he was forced to meet, and to give clear responses to, objections originating in other traditions. Mill's account of cause exemplifies the difference. It is a contribution to a many-sided conversation: in connection with the Canons of Induction, it is a revision, and critique, of Baconianism; against Whewell, it is a defense of induction, and an attempt to draw distinctions between description and explanation and fact and theory which preserve the program of induction. Mill also consciously defended empiricism against various forms of idealism, aimed at the vindication of social inquiry

29

as causal science, and attempted to deal with cause in a way that reconciled
the possibility of social science with common experience. These are concerns that are shared with Comte only in part.

Book Three of *A System of Logic*, in which the Canons of Induction are
presented, was written apart from any influence of Comte. Indeed, as Bain
noted, Mill "tells us how fortunate he was in having finished this book
before reading Comte. That is to say," Bain observed, "unassisted invention
gave a better result than he would have attained by taking Comte into
partnership from the beginning" (Bain, 1882, p. 146). Book Three also has
a reception-history that is distinct from the reception-history of Book Six,
in which Mill's model of social science is presented, and, indeed, many who
rejected the conclusions of Book Six – including Durkheim – found
material in Book Three that could be used in the construction of alternatives to the model of Book Six, alternatives often very far from anything
that Mill himself would have countenanced. The fruitfulness of Book Three
was due to the fact that Mill constructed, or at least characterized and
defined by example, many distinctions that proved useful in later polemics
and applications. Even chance coinages made by Mill in this part of the text
are later found erected into large doctrines. The concept of 'adequate
cause', which will form a large part of the discussion of Weber, is an
example of this.

Mill's discussion of cause begins with the familiar Baconian theme of the
ascent from common sense. The ascent to science by scientific induction
begins not with theology but common experience: "spontaneous inductions…. that food nourishes, that water drowns, or quenches thirst, that
the sun gives light and heat" (1973, p. 318). These inductions are improved
through the mode of "correcting one generalization by means of another,
a narrower generalizaton by a wider," a procedure "which common sense
suggests and adopts in practice" (1973, p. 319), and which is, Mill insisted,
also "the real type of scientific Induction" (1973, p. 319). The basic logic of
induction does not change. "The logic of science" is "that of business and
life" (1973, p. 284), and "all that art can do is but to give accuracy and
precision to this process, and adapt it to all varieties of cases, without any
essential alteration in its principle" (1973, p. 319).

The thesis that the logic of daily life and the logic of science are, at some
basic level, the same, faces some difficulties in connection with causality,
and Mill attempted to resolve them. The drama of *A System of Logic* is in
Mill's pilgrim-like progress through each of these difficulties and problems.
Mill knew this as well. "In the moral and psychological department of
thought, there is hardly an instance of a writer who has left a considerable
permanent reputation, or who has continued to be read by after genera-

tions, except those who have treated or attempted to treat of the *whole* of some great department of speculation" (quoted in Ryan, 1970, pp. x–xi, emphasis in original). He also knew that very few systems had value *as* systems, and that the fragments, "if published separate would probably have attracted little notice" (quoted in Ryan, 1970, p. xii). So he was careful to revise the fragments in response to new issues, whether or not the revisions significantly altered the whole. The fragments, as Mill expected, took on a life of their own. But their peculiarities often derive from the larger systematic purpose, and the enormous influence of the work on cause depended on the larger purpose, and especially on the extent to which Mill succeeded in reconciling scientific usages and commonsense usages.

The most influential of these steps was his handling of the puzzle of the relation between conditions and causes by treating "the cause of a phenomenon ... [as] the assemblage of its conditions" (Mill, 1973, p. 327). His example was not drawn from the advanced sciences, but from commonsense causal reasoning.

If a person eats of a particular dish, and dies in consequence, that is, would not have died if he had not eaten of it, people would be apt to say that eating of that dish was the cause of his death. There needs not, however, be any invariable connexion between eating of the dish and death; but there certainly is, among the circumstances which took place, some combination or other on which death is invariably consequent; as, for instance, the act of eating of the dish, combined with a particular bodily constitution, a particular state of present health, and perhaps even a certain state of the atmosphere; the whole of which circumstances perhaps constituted in this particular case the *conditions* of the phenomenon, or, in other words, the set of antecedents which determined it, and but for which it would not have happened. The real Cause, is the whole of these antecedents; and we have, philosophically speaking, no right to give the name of cause to one of them, exclusively of the others.... All the conditions were equally indispensable to the production of the consequent; and the statement of the cause is incomplete, unless in some shape or other we introduce them all (1973, pp. 327–28, emphasis in original).

Mill went on to respond methodically to other difficulties and objections to which this unified account of scientific usage and the language of 'life' gives rise.

In the causal language of life, as well as in science, it is said that some causes 'counteract' others, and this consideration led Mill to a revision of definition of cause:

The cause, then, philosophically speaking, is the sum total of the conditions, positive and negative taken together; the whole of the contingencies of every description, which being realized, the consequent invariably follows. The negative conditions, however, of any phenomenon, a special enumeration of which would generally be very prolix, may be all summed up under one head, namely, the absence of preventing or counteracting causes (1973, p. 332).

Day invariably follows night as well, and cases of this kind lead to another revision. In the case of day and night, 'day' might be caused by any "sufficiently luminous body," so that the cause of a phenomenon is the "antecedent, or the concurrence of antecedents, on which it is invariably and *unconditionally* consequent" (1973, p. 340, emphasis in original). Similar reasoning should serve to distinguish other cases that are not 'causation' but "conjunctions in some sort accidental" (1973, p. 339).

The basic method of 'correcting narrower generalizations by wider' is most at home in science. In 'life', one rarely engages in the process in an explicit way. Yet in standard cases of scientific reasoning, the process of induction in terms of generalization from particular instances to a class (1973, p. 288) is not free of problems. Such famous cases of scientific reasoning as Kepler's construction of ellipses appears at first to fit the method perfectly. But if all curve fitting is 'induction', puzzles arise that threaten the concept of induction itself. Whewell had suggested that explanation consists in connecting facts by means of a mental conception, and that the only 'process' here is the formulating and testing of explanatory hypotheses, or, as Mill characterized Whewell, "guessing until a guess is found which tallies with the facts" (1973, p. 304). Mill claimed that this account leaves out the elements in which an induction can be said to constitute a 'proof' (1973, p. 305), and the question of whether there *is* inductive proof served as the rhetorical framework in which Mill's treatment of cause was presented.

In retrospect, this is a dispute that Mill lost and the defenders of hypothesis won. An aspect of the dispute, the problem of accidental generalization, remains an open issue in connection with probabilistic causal arguments, as we shall see. Here, and in the case of the problem of distinguishing causes and conditions, Mill supplied much of what was the common language of the later disputes. Mill was concerned to distinguish curve fitting of the Keplerian variety, 'mere' curve fitting, from induction proper. He argued that Kepler's ellipses were a 'description' of the planetary system, not an 'induction' (1973, p. 293), and that Kepler's discovery was merely a matter of "finding a compendious expression" (1973, p. 294). The criterion Mill chose to distinguish mere description is Comte's; Kepler did not "(which is the true test of a general truth) add anything to the power of prediction already possessed" (1973, p. 294). Mill conceded that the process of seeking a 'compendious expression' of a description through hypothesizing and testing is difficult to distinguish from induction; but the similarity, he said, holds only at a certain stage in a larger process of induction.

The larger process of induction was formulated in Mill's Canons of Induction. Whewell gave a particularly succinct characterization of these Canons, which, he noted, "have a great resemblance to Bacon's 'Prerogatives of Instances'" (Whewell, 1984, p. 346).

They are all described by formulae of this kind: – Let there be, in the observed facts, combinations of antecedents, ABC, BC, ADE, &c. and combinations of corresponding consequents, abc, bc, ade, &c.; and let the object of inquiry be, the consequence of some cause A, or the cause of some consequence a. The Method of Agreement teaches us, that when we find by experiment such facts as abc the consequent of ABC, and ade the consequent of ADE, then a is the consequent of A. The Method of Difference teaches us that when we find such facts as abc the consequent of ABC, and bc the consequent of BC, then a is the consequent of A. The Method of Residues teaches us, that if abc be the consequent of ABC, and if we have already ascertained that the effect of A is a, and the effect of B is b, then we may infer that the effect of C is c. The Method of Concomitant Variations teaches us, that if a phenomenon a varies according as another phenomenon A varies, there is some connexion of causation direct or indirect, between A and a (Whewell, 1984, pp. 345–46).

Whewell's objection to the Canons was

that they take for granted the very thing which is most difficult to discover, the reduction of the phenomena to formulae such as are here presented to us.... Nature does not present to us the cases in this form; and how are we to reduce them to this form? (1984, p. 346).

Identifying the conceptual categories that the formulae require is itself the major task of science.

Mill's response to the aspect of this criticism which treats the methods as merely formal and therefore of no value to the scientist was to compare the criticism to the objections made by critics of syllogistic logic in the previous century. "The grand difficulty, they said, is to obtain your syllogism, not to judge of its correctness when obtained" (1973, p. 430). To this Bishop Whately had replied that "their argument, if good at all, was good against the reasoning process altogether; for whatever cannot be reduced to syllogism, is not reasoning" (quoted in Mill, 1973, p. 431). This reply is true to the influence of Mill's methods in the social sciences, for the methods were treated not as an inductive technique or method of proof but as a guide to the formation of causal arguments. As Mill went on to suggest, standard cases of scientific inference could be analyzed as instances of the methods. Thus Kepler's ellipses, "as far as they are a case of induction at all, fall under the Method of Agreement" (1973, p. 432). "Every case without exception of 'chemical analysis' constitutes a well-marked example of the Method of Difference" (1973, p. 432); the list was readily extended.

ULTIMATE FACTS

The claim that the Canons provide an *analysis* of certain patterns of scientific reasoning answers part of Whewell's objection, but leaves open the part involving the problem of discovering categories. Mill had an answer to this question, but it happens to be an answer that creates difficulties for him in connection with social science. Mill treated many cases of scientific reasoning as instances of the Method of Agreement. Several cases that were important to the contemporary social sciences (notably the statistical observations that were becoming fashionable) were placed into this category, which he classed as a method of 'induction'. He argued that, *as* a method of induction, that is, a method of proof of causation, the Method of Agreement is of limited value: where "reversing the proof" by an experiment which produces the effect "artificially" is not possible (1973, p. 389), conclusions about causality must be "subject to very considerable doubt. Though an invariable, it may not be the unconditional antecedent of *a*, but may precede it as day precedes night or night day" (1973, p. 390), i.e. accidentally. Another difficulty with the method as a proof of cause is that "it is hardly ever possible to ascertain all the antecedents" (1973, p. 390). Mill took it that assuring ourselves that we have all the possible antecedents is easier when we are analyzing "a set of arrangements made by ourselves" (1973, p. 390), i.e. constructed experiments. But this is hardly helpful either in astronomy or in the social sciences.

Mill underscored the problem of discovering categories by saying that "the order of nature, as perceived at a first glance, presents at every instant a chaos followed by another chaos. We must decompose each chaos into single facts" (Mill, 1973, p. 379). Successful experiments provide some ground for confidence in our 'decompositions', but this is unhelpful where experiment is not possible. Where the problems are most severe, in the social sciences, Mill failed to take them up at all. The 'must' in the dictum is motivated in part by internal considerations arising in connection with the Canons. As we shall see in connection with Durkheim, the methods may fail if the categories do not correspond to the underlying laws. In the case of the Method of Concomitant Variation, the failure takes the form of producing empirical laws which are 'accidental'. The other methods are eliminative: thus if the true causes are misdescribed, they may be eliminated by the methods, or fail to be included in the list from which the process of elimination proceeds. The problem of ascertaining antecedents arises most visibly in connection with the plurality of causes. Mill's example was of a death that might have been caused by food poisoning or something else – each condition being sufficient to cause death, but neither being necessary. In this case, the Method of Agreement is 'crippled' by the 'plurality of causes', because it cannot *exclude* the possibility that the true cause is other than a given observed antecedent.

The 'must' in the dictum to 'decompose each chaos into single facts' is therefore puzzling, as Mill himself conceded.

If we were obliged to break down what we observe into its very simplest elements, that is, literally into single facts, it would be difficult to say where we should find them: we can hardly ever affirm that our divisions of any kind have reached the ultimate unit (1973, p. 380).

So the concept of simplest facts is a regulative ideal, underwritten by fallibilism about our categories:

It is only essential, at whatever point our mental decomposition of facts may for the present have stopped, that we should hold ourselves ready and able to carry it farther as occasion requires, and should not allow the freedom of our discriminating faculty to be imprisoned by the swathes and bands of ordinary classification (Mill, 1973, p. 381).

Mill concluded from this that social science, which usually lacks the aid of experiment in refining 'divisions', "must be to a great extent, if not principally, deductive" (1973, p. 384). The conclusion is puzzling. It suggests that Mill's response to Whewell was not to solve the issue of the source of categories so much as to run it together with the problems of complexity, for which he believed he had solutions.

Cases of complexity in the natural sciences provide Mill with models of handling complexity and of explanation by derivation which are repeated throughout his discussion of social science. Consider again the invariable sequential relationship of night and day, which is 'accidental', and various cases of concomitant variation which hold only within limits. In such cases, the relation "cannot," Mill said, "be considered to rest on a complete induction" (Mill, 1973, p. 405).

All that in such a case can be regarded as proved on the subject of causation is, that there is some connexion between the two phenomena; that A, or something which can influence A, must be *one* of the causes which collectively determine *a* (1973, p. 406, emphasis in original).

But we can account for them, as a class of uniformities, by a

distinction between two kinds of laws, or observed uniformities in nature: ultimate laws, and what may be termed derivative laws. Derivative laws are such as are deducible from, and may, in any of the modes which we have pointed out, be resolved into, other and more general ones. Ultimate laws are those which cannot (Mill, 1973, p. 484).

Although Mill never said that all empirical laws are ultimately 'derivable' from laws of nature, he clearly supposed that all those regularities that are much more extensive than coincidences must be derivable, or at least that in the presence of an unexplained empirical regularity, derivation will always be a goal of inquiry (cf. Mill, 1973, pp. 482–83).

Mill identified various kinds of derivation or explanation that might serve to account for 'empirical laws' or uniformities: the classic Baconian case of derivation from a wider generalization, cases where an "intermediate link in the sequence" is found, as in the study of the links in the chains that produce sensations (1973, p. 465), and cases where a complex effect is explained by or resolved "into the laws of the concurrent causes and the fact of their coexistence" (1973, p. 464), as where an intermixture of laws explains the effects of planetary motion. In Comte's classification of the sciences, the line between chemistry and physics was the major division within the physical or inorganic sciences, a distinction that was made in terms of the 'organized' character of chemicals. In Mill this division is construed in terms of the a distinction between "modes of the conjunct action of causes" (1973, p. 370). The physical 'composition of causes' is exemplified by the summing of the forces which determine the trajectory of a bullet (1973, p. 372). In the chemical type, summing the effects of causes acting separately does not predict relevant outcomes, such as the new properties of a compound (Mill, 1973, p. 371).

If the empirical laws of social science are the sort of empirical generalizations that come to us described in the "swathes and bands of ordinary classification" (1973, p. 381), and if they are to be derived from ultimate laws that are in closer correspondence with the simplest categories, and if, de facto, most of the explanations of these empirical laws by derivation are to involve composition, the ascent from common experience to causes (that is, to causes in the deeper nomic sense) is to be an arduous affair, in which difficulties deriving from each problem – the discovery of categories, the discovery of ultimate laws, and composition – compound the others. Each problem is nevertheless distinct, and Mill's successors often attempted to avoid this compounding by accepting Mill's account of one while rejecting his account of the other two. 'Chance' adds to the problems.

CHANCE AND CAUSE

Because Mill's eye was on the vindication of induction, he dealt with the problem of ascending from the world as given to the world of causal law by addressing it in the form of the Baconian problem of the probative weight of instances. Thus the question of the number of instances it takes to prove a law by the Method of Agreement was formulated as the question, How is one to conclude that "an observed coincidence between two phenomena is not the effect of chance?" (1973, p. 526). He decided that there is no general answer to the question, but that the frequency of the succession is itself a kind of evidence that the uniformity is a result of law (1973, p. 527). The significance of this step is that it placed frequent coincidences into the same category as empirical laws, which, as he had already argued, science was to explain by derivation from ultimate laws. This seems innocent enough, though Mill's argument in support of the expectation that a given set of coincidences is the result of some unknown law is quite weak. He conceded that "though the probability of a casual coincidence may be capable of appreciation, that of the counter-supposition, the existence of an undiscovered law of nature, is clearly insusceptible of even an approximate valuation" (1973, p. 546). However, he went on to say that if

the number of instances in which a coincidence is observed, over and above that which would arise on the average from the mere concurrence of chances, be such that so great an amount of coincidences from accident alone would be an extremely uncommon event; we have reason to conclude that the coincidence is the effect of causation, and may be received (subject to correction from further experience) as an empirical law. Further than this, in point of precision, we cannot go; nor, in most cases, is greater precision required, for the solution of any practical doubt (1973, p. 547).

The hope concealed in the argument is that the causes can in fact be discovered. In science, Mill said, the "detection of an unknown law of nature – of some previously unrecognised constancy of conjunction among phenomena – is no uncommon event" (1973, p. 547). The question this raises without answering is whether the point has any practical bearing on social science, where it *is* an 'uncommon event'. In short, the existence of a probability gives us no grounds for deciding between the supposition that the causal connection holds between the two phenomena contained in the law, or between some other unknown law. Moreover, of course, the relations expressed in empirical laws may be accidental rather than causal (Mill, 1973, p. 585).

His first pass at the problem of accounting for cases of probable relations was to comment on some relatively simple cases of experiment, where there are interfering or counteracting causes whose existence conceals the law and which we may "deduct from the observed frequency of coincidence" (1973, p. 529) to see if a residue of regularity remains. These cases are contrasted to more complex cases, where the interfering or counteracting causes "are so frequent, or so indeterminate, that we cannot possibly exclude all of them from any experiment, though we may vary them; our resource is, to endeavour to ascertain what is the effect of all the variable causes taken together" (1973, p. 530). Mill commented that the interpretation of these experiments is subject to the statistical proviso that averages of observations be subject to the law of the sum of least squares (Mill, 1973, p. 531). Thus does contemporary statistical thinking first enter *A System of Logic*. Curiously, the example Mill gives here, in which probability figures as a residue that nomic considerations cannot further reduce, is the basic template that is elaborated and expanded throughout Mill's discussions of the role of probability in relation to cause.

Mill changed his views on probability in the course of successive editions of the *Logic*. Indeed, here the changes are frequent and extensive (and much larger than the changes in connection with Comte). The sheer extent of the changes is revealing. They show that Mill was aware of the claims of the statisticians, took them seriously, and did not believe they could simply be argued away, as the claims of a Whewell could.

In the first edition, Mill rejected the 'classical', Laplacean view that probability was a matter of reducing "all the events of the same kind to a certain number of cases equally possible, that is to say, to such as we may be equally undecided about in regard to their existence" (Laplace, 1902, p. 6). Mill's objection was on empiricist grounds; it is fallacious, he thought, to reason from ignorance. "Why, in tossing up a halfpenny, do we reckon it equally probable that we shall throw cross or pile? Because we know that in any great number of throws, cross and pile are thrown about equally often; and that the more throws we make, the more nearly the equality is perfect" (Mill, 1973, pp. 534–35). He soon withdrew this objection, with the remark that

We must remember that the probability of an event is not a quality of the event itself, but a mere name for the degree of ground which we, or some one else, have for expecting it. The probability of an event to one person is a different thing from the probability of the same event to another, or to the same person after he has acquired additional evidence (1973, p. 535).

The concession is a narrow one, however, for only in that class of cases, such as "games of chance, where the very purpose in view requires ignorance instead of knowledge" does this kind of estimate of the probability of an event serve as the stopping point of inquiry (1973, p. 535).

In the normal case, where our knowledge is open to improvement, the importance of other warrants for expectations is overwhelming. Mill used the conventional example of drawing different colored balls from a box to make the point that a "very slight ground of surmise that the white balls were really more numerous than either of the other colours, would suffice to vitiate the whole of the calculations made in our previous state of indifference" (1973, p. 537). Indeed,

a very slight improvement in the data, by better observations, or by taking into fuller consideration the special circumstances of the case, is of more use than the most elaborate application of the calculus to probabilities founded on the data in their previous state of inferiority. The neglect of this obvious reflection has given rise to misapplications of the calculus of probabilities which have made it the real opprobrium of mathematics (Mill, 1973, p. 538).

What is neglected by the statisticians, Mill thought, is the fact that "knowledge of the proportion between the cases in which facts of that kind occur, and those in which they do not occur," can be "either derived from specific experiment, or deduced from our knowledge of the causes in operation which tend to produce, compared with those which tend to prevent, the fact in question" (Mill, 1973, p. 539).

Mill conceived of the relation between the varieties of fact as a kind of contest. "In estimating probabilities, it is not a matter of indifference from which of these two sources [causal reasoning or relative] frequency in past experience" "we derive our experience" (1973, p. 540). The evidence we get by counting relative frequencies is only that of the Method of Agreement, and its conclusions thus can only be an "empirical law" (1973, p. 540). Causal knowledge, he believed, is a stronger ground for expectation.

It is, in fact, evident, that when once causation is admitted as an universal law, our expectation of events can only be rationally grounded on that law. To a person who recognises that every event depends on causes, a thing's having happened once is a reason for expecting it to happen again, only because proving that there exists, or is liable to exist, a cause adequate to produce it. The frequency of the particular event, apart from all surmise respecting its cause, can give rise to no other induction than that *per enumerationem simplicem*; and the precarious inferences derived from this, are superseded, and disappear from the field, as soon as the principle of causation makes its appearance there (Mill, 1973, pp. 541–42).

In the 1851 edition, an early revision, this claim about the general preferability of causal warrants for expectations was expanded by Mill's remarking on why

we feel so much more probability added by the first instance, than by any single subsequent instance... Why, except that the first instance gives us its possibility (a cause *adequate* to it), while every other only gives us the frequency of its conditions? If no reference to a cause be supposed, possibility would have no meaning; yet it is clear, that, antecedent to its happening, we might have supposed the event impossible, i.e., have believed that there was no physical energy really existing in the world equal to producing it.... After the first time of happening, which is, then, more important to the whole probability than any other single instance (because proving the possibility), the *number* of times becomes important as an index to the intensity or extent of the cause, and its independence of any particular time (Mill, 1973, p. 541n, emphasis in original).

Although this passage was deleted in later editions, it had a consequence of historical importance: the terms 'adequate cause' and 'possibility' were adopted by the German probability theorists who were Weber's sources. In Mill, the concepts are scarcely developed at all. But the hint is clear: knowledge of an 'adequate cause', i.e., of the possibility that a given condition *can* cause a particular outcome, weighs much more heavily than additional knowledge of proportions, which cannot substitute for or warrant our knowledge of the existence of a causal relation.

The unusual feature of this reasoning, from the point of view of traditional inductivism, is that the sequence of steps is altered. Cause is not inferred from the collection of instances. We first discover one instance to be a cause, and then refine, by enumeration, our knowledge of the actual proportions. The departure from traditional induction, however, creates its own problems, for it becomes a puzzle as to how one can prove causation in the first instance. As we shall see, the later German theorists of adequate cause resolved this difficulty in a radically un-Millian way. Mill himself changed course. The point that he wished to make in those passages that are retained in later editions is that knowledge of causes, however limited, radically alters our expectations, and this shows the cognitive power of considerations of causation as against knowledge of past frequencies alone.

APPROXIMATE GENERALIZATIONS

Mill's first mention of modern statistical reasoning refers to an experiment. His discussion of nonexperimental cases opens with the example of the discovery of diurnal variations of barometric pressure. He treated this as a 'residual' regularity discovered through the 'elimination of chance'. In this case he did not, as he had in the case of the experiment, treat the 'elimination' as a matter of correcting for errors of *observation*. He reconstructed the 'induction' in this way:

A given effect is known to be chiefly, and not known not to be wholly, determined by changeable causes. If it be wholly so produced, then if the aggregate be taken of a sufficient number of instances, the effects of these different causes will cancel one another. If, therefore, we do not find this to be the case, but, on the contrary, after such a number of trials has been made that no further increase alters the average result, we find that average to be, not zero, but some other quantity, about which, though small in comparison with the total effect, the effect nevertheless oscillates, and which is the middle point in its oscillation; we may conclude this to be the effect of some constant cause: which cause, by some of the methods already treated of, we may hope to detect. This may be called *the discovery of a residual phenomenon by eliminating the effects of chance* (1973, p. 532, emphasis in original).

Although the 'effects of chance' in this case are caused, they are also, like the errors of observation in the case of experiment, local and small in magnitude relative to the large cause and effect relations, which are governed by highly general laws. It is questionable whether Mill ever entirely emancipated himself from the association of the concept of chance effects with cases of minor, local disturbances of general tendencies. In any case, as we shall see, cases that resemble this play a crucial role in his argument.

The cases of frequent coincidence which are central to his account of social science he called "approximate generalizations." These are "truths avowedly not universal; in which it is not pretended that the predicate is always true of the subject" (1973, p. 591). They are first discussed in Book Three, long before the issues of social science are taken up in detail, but they are basic to his reasoning that the phenomena of social life are governed by causal law. The difficulty Mill faced in giving an account of approximate generalizations is this: even if it is conceded that approximate truths or for that matter frequent coincidences suggest the *existence* of a causal law connecting, in some as yet unknown way, the phenomena in question, there is no reason to believe that the laws governing connections are going to be easily discovered. When he characterizes approximate generalizations as "steps towards" universal truths (1973, p. 591), or "as a stage on the road to something better" (1973, p. 592), he must give some sort of account of the road on which the steps are being taken. Half the rhetorical battle is won by calling them 'approximate generalizations', for the examples he was able to think up, such as this one found in the early draft of the *Logic*, "All Hindoos are accessible to bribes" (1973, p. 1100), turn out to be precisely the sorts of things one might regard as true in the main but admitting of individual exceptions which it might be possible to explain. Examples of this sort also make it possible to explain why approximate generalizations prove so useful in action.

Even when science has really determined the universal laws of any phenomenon, not only are those laws generally too much encumbered with conditions to be adapted for every-day use, but the cases which present themselves in life are too complicated, and our decisions require to be taken too rapidly, to admit of waiting till the existence of a phenomenon can be proved by what have been scientifically ascertained to be universal marks of it (1973, p. 592).

Approximate generalizations are pictured as generalizations unencumbered by conditions. Reasons why conditions might be cumbersome fall readily to hand. Even if we possess knowledge beyond the approximate generalization, this knowledge often "cannot be conveniently brought to bear on the particular instance" (1973, p. 594).

One wonders whether there are many approximate generalizations, and whether they look like the sorts of generalizations that might be refined. Mill answered this unstated question in a curious – but significant – way, not by inventorying them, but by stressing the practical situations in which the limitations of approximate generalizations can be largely ignored. Policy, for example, is

principally concerned with the actions not of solitary individuals, but of masses; with the fortunes not of single persons, but of communities. For the statesman ... it is generally enough to know that *most* persons act or are acted upon in a particular way; since his speculations and his practical arrangements refer almost exclusively to cases in which the whole community, or some large portion of it, is acted upon at once, and in which, therefore, what is done or felt by *most* persons determines the result produced by or upon the body at large. He can get on well enough with approximate generalizations on human nature, since what is true approximately of all individuals is true absolutely of all masses (Mill, 1973, p. 603, emphasis in original).

Mill considered this "a sufficient refutation of the popular error, that speculations on society and government, as resting on merely probable evidence, must be inferior in certainty and scientific accuracy to the conclusions of what are called the exact sciences, and less to be relied on in practice" (1973, p. 603). Mill's appeal to this 'refutation' is itself revealing, for it shows that he accepted not only the abstract extension of the principle of causality to the social realm, but accepted the solidity of a large body of quasi-nomic knowledge of the social realm. In itself, the existence of this knowledge suggests that the theoretical inadequacies of the social sciences result from 'complexity', not from the unreliability or unscientific character of the truths themselves: imprecise laws are laws nevertheless.

The existence of imprecise laws, however many, does not in itself show that they are a 'stage on the road' to anything. Mill distinguished the types of generalizations open to improvement. Some imprecise generalizations, which follow the form 'most springs have mineral substances', are not very important for science, for they can ordinarily be replaced by breaking a class down to subclasses of which precise generalizations are true, for example, by distinguishing subclasses of springs. In social science matters are not so easy. With inquiries concerning the actions of classes of human beings, the classification must be grounded on the circumstances of their mental culture and habits, which in an individual case are seldom exactly known; and classes grounded on these distinctions would never precisely accord with those into which mankind are divided for social purposes. All propositions which can be framed respecting the actions of human beings as ordinarily classified, or as classified according to any kind of outward indications, are merely approximate. We can only say, Most persons of a particular age, profession, country, or rank in society, have such and such qualities; or, Most persons when placed in certain circumstances act in such and such a way (Mill, 1973, pp. 593–94).

Part of the problem with these generalizations is practical, and derives from the inaccessibility of the relevant knowledge. "Not that we do not often know well enough on what causes the qualities depend, or what sort of persons they are who act in that particular way; but we have seldom the means of knowing whether any individual person has been under the influence of those causes, or is a person of that particular sort" (1973, p. 594). These difficulties pile up, and as their severity becomes evident, Mill's tone wavers. A matter of convenience becomes a matter of compulsion.

We could replace the approximate generalizations by propositions universally true; but these would hardly ever be capable of being applied to practice. We should be sure of our majors, but we should not be able to get minors to fit: we are forced, therefore, to draw our conclusions from coarser and more fallible indications (Mill, 1973, pp. 594).

Mill did not, as Weber later did, go on to argue that the fact that social science must settle for coarser indications radically alters the *logical* character of causal knowledge in the social sciences by rendering the goal of universally true propositions irrelevant. Instead, Mill treated the limitations as matters of causal complexity (and therefore of degree rather than differences of kind between concepts) and searched for natural science analogs to the kinds of science that the social sciences must be, if they are to be composed of approximate generalizations.

Among the questions that arise in connection with Mill's insistence on the practical value and importance of approximate generalizations is the pragmatic question of *how* they may be used. Given the uncertainty to which all science is prey, one might very well prefer, if this were a possibility, a science composed of a body of rough but useful generalizations, such as statisticians already provide. Mill was eager to close off any such possibility, and employed his stiffest skepticism against it. The basic elements of the argument are found in the earlier section on probability, where Mill was discussing the inferential uses of probabilistic claims. He accepted the claim that if we can count the occurrences of the relevant "local conditions" (Mill, 1973, p. 541) which cause given events, we can use the laws of chance, which govern series of coincidences, and multiply the known probabilities of causes to derive the probability of 'coincidental' outcomes. He pointed out that this multiplication is subject to the supposition

that the probabilities arising from A and C are independent of each other. There must not be any such connexion between A and C, that when a thing belongs to the one class it will therefore belong to the other, or even have a greater chance of doing so. Otherwise the not-Bs which are Cs may be, most or even all of them, identical with the not-Bs which are As; in which last case the probability arising from A and C together will be no greater than that arising from A alone (Mill, 1973, pp. 600–1).

The problem is with the assumption of independence, one aspect of which is the prior distribution. "When the major [premise] is Most B are D, then, even if the minor be Every A is B, we cannot infer that most A are D, or with any certainty that even some A are D. Though the majority of the class B have the attribute signified by D, the whole of the sub-class A may belong to the minority" (1973, p. 592). Characteristically, the lesson Mill drew from this is that the appropriate use of approximate generalizations are dependent on causal knowledge: their result,

like other unresolved derivative laws, can be relied on solely within the limits not only of place and time, but also of circumstance, under which its truth has been actually observed; for as we are supposed to be ignorant of the causes which make the proposition true, we cannot tell in what manner any new circumstance might perhaps affect it. The proposition, Most judges are inaccessible to bribes, would probably be found true of Englishmen, Frenchmen, Germans, North Americans, and so forth; but if on this evidence alone we extended the assertion to Orientals, we should step beyond the limits, not only of place but of circumstance, within which the fact had been observed, and should let in possibilities of the absence of the determining causes, or the presence of counteracting ones, which might be fatal to the approximate generalization (1973, pp. 594–95).

Shutting off the possibility of settling for a discipline composed of approximate generalizations unaided by causal considerations of this broader kind does not solve the problem of how the pursuit of causes is to proceed, however.

Mill made several distinct sets of comments on the subject of how to proceed in the face of causal complexity, each in response to different problems arising in connection with approximate generalizations. The responses to different issues do not always tally very closely, but they do share some thematic features and all bear on, and foreshadow, his account of social science. One set of remarks is in response to the question of "*How approximate generalizations may be converted into accurate generalizations equivalent to them*" (1973, p. 602, emphasis in original). He presented two kinds of case, which are explicitly labeled as "exceptions of the sort which are currently said to prove the rule," in which the approximate generalizations are "capable of being transformed into complete generalizations exactly equivalent" (1973, p. 602). The first kind of case is where

we are cognizant of the character which distinguishes the cases that accord with the generalization from those which are exceptions to it; we may then substitute for the approximate proposition, an universal proposition with a proviso. The proposition, Most persons who have uncontrolled power employ it ill, is a generalization of this class, and may be transformed into the following: – All persons who have uncontrolled power employ it ill, provided they are not persons of unusual strength of judgment and rectitude of purpose (1973, p. 602).

In the second case, where "inquiries ... relate to the properties not of individuals, but of multitudes," where "what is done or felt by *most* persons determines the result produced by or upon the body at large," we can proceed on the principle, "what is true approximately of all individuals is true absolutely of all masses" (1973, p. 603, emphasis in original).

A different set of comments relates to the general question of how one is to take account of exceptions. Mill's strategy here was to make the occurrence of exceptions appear to be an ordinary feature of science with an ordinary remedy. "All laws of causation, in consequence of their liability to be counteracted, require to be stated in words affirmative of tendencies only, and not of actual results" (1973, p. 445). A so-called exception to a principle "is always some other and distinct principle cutting into the former" (1973, p. 445). In the simpler cases, the remedy was to account for the exceptions. When Mill later came to stress that the laws of psychology and ethology are tendencies, this was a useful mental association to have established.

He used the point in connection with the "laws of society in general," i.e. sociology, as well. These, he said, are

in the strictest sense of the word, hypothetical. They are grounded on some suppositious set of circumstances, and declare how some given cause would operate in those circumstances, supposing that no others were combined with them. If the set of circumstances supposed have been copied from those of any existing society, the conclusions will be true of that society, provided, and in as far as, the effect of those circumstances shall not be modified by others which have not been taken into the account. If we desire a nearer approach to concrete truth, we can only aim at it by taking, or endeavouring to take, a greater number of individualizing circumstances into the computation (1974, p. 900).

In each of these sets of comments the theme is "the improvement of approximate generalizations through individualization." Yet Mill knew that, on his own account of the ubiquitous phenomena of the composition of causes, it is an open question as to whether such causal order as is to be found in the social sciences will in fact yield to this strategy. The exceptions, together with the approximate generalizations or frequent coincidences, may themselves be the result of intermixtures of laws and compositions of various minor causes which are not penetrable by way of the strategy of individualizing exceptions.

TIDOLOGY AS A MODEL

The analogies to imprecise natural sciences which Mill developed serve the purpose of making plausible the idea of the role of approximate generalizations. Mill used two examples of imprecise natural sciences. The first, meteorology, was used to show that the lack of predictive power does not undermine the claim that the facts of the social sciences "follow one another according to constant laws" and are therefore "fitted ... to be a subject of science" (1974, p. 844). In meteorology, the complexity and difficulty of procuring data preclude strong prediction. "Yet no one doubts that the phenomena depend on laws, and that these must be derivative laws resulting from known ultimate laws, those of heat, electricity, vaporization, and elastic fluids" (Mill, 1974, p. 844).

Mill made little more of this example. The analogue he made the most of is 'tidology', which, as it happens, was the study to which William Whewell was devoted. "General laws may be laid down respecting the tides, predictions may be founded on those laws, and the result will in the main, though often not with complete accuracy, correspond to the predictions" (1974, p. 845). But we cannot fully explain the results, and there is no autonomous theory of tidology. Whewell had tried to construct such a theory, by working with a number of hypotheses about the tides, including the idea of 'cotidal lines' and had "concluded that no theory of physical astronomy could account for tidal phenomena in a general way. Instead, the variety and multiplicity of the data suggested that detailed study of each individual shoreline was required" (Butts, 1976, p. 293).

Mill took the example over as a paradigm case of a science in which minor local causes are to be found interfering with large general causes.

As much of the phenomena as depends on the attraction of the sun and moon is completely understood, and may in any, even unknown, part of the earth's surface, be foretold with certainty; and the far greater part of the phenomena depends on those causes. But circumstances of a local or casual nature, such as the configuration of the bottom of the ocean, the degree of confinement from shores, the direction of the wind, &c., influence, in many or in all places, the height and time of the tide; and a portion of these circumstances being either not accurately knowable, not precisely measurable, or not capable of being certainly foreseen, the tide in known places commonly varies from the calculated result of general principles by some difference that we cannot explain, and in unknown ones may vary from it by a difference that we are not able to foresee or conjecture (Mill, 1974, p. 845).

Mill's image of the present position of social science was similar: the greater part of the phenomena depends on psychological causes which are largely understood; but 'local or casual' circumstances, some of which are identifiable, some of which are not, make it difficult for us to predict or to remove the differences between the large effects we can predict and the variations we can observe. His problem was to convince us that the body of approximate generalizations we possess – or that Mill acted as though we possess – are causal in the requisite sense, i.e., contain understandable and large causes together with minor local causes.

The analogy with tidology provides an analysis, or perhaps more properly a characterization, of the approximate generalizations we already possess. Mill proceeded by characterizing the relevant observational evidence in ways that are consistent with this larger picture. The observational evidence which pertains to the sciences of human nature, psychology (which contains the laws of mind) and ethology (the science of character) is far removed from ultimate explanations.

We can only make our observations in a rough way, and *en masse*; not attempting to ascertain completely in any given instance, what character has been formed, and still less by what causes; but only observing in what state of previous circumstances it is found that certain marked mental qualities or deficiencies *oftenest* exist. These conclusions, besides that they are mere approximate generalizations, deserve no reliance, even as such, unless the instances are sufficiently numerous to eliminate not only chance, but every assignable circumstance in which a number of the cases examined may happen to have resembled one another. So numerous and various, too, are the circumstances which form individual character, that the consequence of any particular combination is hardly ever some definite and strongly marked character, always found where that combination exists, and not otherwise (Mill, 1974, p. 866, emphasis in original).

The imperfections of our knowledge of the circumstances that go into particular individual cases make positive prediction on the basis of this kind of evidence hopeless. Thus the futility of individual prediction is combined with the practical possibility of rough prediction, and this paradoxical combination is the key to Mill's argument. The force of the predictions is obscure.

If, in the case of any individual, our data could be complete, we even now know enough of the ultimate laws by which mental phenomena are determined, to enable us in many cases to predict, with tolerable certainty, what, in the greater number of supposable combinations of circumstances, his conduct or sentiments would be (1974, p. 847).

Yet this value is limited, in that

the impressions and actions of human beings are not solely the result of their present circumstances, but the joint result of those circumstances and of the characters of the individuals: and the agencies which determine human character are so numerous and diversified, (nothing which has happened to the person throughout life being without its portion of influence,) that in the aggregate they are never in any two cases exactly similar (1974, p. 847).

Nevertheless, despite these limitations,

many of those effects which it is of most importance to render amenable to human foresight and control are determined like the tides, in an incomparably greater degree by general causes, than by all partial causes taken together; depending in the main on those circumstances and qualities which are common to all mankind, or at least to large bodies of them, and only in a small degree on the idiosyncrasies of organization or the peculiar history of individuals; it is evidently possible with regard to all such effects, to make predictions which will *almost* always be verified, and general propositions which are almost always true (1974, p. 847, emphasis in original).

In the case of tidology, the connection between the large causes and basic physical law was relatively close, and the basic physics explain a large part of the effect: prediction and physical law here stand in a close relation. Mill conceived of social science on this model.

It is at least possible to think of the case of the everyday knowledge about action we employ in our own society differently. We may regard the kind of practical knowledge of the social realm we possess as standing largely on its own, and not on any foundation of psychological laws. As Mill admitted, "a very imperfect knowledge of the causes" (1974, p. 869), together with some knowledge of relative frequencies, make it feasible to give predictions that have practical value. If it *were* the case that the body of approximate generalizations to which he has been referring consisted of generalizations whose causal force derived from minor local causes and not larger and more general causes modified by minor local causes, Mill's picture would break down. The best response to this possibility would be for Mill to produce examples of explanations in which the approximate generalizations that do the explaining are shown to divide into these categories and then large causes are shown to correspond to a more general law of some sort. Mill did not do this, of course, so he was limited to conveying the *impression* that this is how the explanations would look, and to making optimistic assertions.

All of the actual generalizations Mill cited are approximate generalizations on the order of 'Youth is impetuous'. Using them to warrant images of ultimate laws is obviously questionable. They served his purposes because of the way he characterized them, and he characterized them in ways that emphasize the similarities between approximate generalizations and ultimate laws. In the first place, practical approximate generalizations are not *merely* approximate generalizations. Practical knowledge consists largely in approximate *tendencies*. For practical purposes, as he said, "it is enough that we know that certain means have a *tendency* to produce a given effect, and that others have a tendency to frustrate it" (Mill, 1974, p. 869, emphasis in original). Presumably the practical usefulness of these tendency statements is a warrant for their validity not merely as empirical laws but as tendency statements: Mill is nowhere explicit about this. What he stressed instead is that the claim that these approximate generalizations are related in a specific way to the real laws of human nature, whose "truths are not, like the empirical laws which depend on them, approximate generalizations, but real laws" (1974, p. 870), which are also 'tendencies'. This is a claim that is central to the characterization, and to the impression Mill sought to convey. But it is not, in itself, easily supported by argument, especially in the absence of any known ultimate laws or 'real' laws of human nature. Mill's argument is that even if the observations concerning human affairs collected from common experience "were universally and exactly true within the bounds of experience, which they never are, still they are not the ultimate laws of human action; they are not the principles of human nature, but results of those principles under the circumstances in which mankind have happened to be placed" (Mill, 1974, pp. 861–62).

The disjunction between the 'circumstances in which mankind is placed' and the principles of human nature is parallel in form to the disjunction between the local causes and large principles of tidology. But we have no clear reason to believe that this disjunction will be reproduced at the level of real laws. The generalizations Mill gave as examples fit the theme of improvement by accounting for exceptions and by individualizing conditions; they do not point very directly to large principles of human nature. So Mill's claims about the form of these ultimate principles depends very much on what Mill told us an explanation of these approximate generalizations *would* consist in. Here, as we have seen, he was highly explicit. The "real scientific truths" are of course not the "empirical laws, but the causal laws which explain them," the empirical laws having "no other function in science than that of verifying the conclusions of theory" (1974, p. 862), and "the *explanation*" of these laws would tell us "the conditions which ultimately determine whether the law holds good or not" (1974, p. 862, emphasis added).

We arrive at this vivid picture more by seduction than by argument. To say that this is how these explanations would or ought to proceed is of course not to say that they *can* in fact proceed in this way, or that our approximate generalizations can be refined in the appropriate way. Why should we believe that they can? Mill's means of supporting this hope is striking. He continued to fend off any expectation that he give serious examples of the real laws of human nature he envisioned by stressing the remoteness of these laws from the approximate generalizations we have. The (mostly fatuous) examples of approximate generalizations we are given indeed have the form of tendency statements for which we may think up exceptions, either classes of exceptions or individual exceptions, for which we can 'assign circumstances' of various kinds. When these examples are discussed as approximate generalizations, we are reminded that they depend on real laws; when they are used as a convenient substitute for examples of real laws, in discussions of the logical properties of real explanations of individual action, the characterization is reinforced, without giving it any more substance. The characterization is sustained by the hope of ultimate explanation, the hope by the characterization.

THE LOGICAL STRUCTURE OF SOCIAL SCIENCE

If we accept the existence of some large class of practical approximate generalizations, and accept Mill's characterization of their relation to the ultimate laws of the science of human nature, something may be said about the relations between these laws and the laws of other sciences well in advance of their full articulation. The logical hierarchy of the sciences is a matter of the relations between the explanatory or quasi-explanatory principles of various sciences *as principles*, that is, as laws that might be used to explain other laws. If we begin with the problem of the logical structure which principles of ethology must have, and then ask how these explanations are explained, and what patterns they might be used to explain, we come to a different arrangement than the simple hierarchical succession found in Comte. For Mill the special social sciences are like separate columns in a structure in which the base is psychology and the roof is sociology. The role of laws of ethology are illustrative of the difference in logical structure.

The laws of the formation of character are ... derivative laws, resulting from the general laws of mind; and are to be obtained by deducing them from those general laws; by supposing any given set of circumstances, and then considering what, according to the laws of mind, will be the influence of those circumstances on the formation of character (1974, p. 869).

The approximate generalizations of ethology, such as 'youth is impetuous', which have already been framed empirically (1974, p. 869), are explained by these laws, and this is a means of 'verification' for the laws of mind. In this scheme, the laws of the general social science come to have the same logical status as *en masse* observations and broad historical patterns: each is to be accounted for by the laws of the special social sciences. Here the picture becomes very muddled.

Mill claimed that observations *en masse* are not a direct solution to the problem of 'verification' because they are so very far removed from the laws themselves (1974, p. 866). The approximate generalizations one obtains through observation *en masse* are thus objects of explanation without being means of *testing* laws: chance and complexity loom so large in the makeup of these observations that they lack probative force. Mill's solution to the twin problems of the difficulty of deduction and the impossibility of the 'direct' verification of causes in the face of chance and complexity is to accept a larger element of apriorism to rely on "collating the conclusions of the ratiocination either with the concrete phenomena themselves, or, when such are obtainable, with their empirical laws. The ground of confidence in any concrete deductive science is not the *a priori* reasoning itself, but the accordance between its results and those of observation *a posteriori*" (Mill, 1974, pp. 896–97). As he described the process, we "begin by obtaining ... [our conclusions] provisionally from specific experience, and afterwards connect them with the principles of human nature by *a priori* reasonings" (1974, p. 897). Because this reverses the usual order of precedence, Mill called it 'inverse' deduction.

Mill's sense of how this process of the building up of the logical structure of social science law would in fact proceed reflected his sense of the state of development of each of the relevant sciences. Mill was quite prepared to say that the basic outlines of psychology were clear, and that "it is at least certain" what general logical form the laws would take (1974, p. 863). Yet he left open such questions as "whether the ultimate laws of our mental nature are few or many" (1974, p. 863), and he was also prepared to concede that the predictive capacity of present psychology is slight. The former question may be thought of as a technical problem of theory construction. The number of 'axioms' is going to be a matter of the extent to which these basic laws prove to be derivable from one another, something that cannot be settled in advance, so it is perhaps of little consequence that he left this question open. The lack of predictive capacity of this psychology is more consequential, but one can see Mill's motivation for the concession.

As Comte had pointed out, political economy is a science whose lack of predictive capacity renders it suspect. Mill needed to exempt it from this kind of criticism in order to fit his own economic writings into his scheme of social science.

'Ethology' he thought to be on the verge of developing an appropriate deductive structure. The maxims which he expected to make up 'psychology' were, he said, "now sufficiently understood ... to render it possible for a competent thinker to deduce from those laws with a considerable approach to certainty, the particular type of character which would be formed, in mankind generally, by any assumed set of circumstances" (1974, p. 873). The task of deriving the *axiomata media*, the laws holding under given circumstances, was now ready to proceed, at least in ethology, by applying the inverse deductive method. As Mill described it, the procedure would be

a double process: first, that of deducing theoretically the ethological consequences of particular circumstances of position, and comparing them with the recognised results of common experience; and secondly, the reverse operation; increased study of the various types of human nature that are to be found in the world; conducted by persons not only capable of analysing and recording the circumstances in which these types severally prevail, but also sufficiently acquainted with psychological laws, to be able to explain and account for the characteristics of the type, by the peculiarities of the circumstances: the residuum alone, when there proves to be any, being set down to the account of congenital predispositions (Mill, 1974, p. 873).

Mill apparently thought that he himself would do this. "In fact," as Bain said, the project of ethology "never came to anything; and he seems shortly to have dropped thinking of it" (Bain, 1882, p. 78). This leaves the matter of explaining *en masse* observations hanging. It is as though Mill thought that once ethology was figured out, the *en masse* observations we possess would, like the various unexplained phenomena of the natural world, be explained at such time as the nomic structure of social science reached them. The problem of the character of sociological laws could not be put off quite so easily, however.

SOCIOLOGY AND THE 'COLLECTIVE ORGANISM'

Mill's account of the general social science, Comte's 'sociology', can best be grasped by a systematic comparison. Mill conceded that "we are able to obtain the best empirical laws" (1974, p. 897), and therefore are able to use Comte's 'method' in precisely those situations "which, from their prodigious complication, the method of direct deduction is altogether inapplicable" (1974, p. 897). These include 'political ethology' and sociology, the "general Science of Society" (1974, p. 906), both of which explain 'aggregate patterns', or 'observations *en masse*', such as the Comtean pattern of the collective organism going through successive 'states.' Mill agreed with Comte that the fact which "essentially determines" the state of society is "the state of the speculative faculties" (Mill, 1974, p. 926). The historical evidence strongly supports the conclusion "that the order of human progression in all respects will mainly depend on the order of progresssion in the intellectual convictions of mankind, that is, on the law of the successive transformations of human opinions" (Mill, 1974, p. 927).

Mill wished to claim that the explanation of the process of the patterns of 'dynamics' or successsion, and the patterns of 'statics' or coexistence, are not, as Comte believed, autonomous laws, but that instead "the mode of production of all social phenomena is one great case of Intermixture of Laws" (Mill, 1974, p. 899). Thus Mill insisted that the law that states that human progression depends on intellectual progression is an 'empirical law' that needs explanation, by derivation from the genuinely explanatory laws of psychology and laws governing local conditions found in the special social sciences. 'Ethology', and specifically political ethology, he believed, would contribute "the most important class of sociological laws" (1974, p. 905) and thus provide much of the immediate foundation for the general social science (1974, pp. 906–7).

He nevertheless found this difficult to maintain, and frequently slid back to a recognition of the *de facto* autonomy of sociological laws, especially when he concerned himself with characteristically Comtean problems, and when he attempted to reformulate Comtean ideas. The Comtean notion of consensus reappears in Mill in the form of the idea that intermixture is a causal feature of the domain of sociology understood as the science of states of society: "There is no social phenomenon which is not more or less influenced by every other part of the condition of the same society, and therefore by every cause which is influencing any other of the contemporaneous social phenomena" (1974, p. 899), which is to say that there is a 'consensus' among the causes such that the same cause has different effects in the different causal contexts of different 'states of society' (1974, p. 899), and this assures the independence of sociological laws.

Comte's approach was to start with the laws of a complex phenomenon, the collective organism, and seek the laws relating its constituent parts to the whole. Comte's use of the concept of the collective organism is taken up by Mill in *A System of Logic*, and the general contrast between mechanical and organic conceptions of society is taken up in 'Representative

Government' (Mill, 1910). The same two related but distinct themes, the 'harmony' that results from the causal fact of the interdependence of a large number of causes, and the fact which Mill called 'social stability' and Comte called 'order', figure in both Mill's and Comte's uses of the notion of the organism. For Mill, the list of interdependent causes included

the degree of knowledge, and of intellectual and moral culture, existing in the community, and in every class of it; the state of industry, of wealth and its distribution; the habitual occupations of the community; their division into classes, and the relations of those classes to one another; the common beliefs which they entertain on all the subjects most important to mankind, and the degree of assurance with which those beliefs are held; their tastes, and the character and degree of their aesthetic development; their form of government, and the more important of their laws and customs (Mill, 1974, pp. 911–12).

The observed "Uniformities of Coexistence" between various facts of this type "must ... be corollaries from the laws of causation by which these phenomena are really determined. The mutual correlation between the different elements of each state of society, is therefore a derivative law" (1974, p. 912).

The "*consensus* of the various parts of the social body" is understood to mean "the influence exercised by every one of those phenomena over every other" (1974, p. 912, emphasis in original). Mill's analysis of this consensus is causal throughout. He gave even less justification than Comte for usages like 'social body'. He was sparing in appealing to them, but when he did, he used them interchangeably with the notion of 'society', and without seeming to give it any special ontological or explanatory force. Nothing causal was meant to follow from the concept, for it was presumed that the explanations of states of society would be by causes, and the composition of causes, and that the nomological force of the causal explanations would come by way of derivation from the laws of psychology, a derivation to be mediated by the *axiomata media* of the special social sciences with their various domains of causes.

Despite the practical political importance of social stability, the problem was not theoretically central for Mill; it arose only incidentally to the study of coexistences. Stability is an aggregate fact about 'society', a 'state'. Thus, social stability is not implied by the consensus of causes, or by some teleological concept of the social body, but is one of the aggregate consequences that is explained by the Uniformities of Coexistence one discovers with the principle of consensus of causes in hand. Mill had his own suggestions about the conditions of social stability, which included such things as a sense of loyalty to the regime, to a common God, or to the protectors of the state (1974, p. 922), "a strong and active principle of cohesion among the members of the same community or state" (1974, p. 923), and

for all who were not slaves, kept down by brute force ... a system of *education*, beginning with infancy and continued through life, of which whatever else it might include, one main and incessant ingredient was *restraining discipline*. To train the human being in the habit, and thence the power, of subordinating his personal impulses and aims, to what were considered the ends of society; of adhering, against all temptation, to the course of conduct which those ends prescribed; of controlling in himself all feelings which were liable to militate against those ends, and encouraging all such as tended towards them.... (Mill, 1974, p. 921, emphasis in original).

These conditions often do not obtain. So with the principle of consensus one also discovers the conditions of *in*stability, and of other 'states' of society.

STATISTICS AND HISTORY

Mill's discussion of chance began with skepticism about the application of the most simple of the deductions that may be performed on the basis of knowledge of dependent probabilities, and stressed the relative importance of knowledge of causes. The model of tidology, i.e., of large effects that are modified by local causes, served him as a model in which approximate generalizations could be underwritten by basic causal principles. These are 'approximate' or 'imprecise sciences'. They are sciences that have some deductive structure but are made up of approximate generalizations: the special social sciences fall into this category. The larger deductive structure in which these generalizations fit is one in which the approximate generalizations of the special social sciences are explained by the tendency statements of psychology together with conditions, and where the patterns at the highest level, i.e. of sociology, are explained by the laws of the intermediate social sciences, to which they are to be linked by such devices as the composition of causes.

If we return to earth – to the *en masse* observations that empirical social science has in hand – the radical utopianism of this vision becomes apparent. As we have seen, these observations get lost in the shuffle when Mill depicts this structure of deductively and compositionally linked tendency statements. They are too distant from the explanatory tendencies to serve to verify them, so they must wait in the antechamber of social science until nomic science is ready for them.

When Mill was forced to make sense of the role of these *en masse*

observations, he did so by arguing that the preliminary work of the general
social science consists "in finding general propositions which express con-
cisely what is common to large classes of observed facts" (Mill, 1974,
p. 907). History and statistics supply examples of this work, and Mill
accounted for the case of historical pattern by analogy to his treatment of
statistics. The role of statistics is strictly limited. "In statistics," he said, "it
is evident that empirical laws may sometimes be traced" (1974, p. 907), and
sometimes statistical inquiry will give surprising results, as might an inquiry
into the distribution of causes of bankruptcy. But the empirical laws to be
discovered by statistical inquiry are to be handled with caution. Statistics
is at most "a means (happening accidentally to be the only, or the best,
available) for obtaining the necessary data for the deductive science" (1974,
p. 908). We must keep in mind that

When the immediate causes of social facts are not open to direct observation, the empirical
law of the effects gives us the empirical law (which in that case is all that we can obtain) of
the causes likewise. But those immediate causes depend on remote causes; and the empirical
law, obtained by this indirect mode of observation, can only be relied on as applicable to
unobserved cases, so long as there is reason to think that no change has taken place in any
of the remote causes on which the immediate causes depend (Mill, 1974, p. 908).

This means that "even where conclusions derived from specific observation
are available for practical inferences in new cases, it is necessary that the
deductive science should stand sentinel over the whole process; that it
should be constantly referred to, and its sanction obtained to every
inference" (1974, p. 908).

   This accomodation to statistics reflects a deep suspicion of the claims
of the statisticians, and these claims continued to make Mill uneasy. In a
chapter added to the last four editions of *A System of Logic*, Mill discussed
Henry Thomas Buckle's *History of Civilization in England*, which made a
strong case for the importance of statistical regularities. Mill endorsed this
case, and repeated Buckle's insistence on the conflict between our commonsense views of moral responsibility and the remarkable uniformity of
social statistics.

What act is there which all would consider as more completely dependent on individual
character, and on the exercise of individual free will, than that of slaying a fellow creature?
Yet in any large country, the number of murders, in proportion to the population, varies ...
very little from one year to another, and in its variations never deviates widely from a certain
average. What is still more remarkable, there is a similar approach to constancy in the
proportion of these murders annually committed (Mill, 1974, p. 932).

Mill was quick to put this to use in support of his own views. "This singular degree of regularity *en masse*, combined with the extreme of irregularity in the cases composing the mass, is a felicitous verification *a posteriori* of the law of causation in its application to human conduct" (1974, p. 933). But he gave the causal character of these facts a specific reading, in line with his working distinction between general causes and local conditions:

Every human action, every murder for instance, is the concurrent result of two sets of causes. On the one part, the general circumstances of the country and its inhabitants; the moral, educational, economical, and other influences operating on the whole people, and constituting what we term the state of civilization. On the other part, the great variety of influences special to the individual: his temperament, and other peculiarities of organization, his parentage, habitual associates, temptations, and so forth. If we now take the whole of the instances which occur within a sufficiently large field to exhaust all the combinations of these special influences, or in other words, to eliminate chance; and if all these instances have occurred within such narrow limits of time, that no material change can have taken place in the general influences constituting the state of civilization of the country; we may be certain, that if human actions are governed by invariable laws, the aggregate result will be something like a constant quantity. The number of murders committed within that space and time, being the effect partly of general causes which have not varied, and partly of partial causes the whole round of whose variations has been included, will be, practically speaking, invariable (1974, p. 933).

The invariability of the rate thus is not granted the *de facto* autonomy of sociological tendencies, or, for that matter, of the practically valuable approximate tendency statements he discussed at such length earlier. The stability of rates is contingent upon the continuation of the general influences, and on the 'local' causes, at least the independence and randomness of the local conditions in relation to the general causes.

All this one would expect. But the analysis also shows the distance between these *en masse* observations, which are the largest kind of systematic data then or now possessed by social science, and the laws that are to explain them. In this respect, matters are far worse than in tidology. In tidology the basic principles are known, and the complexity arises with the local causes. With murder rates, one has no approximate generalizations that resemble anything that one might take to be closely related to a basic psychological principle. There *are* no large effects to be distinguished from local effects – the opacity of the local causes, the sheer complexity which makes it so extraordinarily difficult to turn tidology into a precise science, is not limited to a relatively small *residue* of variation, but extends to the whole of the rate. To say that one will take the two sets of causal influences of which Mill spoke – the 'general circumstances of the country' and the 'great variety of influences special to the individual' – and reduce them to a deductive, compositional causal explanation is to retreat from the world of the possible to the world of speculative philosophy in the pejorative sense of the phrase.

It will suffice to observe the highly promissory character of this accomodation to the explanatory and predictive claims made for statistical rates. Mill's remark that "deductive sciences should stand sentinel" over the application in new circumstances of conclusions drawn from statistics is telling. The remote causes and laws with which we are supposed to ultimately explain (and govern the use in new circumstances of) the statistics are remote indeed, both in the sense that a great many deductive steps would be required to link the causes with the rates and in the sense that the time at which such laws might conceivably be available is the remote future. The largely complete laws (and laws of composition) of several sciences admittedly in their infancy would be required to give an explanation of an aggregate fact like a murder rate, which is, after all, a simple example.

The historical implausibility of this accomodation may be seen in terms of the problem of 'ascent'. For Bacon, the ascent was a process of building universals on the collection of particulars and on prerogative instances that point to universals; for Comte, it was the gradual remodeling of a structure already built, by replacing metaphysical elements with positive ones. For Mill, the structure is based on a solid but rough foundation of approximate psychological truths, on which another rough structure of approximate ethological truths is built. On this structure large-scale historical patterns of social development will ultimately rest. At present, however, the elements of the structure which connect the laws to the patterns is no more than a huge scaffolding, made largely of rather flimsy a priori material, its apriorism dignified as science by the imprimatur of the Inverse Deductive Method. The Inverse Deductive Method is, one might say, a method of building theories with a large scaffolding connecting statistical and historical patterns to remote causes. This scaffolding is to hold the laws of the special sciences until they are refined to the point that they stand as laws, and, by the composition of causes, are able to hold the en masse statistical observations up directly. The flaw here is that building such a scaffolding is itself far more difficult than Mill imagined. The enormous deductive distance between laws and en masse observations is key. The Inverse Method amounts to a license to use whatever a priori principles can be invented that more or less fit with what Mill called 'common experience' to 'collate' or 'connect' the laws of human nature with the kind of complex, mixed aggregate facts which are the en masse observations of social science.

Mill apparently thought that the principles that were useful in making one 'connection' could be made to square with the principles that were useful in making others – that the pieces would begin to fit together, like a puzzle. For this hope he had no basis. In the absence of a highly developed framework of such principles, including principles of composition, the notion of these sciences 'standing sentinel' over statistics is without practical meaning. One can scarcely be a sentinel over what one cannot reasonably hope to reach in the foreseeable future.

Infant sentinels are not likely to be very effective ones. By the time of the later editions of *A System of Logic*, the study of statistical rates was no longer in *its* infancy. So Mill's vision of deductive science standing as a sentinel over the process of using and generalizing from the empirical laws discovered by statistical methods was out of date by the time it was formulated. What occurred was this: *en masse* observations accumulated rapidly, without being integrated into any substantial theoretical structure, like bricks piled at a building site. Others chose to do what they could with the bricks.

CHAPTER FOUR

QUETELET: RATES AND THEIR EXPLANATION

Comte's disdain for statistics had resonance beyond its echoes in the milder criticisms made by Mill in *A System of Logic*. Claude Bernard, the influential biologist and philosopher of experimentalism, who carefully distanced himself from Positivism in the course of the dispute over vitalism which pitted Pasteur against Comte's followers (Virtanen, 1960, pp. 2–4), shared in Comte's and Mill's suspicion of the claims of the statisticians.

Statistics ... is of use only in directing the observer toward the research for this undetermined cause, but it can never lead to any real law.... By basing itself on statistics, medicine could never be more than a conjectural science; it is only by basing itself on experimental determinism that it will become a true science.... (quoted in Virtanen, 1960, p. 21; cf. Bernard, 1952, pp. 194–95).

Was this a misunderstanding of the claims of the statisticians? Or did the temptation to close off inquiry prematurely and the notion that statistics provided a substitute for 'real law' lurk in the assertions and practices of contemporary statisticians?

The statistician whose concerns and claims come closest to Mill's and Comte's was Adolphe Quetelet, a figure who appears in a curiously varied collection of intellectual environments. Quetelet was trained in mathematics, which he taught in a private school from the age of seventeen. He later became an instructor at the new University of Ghent, where he earned a doctorate in mathematics from a Frenchman who had fallen from favor with the Paris authorities. During the twenties, he was in Brussels, where he was exposed to more French refugees, marrying into a refugee family in 1825. During the same year he formed the 'Society of Twelve', and in the following year created 'La Société Belge pour la Propaganda de l'Instruction et de la Moral', whose aim was to promote tolerance and mass education. These groups were Saint-Simonian in inspiration, and despite the efforts of the authorities of the new Kingdom of the Netherlands, who promptly suppressed the society and imprisoned some of Quetelet's friends, Saint-Simonianism grew in influence among Belgian intellectuals. Thus, like Mill, Comte, and of course Marx – whose father participated in a Saint-Simonian study group when Marx was a youth – Quetelet's thought was a product of Saint-Simonianism (Diamond, 1969, pp. v–vi).

Quetelet retained and extended the Saint-Simonian language of social physiology, and added to it with such notions as social 'mechanics', 'social physics', and the like. Comte had no monopoly on these terms, and the fact that he shared them with Quetelet doubtless added an edge to his denunciations of statistics. The two careers progressed very differently: where the hubristic Comte struggled, the modest, gregarious, and equally industrious Quetelet thrived, becoming friendly with many of the great scientists and intellectuals of the day, including the circle of mathematically oriented Cambridge-trained physicists and philosophers, a group that included Herschel, Whewell, and Babbage.

The 'external' fact that was the basis of Quetelet's importance was the rapid development of interest in official enumerations of various kinds, such as the censuses of Paris of the twenties. Little of the sort of data which the statisticians in these societies studied had been systematically collected fifty years earlier. The first modern British census was carried out in 1801. Physical measurements such as those analyzed by the anthropometers of the century were not collected prior to the development of the modern mass army. These newly gathered materials supplied one of Quetelet's pet examples – the chest measurements of Scottish recruits. In 1833, these developments, and others like it, led to the creation of a section on statistics in the British Association for Advancement of Science, and in 1834 to the founding of the Statistical Society of London (Hankins, 1908, pp. 29–30). Quetelet was present at each founding, and was an active figure in the international movement for the collection of comparable statistics.

The ordering of these large masses of data into an intelligible form was a formidable practical task, and the ways in which it was accomplished reflected the needs of those who had uses for the data. The methods of organizing data that were developed at this time, as well as many of the basic modes of analysis, have remained standard practice to the present day. The methods were tabular, and problems of life insurance were the primary practical inspiration and the primary beneficiary of the new statistical data and methods. The textbooks of the day which purport to apply the concepts of probability to the moral and political sciences (e.g. Laplace, 1902) typically devoted the bulk of their discussions of applications to life insurance and annuities.

By this time, the large insurance companies had acquired enough data in their own records to construct mortality rates for various categories of the population, such as occupation (Farr, 1885). To write insurance, it was of course useful to know the probability of the event that was being insured against. As the probabilities varied according to the categories into which individuals fell, estimation depended on selecting categories, on the 'art' of constructing tables that were simple enough to be used, but that subcategorized in the ways that captured important differences in rates of occurrence of outcome events. When the categories were continuous variables, such as age, these purposes were best served (and, in modern terms, the least 'information lost') by reducing the relationships within categories to an algebraic formula.

William Farr, who was superintendent of the British Statistical Department, constructed life-tables for the Registrar General's Office, and his introduction to the life-tables published in the 1843 annual report of that office deals with the general construction of these formulae. A colleague later recalled "the expression of his countenance, beaming with pleasure and triumph, almost childlike in its unaffected simplicity, when (during the progress of the Life Table, No.3,) he reached the office one morning with a small page or two of MS., containing *one* of those formulae which had taken him *all the night* to work out" (Humphreys, 1885, p. xvi, emphasis in original). The mathematical work was curve fitting, and it resembled the curve fitting of other areas of science. If we see Farr in the discourse of his time, locate his statistical interests within his other scientific interests, compare his biography with the biographies of his contemporaries, and place him within the intellectual circles of the time, we can see how statistical practice developed autonomously and without the 'sentinel' of nomic social science standing over it. Farr was trained as a physician (in Paris, where the disturbances of 1830, in addition to presenting him with a vivid introduction to the people, gave him the opportunity to see many gunshot wounds). Thus he was himself a 'scientist'. He saw no fundamental distinction between his statistical work and other areas of science.

When he wrote on medical subjects, he presented his formulations as 'laws', as in 'The Law of Recovery and Mortality in Cholera Spasmodica', published in 1838 in the *Lancet*. In the same year, the *Lancet* published his 'Benevolent Funds, and Life Assurance in Health and Disease'. Among his other papers, were 'The Mortality of Lunatics', in 1841; 'Influence of Scarcities and of the Prices of Wheat on the Mortality of the People of England', read in 1846; 'Influence of Elevation on the Fatality of Cholera', in 1852; 'Income and Property Tax', in 1853; 'On the Pay of Ministers of the Crown', in 1857; 'Mortality of Children in the Principal States of Europe', in 1866; 'Valuation of Railways, Telegraphs, Water Companies, Canals, and Other Commercial Concerns, With Prospective, Deferred,

Increasing, Decreasing, or Terminating Profits', first read in 1873; 'Some Doctrines of Population', 1877; 'Babbage's Analytical Machine', in 1878; and 'Density or Proximity of Population: Its advantages and Disadvantages', also in 1878 (Humphreys, 1885, pp. xiii, xv, xviii).

The sheer range of these papers is suggestive: the statisticians were not shy about pushing into new topics. The use of the term 'law' is equally suggestive. There is a natural extension from its uses in medical contexts, such as the rates of death and recovery in cholera, to social contexts: the medical and social categories overlap, and the technical problems of curve fitting are precisely similar in the various cases. Statistics practiced in this way begins to look like an inductive machine: a given table more or less represents a distribution within a relatively stable universe, and one can produce a predictive 'law' to fit the curve of values in the table. The similarity of the mathematical work to the curve fitting of the physical sciences is at the same time vaguely threatening, and the use of the term law underlines the threat. Here we can begin to see the sources of Comte's and Mill's anxieties: not only can these laws be treated as a stopping point for inquiry; it is difficult to see what it would be to 'go beyond', or to explain these laws by reference to more general laws.

Mill's discussion of explaining the *en masse* observations of political ethology by composition, which is an attempt to answer this question, is clearly not feasible: only if the number of relevant causal principles were small and the 'local causes' relatively weak could such a process of explanation by derivation hope to succeed. Complexity, however, is admittedly a prominent causal feature of the social world, and the causal principles relevant to these explanations should be hidden by this complexity. The ease with which a statistician like Farr could construct 'laws' seems to suggest that the products of this inductive machine are radically unlike other sorts of inductive generalizations.

The term cause, and the concepts associated with it, are symptomatic. The use of terms like 'influence' in Farr's titles seems unobjectionable. The cholera study, which described "its sudden outbreak, and its as sudden cessation when the supply of polluted water which was its cause ceased" (Humphreys, 1885, p. xxii), was classic epidemiology, and the kind of knowledge that anyone would regard as a triumph of science. The conceptual categories that Farr introduced in his statistical inquiries – e.g. the distinction between healthy and unhealthy counties – advance our causal understanding, but in a peculiar way. They point toward the possibility of a more general set of properties under which healthy and unhealthy might subsumed, and in themselves hold out some assurance that there are causes for the unhealthiness of some counties, and causal relations between some properties of the county and 'health'. But the conceptual categories have an indeterminate relation to what as scientists we would ordinarily regard as causal concepts, and there is little either in the concepts or the form of the 'law' which serves us in what Mill called "the ascent to causes."

The categories 'healthy county' and 'polluted water' are a case in point. The conceptual difference between the two is at best a matter of degree. Cholera is an infectious disease. 'Polluted water' is not what one would now call its cause: the infectious agent is the cause. The difference between Farr's cruder category of 'polluted water' and present causal categories is that a set of mechanisms has been specified that corresponds to present categories. In connection with cholera outbreaks, historical hindsight allows us to say that the concept 'polluted water' has been successfully refined into causal categories with a 'mechanism' and 'unhealthy counties' has not. But hindsight is not methodology: there is nothing on the face of the concepts that marks the one as causal and the other as noncausal, much less which distinguishes the one category as 'refinable' into causes and the other as a dead end.

Statistics as Scientific Method

Farr was cosmopolitan and technically sophisticated, but he was not methodologically sophisticated; Quetelet was both cosmopolitan and methodologically sophisticated. He had met and befriended Gauss (Dunnington, 1955, p. 154), and his relations with the circle of Herschel and Whewell went beyond mere acquaintance. He supplied notes for a translation of Herschel's famous book on light, and contributed data to Whewell's study of the tides. Quetelet's ambitions were correspondingly more elevated. Farr is not central to the story of the problem of cause and probability, but he can serve as a point of departure and comparison: we can see how Quetelet built on the body of practices found in practicing statisticians such as Farr, but he embedded these practices in a larger conception of the character of sociological laws – a conception that parallels and competes with those of Mill and Comte.

Farr and Quetelet share an impulse that is not to be found in Mill or Comte. The quotation on the title page of *Sur l'homme et le développement de ses facultés; ou Essai de physique sociale* (1835) is from Laplace:

Appliquons aux sciences politiques et morales la méthode fondée sur l'observation et sur le calcul, méthode qui nous a si bien servi dans les sciences naturelles.

This is an analogue to the arguments for the extension of the concept of causal law found in Comte and Mill. But it is not the same argument, as another quotation, *"Mundum numeri regunt"* (quoted in Hankins, 1908, p. 17), placed on the title page of a set of Quetelet's popular lectures on probabilities, suggests. *Number*, not nomic form, is the 'method' that is to serve moral and political science as it served natural science, and this is an important difference. For Quetelet and a long series of successors, the preference for that which is countable and measurable stands on its own as a cognitive value. The publisher's preface to the English translation identifies a related cognitive value: Quetelet shows "that he is no theorist or system-maker, but simply wishes to arrive at truth by the only legitimate way, namely, the examination of *facts* – the incontrovertible facts furnished by statistical data" (Quetelet, 1842, publisher's notice, emphasis in original). Quetelet himself made similar comments. "It is not so much a method which we want, when endeavouring to appreciate the development of moral qualities, as sufficient and trustworthy data" (Quetelet, 1842, p. 78). In the preface to the 1842 English 'People's Edition' of the *Treatise on Man*, Quetelet described his own efforts as "the observation and exhibition of man," comparing himself to Durer (Quetelet, 1842, pp. v–vi), and disclaimed any theoretical ambitions. "My aim is not to defend systems, or bolster up theories; I confine myself to the citation of facts, such as society presents to our view" (1842, p. vii). Furthermore, he said, "I am less desirous to explain phenomena than to establish their existence" (1842, p. vii).

In one sense this profession is unambiguously true. Quetelet and contemporary statisticians were extremely interested in the accumulation of statistical information, much of it quite trivial. Quetelet quoted with approval a letter from his peer M. Guerry:

I am now occupied, along with M. le Docteur Esquirol and M. le Docteur Leuret, with the statistics of insanity. We measure the head, in every direction, of every person at Charenton, the Bicêtre, and the Salpêtrière. We also measure the cerebrum and cerebellum of those who die. I have thus been led to undertake the *Histoire du Developpement de la Tete Humaine Moyenne*. I have been led to it entirely from having read your excellent Memoir on the Stature of Man. Fifteen days ago, we noted the state of the pulse of ninety maniacal persons, between five and seven o'clock in the morning, and whilst they were at breakfast. We already have found certain periodic returns in the number of the pulsations; these observations will be continued to the end of the month (Quetelet, 1842, pp. 98–99n).

At times, Quetelet wrote as though the numbers speak directly, and that his own conclusions could be read directly from the numbers, without going through any elaborate stage of theoretical interpretation or ratiocination. But Quetelet's conclusions, e.g. on crime, were nevertheless large.

From the examination of numbers, I believed myself justified in inferring, as a natural consequence, that, in given circumstances, and under the influence of the same causes, we may reckon upon witnessing the repetition of the same effects, the reproduction of the same crimes, and the same convictions.... Now, what do these facts teach us? I repeat, that in a given state of society, resting under the influence of certain causes, regular effects are produced, which oscillate, as it were, around a fixed mean point, without undergoing any sensible alterations (1842, p. vii).

He contrasted this kind of reasoning with "system-building" on the grounds that the causal relations in question are already enshrined in common sense: "we are thoroughly convinced that laws, education and religion, exercise a salutary influence on society, and that moral causes have their certain effects" (1842, p. vii). All statistics does is to "give more precision" to these ideas (1842, p. 96). The ascent from common sense, for Quetelet, at this first stage, is thus an ascent from the previous established causal reasoning given in common sense to the more precise, data-based, results of statistics.

Refinements of commonsense causal ideas take a characteristic form in Quetelet's writings. In his three major books on social topics, data is presented in the same tabular form as mortality tables. The 'penchant' for crime, for example, varies according to age and sex, and differs for city-dwellers and other such categories. The same kinds of ratios of the number of crimes performed by members of those other categories can be calculated, and these ratios can be compared to one another, and, when the categories are themselves numerical, can be placed in series, e.g., by increasing age. Formulae, of the same kind that kept Farr awake at night, can be fit to these series. Quetelet called these formulae 'laws', and he produced many such series, by age, of such diverse properties as height, weight, strength, pulse-rate, and other physical properties, as well as such intellectual and moral facts as the ages at which authors produce and actors perform their principal dramatic works, the ages of admission to insane asylums, of suicide, and, of course, crime. The explanatory force of these series, and of the curves that could be fit to them, is puzzling. Their legitimacy as 'causes' is established by reference to common sense. But if the descriptions are to be taken as something more than a mere summary of the data included in the table, as 'propensities' which can support predictions for the future, generalizability or representativeness become issues. These problems are ubiquitous in practical statistical reasoning. We can see a simple example of the problem in Farr, whom we find defending certain general conclusions about Welsh mortality which he based on 1830 figures by the comment that 1830 was an average year. This means 'representative', but it also suggests something more, that the causal situation itself could be generalized. Farr's use of the term reflects this consideration: if Wales had been subject to famines for a half-dozen years in the same decade, mortality rates would not be a useful basis for the predictions made by insurance companies or governments. By the same token, stability makes possible quite precise predictions. One of Farr's followers observed that "The proportions of sex, age, and conjugal condition change so slowly that it may be assumed, without affecting the trustworthiness of the calculations based upon such assumption, that the *proportions* found to exist at the last Census will be maintained until 1891" (Humphreys, 1885, p. 6, emphasis in original), and this means that the numbers of persons in these categories may be projected, for intercensal years as well as for the future. Thus the *stability* of rates over time is a central and inescapable issue for the users of statistics, even for these very simple predictive purposes. The dependence of the outcomes on causes pushes questions about stability one step back – by substituting questions about the stability of *causal circumstances*. Rates, however, have a kind of remoteness or autonomy from circumstances, and this suggests an alternative approach to the problem of stability.

Quetelet's response to the issue of stability took this alternative. He argued that features of the rates themselves marked them as 'facts'. The reasoning derives from the century before, when various writers, impressed that many statistical ratios were stable over time, claimed that this furnished proof of the divine order working through human affairs (Walker, 1931, p. 17; Lottin, 1912, pp. 368–71). Quetelet himself was not above making theological remarks of the same species (e.g., 1842, p. 7). But his account of the facticity of rates rests on a nontheological basis.

The rhetoric Quetelet used in these discussions is memorable and picturesque.

In every thing which relates to crimes, the same numbers are reproduced so constantly, that it becomes impossible to misapprehend it – even in respect to those crimes which seem perfectly beyond human foresight, such as murders committed in general at the close of quarrels, arising without a motive, and under other circumstances to all appearance the most fortuitous or accidental (1842, p. 6).

There is, he went on to say,

a *budget* which we pay with frightful regularity – it is that of prisons, dungeons, and scaffolds. Now, it is this budget which, above all, we ought to endeavour to reduce; and every year, the numbers have confirmed my previous statements to such a degree, that I might have said, perhaps with more precision, "there is a tribute which man pays with more regularity than that which he owes to nature, or to the treasure of the state, namely, that which he pays to crime" (1842, p. 6, emphasis in original).

The imagery is underscored by a particular, recurrent trope. After one particularly lengthy discussion of crime rates in *Social Physics*, he remarked that he

cannot conclude this chapter without again expressing my astonishment at the constancy observed in the results which the documents connected with the administration of justice present each year (1842, p. 96).

'Astonishing' is the key word. It marks a distinction between the unastonishing world of common sense and a new order of facts. The theological tradition of Süssmilch depends on the notion of astonishment to make the point that this new order is divine. As we shall see, Quetelet used it in a way that connects his views to the methodological writings of such contemporaries as Whewell.

Quetelet's conclusion from the astonishing regularities, that "moral phenomena, when observed on a great scale, are found to resemble physical phenomena" (1842, p. 6), and "that *every thing which pertains to the human species considered as a whole, belongs to the order of physical facts*" (1842, p. 96, emphasis in original), was usually expressed in conjunction with a particular interpretation: "the greater the number of individuals, the more does the influence of individual will disappear, leaving predominance to a series of general facts, dependent on causes by which society exists and is preserved" (1842, p. 96). Sometimes Quetelet's point is that "the laws which relate to the human species" can best be observed at the aggregate level,

for, by examining ... [individual cases] too closely, it becomes impossible to apprehend them correctly, and the observer sees only individual peculiarities, which are infinite. Even in those cases where the individuals exactly resemble each other, it might still happen that, by examining them separately, some of the most singular laws to which they are subject, under certain influences, might escape for ever the notice of the observer (1842, pp. 5–6).

Sometimes the thought is of

the fundamental principle, that *the greater the number of individuals observed, the more do individual peculiarities, whether physical or moral, become effaced, and leave in a prominent point of view the general facts, by virtue of which society exists and is preserved* (1842, p. 6, emphasis in original).

The idea that these facts have a special significance in connection with the existence of society itself Quetelet left largely unelaborated and unexplained in his *Social Physics* and his *Letters*. He explored them in more detail in his final major sociological work. The idea that individual differences are effaced at the level of *en masse*, aggregate statistical observation is the one that he gave the greatest technical elaboration. The argument is the key to his case for the famous concept of the *homme moyen*, or average man. Both the idea of cancellation and the idea of the basic causes of societal preservation, we shall see, reappear in Durkheim.

THE AVERAGE MAN

Gauss's paper on least squares was concerned with a particular kind of error, the observational errors of astronomy; Quetelet observed the same distribution, the same 'curve of possibilities', in other contexts. He reasoned about occurrences of these similar distributions by analogy.

We aim at a target – an end – marked by a point. The arrows go to right and left, high or low, according to the address of the shooters. In the mean time, after a considerable number of trials, the butt, which has not yet been touched, perhaps, a single time, becomes so well pointed out by the marks around it, that they would aid at once in rediscovering it, if it should chance to be lost sight of. Nay, more than this; even aims the most unfortunate may be made to conduce to this end; commencing with those marks which are farthest away, if they be sufficiently numerous, one may learn from them the real position of the point they surround.

This figurative reasoning is applicable, it may easily be conceived, to all inquiries into the physical sciences, and even the moral also, where the point in view is to arrive at means or averages (Quetelet, 1842, p. x).

He conceded that this extension to the means or averages of the moral realm is based on the questionable presumption

that human nature, in its aberrations, has not a tendency to deviate from the mean in one sense in preference to another, as those who aim at a mark might have a tendency to shoot always too high or too low (1842, p. x).

But the question of the shape of actual distributions is one that can be approached 'empirically', by showing that the distribution of observations in both cases has the regularity of the bell curve.

In the *Letters*, this analogical argument is presented fully. He considered the Roman statue 'the Gladiator', and asked what would happen if its dimensions were measured five hundred times. The measurements would, he suggested, be distributed according to 'the curve of possibility'. If a thousand sculptors were commissioned to copy the statue, the probable errors would increase, but, if the copyists have not worked with preconceived ideas, in exaggerating or diminishing certain proportions, according to the prejudices of their particular school, and if their inaccuracies are but accidental, the thousand measurements grouped in order of magnitude would still present a remarkable regularity, and would succeed each other in the order assigned by the law of possibility (Quetelet, 1849, pp. 91–92).

Similarly for the 5,738 chest measurements of the soldiers of the Scotch regiments. "The difference which Nature makes in the heights of men is not greater than that which inexperience would produce in the measurements taken on one individual man in an attitude more or less curved" (1849, p. 95). The conclusion is presented as obvious.

If there existed no law of possibility which presided over the development of man, if all were chance, I (in my turn) ask how much should we not have to wager against 1 that 5,738 measurements, taken on as many chests, would range themselves in an order quite different from that determined by the law of possibility? (1849, p. 93).

Had the same measurements been performed on a 'mixed' group, Quetelet reasoned, one could have derived an arithmetic mean, but not a bell curve. As he expressed it, the 'law of possibility' governing this curve is verified for the Scotch soldiers, and would presumably not be verified for the mixed groups, which would contain an unknown mixture of types.

The distinction between mere arithmetic means and true means or true values has a clear sense in connection with observational error, where it can be assumed first that there *is* a true value and second that the means of given sets of observations will be distributed around this value. The mean for any set of *observations* cannot be assumed to *correspond* to the true value, for the means of observed distributions are also distributed according to a curve of errors. In the case of 'values' of the sort Quetelet had in mind, the true values are values of a 'type', and matters are more obscure. Quetelet wished to treat the existence of an appropriately shaped distribution as evidence of the *existence* of the type. The question, raised later, in different ways, by John Venn and the Durkheimian Maurice Halbwachs, among many others, is whether there is anything added by appealing to such 'types'.

In one scientific context, Quetelet's use of the concept of type served a purpose. The nineteenth-century pre-Darwinian concept of race had been bedevilled by puzzles over racial types, and the concept of a 'perfect representative' of a race was the source of many of the difficulties. If no actual perfect examples existed, did the racial type itself exist? Did the perfect examples formerly exist, and do 'imperfections' or deviations mean that mongrelization or degeneration has set in? To think of a racial type as a matter of the actual distribution of various physical and physiognomic properties answers these questions, by explaining how a type can exist without, so to say, any perfect tokens.

To think of social and moral properties analogously suggests a particular kind of reasoning: that types, not just individuals, can be treated as the subject of causal influence, and, to the extent that 'types' may be said to determine the actions of properties of the individuals of the type, the type may be treated as a *source* of causal influence. This serves to make the two levels of *description*, individual and *en masse*, into two levels of *explanation* as well – an extremely significant step, for it raises the possibility of a more or less systematic set of causal principles operating at the level of *en masse* facts, whose relation to individual actions and properties is mediated by the 'types' which individual explanations directly appeal to. This bi-level explanatory structure opens up the possibility that the form of the causal relations governing types may have no analogues on the individual level, and no systematic relation to common-sense explanations.

THE LAW OF ACCIDENTAL CAUSES

Quetelet came to this bi-level structure of explanation gradually. His own ordering of his texts is formulated in his final and most 'sociological' work, *Du Système social et des lois qui le régissent*. In *Social Physics*, he established the theory of the average man, and the necessity of thinking of the average in terms of the distribution around a mean. In the *Letters*, he used the law of accidental causes to account for the causal relation between the average man understood as a *'type'* and the instances of the type. The type, plus the law of accidental causes, over a sufficiently long period of time, predicts the distribution (Quetelet, 1848, pp.ix–x). The last book, the *Système Social*, is an inquiry into the laws that operate at the highest "dégres d'agrégation" (1848, p. xii). This self-periodization is misleadingly simple, for much of what is said in the later books is foreshadowed in *Social Physics*.

The progression is, however, true to the logic of Quetelet's approach. One observes *en masse* and discovers astonishing regularities. The stability of these regularities suggests that they are facts, to be treated as objects of inquiry on the same order as the facts of physics. The predictive and explanatory significance of these facts depends on separating out their influence from the various accidental causes which also bear on individual cases, and ultimately on discovering the principles governing the aggregate facts.

The 'law of accidental causes' is a bridge from the notion of averages to the causal reasoning that follows. The style of Quetelet's discussion of the law is characteristic: he does not formulate a basic conception and reason from it, but rather explicates a given concept in a variety of ways, usually leaving it unclear as to what is derived and what is assumed, and therefore leaving the logical status of the concept unclear. The links between concepts are analogical, as where the concept of type is explicated in terms of statues of gladiators and arrows landing in a pattern around a mark. The concept of the law of accidental causes is explicated similarly, and here the analogy brings Quetelet to some conclusions about cause which would have been difficult to reach in any other way. If the 'law of least squares' is a law governing the distribution of observational errors, and errors are caused, the causal meaning of the law is that the various causes of error balance one another out over the long run. Just as the fact that observations are distributed normally around a mean value shows that there is a 'true value', it shows that the causes of deviations are equivalent, or cancel one another's effects over the long run. If the distribution is skewed, this shows that these causes do not cancel one another out, but that the causes in one direction are stronger than those in the other.

The idea of causes cancelling one another out may be used to revise the conventional distinction, which Quetelet himself appealed to in *Social Physics*, between natural and disturbing causes. A given observation may be said to be jointly determined by accidental causes, governed by the law of accidental causes, variable causes, such as those to which curves might be fit, and constant causes, such as those which produce stable equilibria.

Classifying causes in this fashion is a more radical step than it at first appears. The law of accidental causes is not, as Quetelet sometimes described it, a law of nature. In this classification, the category serves as a conceptual device for dealing with causes left over when the effects of constant and variable causes have been taken into account. In this respect it resembles Mill's category of local causes. But Quetelet's classification enabled him to handle these causes in a new way. The existence of the bell curve indicates that, within limits and in the long run, predictions can be made which ignore accidental causes. This use is empirical, based only, as Mill would say, on the Method of Agreement. The problem it solves is a problem having to do with the grounds for selecting categories in the face of the infinity of causes: it warrants particular selections by showing that given selections of categories yield rates that are, within limits, stable, and that one can, at least for purposes of prediction, ignore other causes. In practice, stability is used as a substitute for a curve: there is no 'distribution' of observations for the kinds of facts Quetelet was primarily concerned with, such as the population of a given province on a given date or the number of criminal offenses in a given year; there is only one 'observation': so the relative stability of a rate over the years is treated as a warrant for the assumption that the 'accidental' causes which bear on the rate 'cancel one another out'.

Once this step – of ignoring the infinity of causes – is made, it is a short step to the philosophical view that there is a significant *irreducible* element of contingency in nature – to the doctrine, as Pearson was to state it, that "variability is the law of nature." As we shall see shortly, it is also a short step to a particular practical concept of causality, in which the test of causality is the existence of a stable difference in proportions or rates between categories. The statistical commentary of Farr and its looser, medical notions of causality relied on this test.

Quetelet's unwillingness to clarify the logical status of the law of acciden- tal causes created difficulties that become apparent in Venn's critique of Quetelet, which will be examined shortly. Venn showed that it is a very early step in Quetelet's analogizing about error distributions and types that is at issue. If we set these issues aside for the moment, we can see how the practice of statistical analysis can proceed from that of treating any more or less 'stable' ratio as a case governed by the law of accidental causes, and that Quetelet's practice largely corresponds to the statistical commentary practiced by writers like Farr, and that the objections that may be made against Farr's causal reasoning arise for Quetelet's practical causal reason- ing as well.

PRACTICAL CAUSAL REASONING

The starting point of Quetelet's practical reasoning is the concept of stable rates construed as 'penchants', or propensities. Quetelet defined the terms in this way:

Supposing men to be placed in similar circumstances, I call the greater or less probability of committing crime, the *propensity to crime*. My object is more especially to investigate the influence of season, climate, sex, and age, on this propensity (Quetelet, 1842, p. 82, emphasis in original).

When Quetelet spoke of the influences on the propensity to commit crimes, it was in terms such as this: "From the data of the preceding tables, it is scarcely possible not to perceive the great influence which age exercises over the propensity to crime, since each of the individual results tend to prove it" (1842, p. 94). 'Causes' and 'influences' are used interchangeably in these contexts (e.g. 1842, p. 92). Quetelet had little anxiety about the problems of the causal mechanisms of these relationships. His own statistical commentaries, as his comments about statistics as a matter of "giving more precision" to established ideas would lead one to expect, typically are either descriptive – "The higher we go in the ranks of society, and consequently in the degrees of education, we find a smaller and smaller proportion of guilty women to men; descending to the lowest orders, the habits of both sexes resemble each other more and more" (1842, p. 96) – or else not very far removed from common sense – "Of 1129 murders committed in France, during the space of four years, 446 have been in consequence of quarrels and contentions in taverns; which would tend to show the fatal influence of the use of *strong drinks*" (1842, p. 96, emphasis in original). The novelty is in the ways in which these prosaic explanations are tested and related to one another.

Consider this discussion of mortality rates, in the *Letters*: he begins with the rates for three periods. "The mortality for the first and third period was the same; but it was less during the second, which comprises the years 1834, 1835, and 1836. If we seek a cause for this inequality, we shall probably find it in the price of provisions" (Quetelet, 1849, p. 135). Quetelet showed, through the use of a table, that the death rates varied, with a slight lag, with the price of grain. "We see that during the years 1833–4–5, the prices of wheat and rye were less than during the two other triennial periods. It would therefore appear that the actual cause of the diminution of the mortality during this same period was the reduction in the price of grain" (1849, p. 135). The method here, as Quetelet explained it,

is to divide into groups or series the objects supposed to be under their influence. When these groups are formed in the same manner, and are in all respects comparable, they will be successively equal one to another, if the causes which have given them birth be constant. On the contrary, they will be unequal if the causes be variable (1849, p. 134).

Thus a 'causal' relation for what Quetelet called a variable cause, in practice, is shown by the disappearance of a difference in rates when the rates are based on data grouped according to the categories represented by the cause. This was not meant to be used as a procedure by which 'variable causes' may be *discovered*; the statistician must be the source of the categories, and this means that the categories will be selected from a set of categories which for some reason are regarded as possible causes, and which thus have, in some sense, a 'causal character'.

The categorizations thus are hypotheses, and the criterion by which they are tested is statistical relevance: any kind of change in the rates as a result of a subcategorization is evidence that the categories used to define the subcategories are statistically relevant to the outcome. When the rates for the subcategories are the same as the rates for the categories from which they are taken, the categories used to define the subcategories are statistically *irrelevant* to the outcome, and therefore eliminated as causes.

Unlike present-day writers such as Salmon, or later nineteenth-century writers, such as von Kries, Quetelet did not give any argument to the effect that explanations consisting of a showing of statistical relevance plus a claim of some variety of causal relevance involve a distinct variety of probabilistic, non-nomic cause. Instead, he used the distinction between constant, variable, and accidental causes to assimilate this practical procedure of causal hypothesis testing to the general framework of the conception of cause found in conventional scientific practice. Philosophers' questions about necessity and invariance did not trouble him. In the case of the variations of grain prices and death rates, the distinctions would work like this. The death rate as a whole is determined by a great variety of causes, some of which 'cancel one another out' over the long run, and are thus 'accidental'. The rate is also determined by a number of 'constant causes', including the basic physiology of the particular human type in question, such as male Scots or Frenchmen. The theory of the *homme moyen* deals with this pair of concepts. Variable causes are those which have effects on rates that can be shown by differential rates in subcategorizations, such as 'years in which the cost of provisions is high'.

The characteristics of a type itself are determined by constant causes that are themselves inaccessible to analysis, simply because they do not vary. Quetelet noted some exceptions to the fixity of types and the inaccessibility of the causes of types, a point which has bearing on his social theory. However, in his own practice, the type, in this instance the usual death rate, is the stopping point for analysis. Variations around the type, such as differences in death rates corresponding to prices of provisions, may be governed by variable causes. As we have noticed, the 'law of accidental causes', which Quetelet discussed as though it could be empirically confirmed for a given type by inspecting a distribution, is ordinarily not treated in this way. There is, for example, no 'distribution' of annual death rates to inspect. It is simply assumed that any relatively stable rate, such as a death rate, is governed by the 'law of accidental causes' and that the various 'variable causes' in fact 'cancel one another out' and are, taken together, statistically irrelevant to the rate. Thus, in practice, the only means of

disconfirming the assumption is to produce a variable cause that systematically relates to the rate, as 'price of provisions' does. This does not disconfirm the 'law of accidental causes' as a law of nature, of course, but shows
its inapplicability. But once this variable cause is taken into account, the
law of accidental causes is assumed to apply to the rates *within* the subcategories defined by the variable cause, so that, e.g. the rate during years of
high prices for provisions is assumed to be stable, and causes not taken into
account are assumed either to be constant or to 'cancel one another out'.

In the absence of actual distributions of observations that correspond to
'the curve of possibility', it is assumed both that any relatively stable rate
is governed by the law of accidental causes and that a set of constant causes
compose to determine the rate. As we have seen, these constant causes are
inaccessible to further analysis by statistical means. If a particular categori-
cal distinction, which is a putative 'constant cause', when used to subcate-
gorize, produces a difference in rates, it can no longer be regarded as a
constant cause. If, as in the case of 'price of provisions', it indeed varies,
it becomes a variable cause. If the category that produces these differences
in rates is a property, such as ethnicity, which distinguishes groups, it is
handled differently. The existence of ethnic variations in rates becomes a
basis for regarding the rate for the total group from which it was originally
subcategorized, e.g., France, as 'mixed', and for regarding the group as
composed of more than one 'type'. Thus a population of a particular
country may have a mixture of ethnicities, with different death rates for
each group. Quetelet would proceed as follows: he would first assume that
the national death rate represented a 'type'; when shown that the rates
differed by subcategory, he would say that there is a mixture of types; if
the rates within the categories were relatively stable, and no further ethnic
subcategorizations produced additional differences, he would then treat
the ethnic categories as corresponding to 'types', each type determined by
its own particular composition of constant causes.

The problem of category selection is a peculiarity that distinguishes this
method from the practice of the physical sciences. Where a physicist
aspiring to laws of nature gets the concepts of a hypothesis wrong, the laws
he forms with these concepts are likely to be empirically inadequate. To be
sure, some categories proposed by statistical analysts prove to have *no*
statistical relevance to rates: when one subcategorizes using them, no
differences in rates appear. But this test is drastically less severe than the
tests of physicists' hypotheses, so much so that it is questionable that it has
much significance as a conceptual sieve.

The difficulty here may be seen in Farr's concept of polluted water as the statistical category which represented the cause of cholera, or his concept of 'healthy counties'. If one had a variety of possible explanations in mind – 'hypotheses', each of which could be treated as a cause, in the looser sense of this word found in connection with, e.g. medical statistics – what would this technique (of subcategorizing and seeing whether the difference remained or vanished) yield? If the partitions of the universe defined by each categorization were not independent, that is, if there were any degree of intercorrelation between the 'variables', the true cause of cholera, as well as all the sorts of things that were not independent of this category, would, by this criteria, prove statistically relevant to the outcome. If Farr had tried, for example, to evaluate the hypothesis that cholera was a disease associated with religious confession, education, or crime, he could not have excluded these hypotheses using this test, for they would have correlated, in some degree, to the variable causes. Nor would such categories as polluted water, which are conceptually related to the causal mechanism of cholera as we now understand it, necessarily make for *more* of a difference in the rates than these other categories.

It might be, for example, that the category 'polluted water' (which, in retrospect, we see had pointed to the modern notion), in fact corresponded so imperfectly to the 'true causes' in these particular circumstances that other 'variable causes' produced higher correlations (but, in retrospect, were dead ends, pointing to no 'better' concepts).[1] It might also be that susceptibility to cholera is a constant, and that the rate of susceptibility is low, so that *no* discoverable probability will be especially high. As the negative standards for what can count as a cause are relaxed, the range of easily conceivable hypotheses consistent with the data drastically increases. And this creates a situation for the practicing statistician that is drastically different from that of the experimental physicist.

One of the set questions produced by this problem over categories was Is statistics an art or a science? The answer Quetelet gave is that

the complete enumeration of the influencing causes is nearly impossible in the greater part of social phenomena, because those causes are not only very numerous, but sometimes they are so indirect, and at the same time so feeble as to elude all investigations. The property of an observing genius is to know how to seize upon the most influential causes, – those which sensibly modify phenomena, – those, especially, which act in a continued or periodical manner; and to abandon the others as not necessary to be regarded, and as ranging among the accidental causes, whose results are inappreciable when the trials have been sufficiently repeated (Quetelet, 1849, p. 130).

The observing genius, faced with the near impossibility created by the feebleness of influences, their indirectness, and the fact of the "infinity of causes which give rise to an event" is thus limited to introducing "a greater degree of order" (1849, p. 107).

THE TWO-TIER MODEL

The primary means of introducing order is the application of the distinction between constant, variable, and accidental causes, an application which, as we have seen, is based on empirical evidence and a number of assumptions. Quetelet also embraced a number of intuitive principles, notably "that *effects are proportionate to the causes which produce them.* This fertile principle serves (so to speak) as the foundation of all the sciences of observation" (Quetelet, 1849, p. 128, emphasis in original). The principle has important implications in connection with aggregate social patterns, for a cause which is 'proportional' to these must be suitably 'large'. The model of the logical structure of social science that Quetelet constructed is based both on the notion that rates are for the most part determined by constant causes and that the causes that explain these constants are different in character – 'larger' and more closely bound to the constitution of society – than the determinants of individual action.

The procedure is based on the idea that while it is not practically feasible to add up the contributory effects of the infinity of causes that compose to produce the rate, it is often possible to work in the other direction. Determining what part of the whole is contributed by a given cause is possible by subtracting its effect, i.e. by partially grouping the numbers and showing the degree of difference to be attributed to the cause in terms of which the grouping is done. In the case of the mortality rate, times of expensive and cheap provisions can be compared, and the difference attributed to the price of provisions. This method, 'partialling', is basic to twentieth-century multiple correlation techniques.

The 'order' that is imposed by methods of partialling, i.e. by seeking proportional causes and ignoring causes that 'cancel one another out', is in many respects, reminiscent of Mill's 'tidological' model of large tendencies and local causes. But Mill's version of this approach is based on the idea that the causal laws governing broad tendencies may be identified and understood in the early stages of analysis, then improved through the addition of local causes. Quetelet shares the language of tendencies and shares the general strategy of starting with the large causes. "In statistical researches, our object is generally to discover the causes which influence social facts, and to determine the degree of their energy. These appreciations, especially the latter, sometimes become impossible; and we must confine ourselves to the study of the causes, and their tendency" (Quetelet, 1849, p. 147). But they part company on the question of where the larger causes are to be sought. Mill's notion was that tendency statements were to be grounded in general psychological principles, and applied to the explanation of sociological or ethological tendencies operating at higher levels of aggregation. Quetelet's strategy was the two-tiered approach of identifying the constants and explaining them. The 'constants' vary between social circumstances, so to explain the constants by subjecting them to laws would be to construct explanations on this higher, social level, which are autonomous. These laws would not necessarily owe anything to common sense – indeed, they are about objects that are themselves not known to commonsense discourse.

The reasoning gives us a different picture of the ascent. The first-order study of statistics, as Quetelet put it, "has then for its object that of presenting a faithful representation of a state at a determined epoch" (1849, p. 179). It is analogous to "Botany at its birth," when "it was limited to the collection of plants, to their recognition, to their enumeration, and to the description of them in a more or less complete manner" (1849, p. 179). To limit statistics to this kind of activity would, however, be the same as limiting astronomy to describing the paths of the planets. The second level is concerned with laws analogous to the physical laws governing the solar system, and its laws determine modifications from country to country in the first order 'laws', such as the 'law' that produces the distribution of suicides. Quetelet's first-order description, the curve fitting that takes up much of *Social Physics*, is thus understood in the light of this larger task.

The source of the notion that the strongest causes man is subject to as a member of the social body are "morals and institutions" (1848, p. 88) and the related idea that these are the determinants of the order of facts represented by stable rates is obscure, but not because there is any lack of candidates. At one point Napoleon is quoted to the effect "that under whatever relation we may view man, *he is as much the result of his physical and moral atmosphere as of his own organisation*" (Quetelet, 1842, p. 82n, emphasis in original). This kind of remark was found so frequently in the French literature of the day that Quetelet may well have regarded it as a matter of common sense for which no theory was needed. The intellectuals who advanced this view included the physicist J. B. J. Fourier, whose study of various demographic characteristics of Paris in the 1820s "states repeatedly that average values depend on general causes, and change only very slowly 'by the secular progress of institutions and customs'" (Hankins, 1908, p. 49). The natural theologian Süssmilch made similar remarks. Whatever the source, however, the use of these notions places Quetelet squarely in the rhetorical space occupied by other pretenders to the science of society.

Astronomy is Quetelet's model, and the analogy Quetelet had in mind is to the Laplacean account of the solar system: the planets have their own laws, governing their paths, just as the penchant for committing various types of crime can have curves fit to them for each society; the planets deviate from their paths, within statistical limits, and these 'perturbations' are analogous to the statistical variations year to year around crime rates. The concept of 'perturbations' provided Quetelet with a device for resolving one of the chief bugaboos of the day, the problem of the influence of great men, a problem then usually seen in light of the problem of free will and determinism. If Quetelet's account of the stability of the *homme moyen* is correct, it would be difficult indeed to envision successful changes in the basic features of the human condition in a given society, and if this is the mark of greatness, it is obscure as to how greatness is possible. Quetelet's response to this was to use the notion, familiar to followers of Victor Cousin, that all "history, not that of one people or one epoch only, but that of all epochs and all human nature, is represented by ellipses great men" (Quetelet, 1842, p. 101) to argue that "the great man, in his individuality, is the best representative of the degree of development to which human nature has attained in his times" (1842, p. 101). Greatness becomes a matter of representativeness, together with harmony between elements. Representativeness is, Quetelet thought, necessary for great influence.

A man can have no real influence on masses – he cannot comprehend them and put them in action – except in proportion as he is infused with the spirit which animates them, and shares their passions, sentiments, and necessities, and finally sympathises completely with them. It is in this manner that he is a great man, a great poet, a great artist. It is because he is the best representative of his age, that he is proclaimed to be the greatest genius (1842, p. 101).

The works of the great man can introduce 'perturbations' into the social system, which, in the long term (as "secular perturbations"), alter its laws, but only in a limited way (Quetelet, 1842, pp. 6–8). His limitations are a result of the limited modifiability of the social state and the fact that "as a member of the social body, he is subjected every instant to the necessity of these causes, and pays them a regular tribute" (1842, p. 7). He can succeed when, "as a man, employing all the energy of his intellectual faculties, he in some measure masters these causes, and modifies their effects, thus constantly endeavouring to improve his condition" (1842, p. 7). 'Free will' seems to gain a purchase, however limited, in this reasoning – responsible for some of the fluctuations one finds in rates, but not with much efficacy in changing the types (Quetelet, 1842, p. ix).

THE 'FICTIVE BEING' AND THE SOCIAL SYSTEM

Quetelet himself identified 'constants', or types, with the stable laws of the paths of planets. The question this raises is, "Having thus observed the progress made by astronomical science in regard to worlds, why should not we endeavour to follow the same course in respect to man?" (Quetelet, 1842, p. 9). 'Following the same course' depends on finding appropriate analogues in the social realm. The problem in making the ascent by this route is that the planets are a great deal more tangible than the aggregate objects of sociology, such as the collective organism. The device Quetelet substituted for the planets is the "fictive being" of the *homme moyen* (1848, p. 14) – a 'thing' whose properties have some scientifically valuable features which Comte's and Mill's collective organisms do not. Quetelet's *homme moyen* is a type that is describable by 'laws' and that in turn predicts individual outcomes. When he said "that *every thing which pertains to the human species considered as a whole, belongs to the order of physical facts*: the greater the number of individuals, the more does the influence of individual will disappear, leaving predominance to a series of general facts, dependent on causes by which society exists and is preserved" (1842, p. 96, emphasis in original), however, he was making the different point that rates are facts, and therefore open to *explanation*. Quetelet repeatedly insisted that they also represent *determinants* of action (in the strong sense that their stability is evidence of the negligibility of free will – "that those who are guilty, are sometimes obliged in an irresistible manner, not having the free command of the will" [Quetelet, 1842, p. 22]). This raises the question of the logical role, and the dispensability of, the *homme moyen*. If the two-tier model can stand as a nomic structure, built of constants, variable causes, and accidental causes, without any ontological reliance on the conceptual device of the *homme moyen*, the device may indeed be dispensable. Quetelet raised the question himself by his unexplicated insistence on the 'fictive' character of the *homme moyen* as a 'being', which seems to suggest that he wished to

leave the question of its ontological character open. Yet he made other
remarks that suggest some much more radical claims. Phrases such as the
"causes by which society exists and is preserved," however, suggest a kind
of reality for society that goes far beyond the modest idea that the *homme
moyen* is a determinant of action, and toward a strong form of 'social
realism'.

We are, however, left with vague suggestions. The substantive remarks
Quetelet made on social development are only loosely integrated with his
remarks on the *homme moyen*. Indeed, his substantive explanations of the
development of the *homme moyen* are not easily distinguished from Comte
and Mill. Quetelet's human finds that "as his reason becomes developed,
a new world is unrolled before his eyes, contracting the limits of the former
one; and it is this continually increasing triumph of the intellectual man,
which the history of the arts and sciences presents to us at every page"
(Quetelet, 1842, p. 100). Quetelet went so far as to say that "science only
is truly progressive" (1842, p. 101). So the novelty of Quetelet's discussions
of the laws of social development is found primarily in the explanatory
imagery he borrowed from astronomy and physics.

The key terms for Quetelet, at what I am calling the 'second tier', the tier
of the explanation of rates, are 'equilibrium', 'conservation', and 'perturbations'. The imagery itself has a politically conservative air, which
Quetelet exploited in a few remarks on revolution. He did not apply these
images consistently, and indeed used images of the social body, the notion
of social physiology, together with the idea that it has "principles of conservation" (1842, p. 7). However, the main strand of usages are physical and
astronomical.

The *homme moyen*, "the *social* man" is said to resemble "the centre of
gravity in bodies: he is the centre around which oscillate the social elements," so that in social system explanations "we must follow the progress
of the centres of gravity in each part of the system" (Quetelet, 1842, p. 8,
emphasis in original). As with planets, the movements may be perturbations, movements toward equilibrium, or movements which are part of
the movement of the system. What is part of the system and what are
'perturbations' must be determined by fitting curves mathematically; but
even here Quetelet managed to find a starting point in common experience.

What we see daily proves to us sufficiently the effects of internal actions and forces reacting
on each other; but the centre of gravity of the system, if we may so say, and the direction of
the movement, are unknown; it may even happen, that whilst the motion of all the parts of
the system is progressive or retrograde, the centre may remain unvaryingly in equilibrio
(Quetelet, 1842, p. 8).

One may note that this use of the term system remains in the realm of astronomic imagery. When Quetelet turned to politics, the imagery became mixed between the physical and the physiological (Quetelet, 1842, pp. 100–02; see also 1848, pp. 235–36). The stress is on the various "principles of conservation" which limit change, and on the slowness of change. Genuine change is slow: "a moral power capable of modifying the laws which affect" man "acts in the slowest manner, so that the causes influencing the social system cannot undergo any sudden alteration" (Quetelet, 1842, p. 96). On the other hand, "Revolutions ... are never accomplished without certain actual sacrifices; as sudden changes, in a corporeal system, never take place without a certain loss of vital power" (Quetelet, 1842, p. 102). The less violence the better, for "where states of equilibrium and motion are possible, in physical phenomena as well as in political facts ... *the action is equal to the reaction*" (1842, p. 102, emphasis in original).

The social body is like an elastic body in which its particles return to the same place after a blow. "If each one is fully imbued with a knowledge of his rights and duties – if he invariably desires to do that which is just – if he energetically strives to re-enter the course he has traced out as soon as any one attempts to make him swerve from it – and if the reaction be allowed to manifest itself immediately after the action, both will be very *evidently* equal" (Quetelet, 1842, p. 102). Revolutions are reactions, cases where governments return to equilibrium.

Stable equilibrium exists, when, in consequence of action and reaction of every kind, a government constantly regains its normal state; if, on the contrary, under the action of slight causes, a government tends to diverge more and more from its normal state, and if, each year, it change its form and institutions without adequate motives, its downfall is at hand, and it will infallibly sink, unless it finds assistance in the adjacent governments; but even then its fall cannot be long retarded (Quetelet, 1842, pp. 102–03).

In *Social Physics*, passages like these, which bear on contemporary social and political life, are not very long, and the general problem of the character of laws on the 'second tier' is discussed only sparingly. In his *Social System*, the nomic structure of the second tier is discussed at greater length, but not at much greater depth. One suspects that, like Mill, Quetelet found the going more difficult than it first appeared.

In *Social Physics*, the various interactive 'elements' in society, and the principles of motion, conservation, and equilibrium governing them, are spoken of, but not specified. In the *Social System*, Quetelet saw how distant the goal of ascertaining their laws is. Public opinion, he noted, has, since Rousseau, been held to be a major force in society, but its 'laws' are unknown (1848, p. 201). Nevertheless, we can, he thought, extend the lessons of stable equilibria which can be learned from the experience of revolutions, particularly the French Revolution, to identify various kinds of equilibrium between 'elements': the harmony or *"juste équilibré"* (Quetelet, 1848, pp. 197–98) which holds between law and morals, between the various human faculties (1848, p. 278), between the states of man as an individual and man as an element of a collectivity (like the savage stage of tribal and family attachments on the one extreme, egoism on the other [1848, pp. 296–97]).

One implication of these remarks is normative: the Aristotelean lesson of the special virtue of the mean, an association which, curiously for a nineteenth-century scientist, he embraced (1848, p. 303). He credited God with the creation of a material world without perfect equilibrium, and went on to observe

C'est par des lois semblables que sa divine sagesse a tout équilibré aussi dans le monde moral et intellectuel; mais quelle main soulèvera le voile épais jeté sur les mystères de notre système social et sur les principes éternel qui en règlent les destinées et en assurent la conservation? Quel sere l'autre Newton qui exposera les lois de cette autre mécanique céleste? (Quetelet, 1848, p. 301).

Another Newton was not to be found among Quetelet's contemporaries. It was not until Durkheim wrote on these subjects forty-five years later that anyone was to attempt to make much of these notions of equilibrium.

QUETELET AND CONTEMPORARY METHODOLOGY: HERSCHEL AND WHEWELL

As we shall see, Durkheim attacked the concept of the *homme moyen*. One of the earliest works of Maurice Halbwachs, a central member of the Durkheimian group, was a critical essay on Quetelet from a Durkheimian point of view. Halbwachs later wrote that Quetelet's doctrine of the *homme moyen*, "as a pioneering conception … was inevitably couched in metaphysical terms – as a theory of social determinism through an hypostatized abstraction. It thus laid itself open to valid criticism by statisticians and philosophers" (1934, p. 23). What Quetelet himself believed about the character of this 'abstraction' is something of a puzzle, for two reasons. One is that Quetelet did not in his writings on social science make an explicit appeal to the contemporary methodological literature on hypothesis. However, there are some strong clues that can be followed up, notably his characterization of the *homme moyen* as a fictive being and his relationship to certain contemporaries, notably Whewell and Herschel, who played leading roles in Britain as spokesmen for science. Herschel critically but rather favorably reviewed Quetelet's *Letters* in the *Edinburgh Review*. The second source of obscurity over the concept is that while his later critics repeatedly dismissed the concept as metaphysical and overstressed, Quetelet was rather diffident about the ontological significance of the *homme moyen*. *Pace* Halbwachs, the term 'fictive being' hardly indicates 'metaphysical hypostatization'. As we have seen, Quetelet thought that the attributes of the types that can be discovered in society were straightforward empirical facts, proved beyond any question by the repeated empirical observations in many domains which he recorded in *Social Physics*; in the same early text he also said repeatedly that the values of the types are themselves determined by the state of society, and that the 'laws' that describe the relationship between age and such things as the penchant for crime are laws of the social system.

The nomic structure he envisioned is fully explained only in his later book, *Social System*, and this may account for the later perception. This book, with its argument that the social body, like a physical body, has a center of gravity and an equilibrium which it returns to after revolutionary 'perturbations', was published at the worst possible time. Quetelet's introduction is dated January 14, 1848. The revolutionary upheavals followed in a few months. Marx was luckier: his *Manifesto* was buoyed into prominence by the same forces that rendered Quetelet's book irrelevant. Yet time proved that Quetelet had the better prognosis: the events were not the herald of the classless society and the end to the exploitation of man by man, but were no more than an important 'perturbation'.

Clues to Quetelet's conception of hypothesis can be found in his earliest works. The strand of argument that is shared with Herschel and Whewell is a particular insistence on the cognitive importance of surprise. This is implicit in Quetelet: it was his point when he insisted on the astonishing regularity of this or that rate. Herschel was also fond of the notion of what he called, alluding to Bacon's notion of prerogative instances, *instantiae luciferae* (Herschel 1850, p. 28), and held that unless a theory enables "us to extend our views beyond the circle of instances from which it is obtained ... we cannot rely on it" (quoted in Laudan, 1981, pp. 130–31, see also pp. 167, 172, 203). Whewell built this into an elaborate theory of what he called the consilience of inductions: the idea that the independent support for a hypothesis given by a successful prediction of phenomena in domains the hypothesis was not originally devised to explain is a source of special confirmatory weight in favor of a hypothesis (cf. Laudan 1981, pp. 130–36).

The word 'astonishing', however often it is repeated in Quetelet, may seem like a weak strand on which to hang an interpretation, but there is more to it than this, and the personal relationship between the three men is highly suggestive.

Herschel's relationship with Quetelet is alluded to in his review of the *Letters*, where he expressed his gratitude for Quetelet's assistance, in his capacity as "perpetual Secretary to the Belgian Academy of Sciences, as well as that of Director of the Royal Observatory at Brussels." Herschel also described him as the "centre of an immense correspondence" (Herschel, 1850, p. 8). The expression of gratitude is for help in international work in astronomy.

No one threw himself with more entire devotion into the system of combined magnetic and meteorological observations set on foot by the British and other governments, and which has been productive of, and continues to produce, such useful and valuable results to science (Herschel, 1850, p. 8).

France, he noted "stood aloof and furnished not one solitary instance of co-operative observation (thus interposing herself as a desert might have done between England and the rest of the Continent)" (1850, p. 8). Quetelet performed a similar service for Whewell in connection with his studies of the tides. As these relationships were based on data collection, it might be supposed that there is no reason to think that Quetelet felt any sense of methodological community with them. Yet the task Quetelet performed for Herschel, supplying notes for the translation of the book on light, belies this. The problem of the logical status of the wave theory (which Herschel warmly defended) was the central problem of the contemporary methodological dispute over hypothesis. As Laudan points out, "the wave theory itself ... served as an epistemological archetype for such philosophers as Herschel and Whewell" (1981, p. 136). Mill and – in a more equivocal way – Comte came down on the other side of this dispute (cf. Laudan, 1981, p. 128).

If we apply Whewell's methodological notions to Quetelet's work, we get some interesting results. Begin with a few sayings of Whewell. "The two processes by which we arrive at science" Whewell called "*the Explication of Conceptions* and *the Colligation of Facts*" (1984, p. 205, emphasis in original). The former is the process "by which *conceptions* are *made more clear* in themselves" (Whewell, 1984, pp. 204–5, emphasis in original), the latter the process "by which the conceptions more strictly *bind together the facts*" (Whewell, 1984, p. 205, emphasis in original). The two processes proceed in close association. "Inductive truths are of two kinds, *Laws of Phenomena*, and *Theories of Causes*. It is necessary to begin in every science with the

Laws of Phenomena; but it is impossible that we should be satisfied to stop short of a Theory of Causes" (1984, p. 259, emphasis in original). Discoveries "are not improperly described as happy *Guesses*" (1984, p. 211, emphasis in original). "Hypotheses may be useful, though involving much that is superfluous, and even erroneous: for they may supply the true bond of connexion of the facts; and the superfluity and errour may afterwards be pared away" (1984, p. 256). "It is a test of true theories not only to account for, but to predict phenomena" (1984, p. 256). "*The Consilience of Inductions*" is a particular kind of prediction which "takes place when an Induction, obtained from one class of facts, coincides with an Induction, obtained from another different class. This Consilience is a test of the truth of the Theory in which it occurs" (1984, p. 257, emphasis in original). A surprising fit between results in different realms is thus a case of consilience.

Had Quetelet been familiar with these general ideas, as he almost certainly was, he would have found them comforting. The theory of *homme moyen* is a self-proclaimed hypothesis, an *être fictif*. The main confirmatory support for the conception is the astonishing consilience between the many 'laws of phenomena' Quetelet described. If we think of these laws taken together as attributes of the *homme moyen*, if we, to use Whewell's language, "superinduce" "the new mental element" of the concept of the *homme moyen*, "the Facts are not only brought together, but seen in a new point of view" (Whewell, 1984, p. 257). And the hypothesis leads us to look for yet other attributes of the *homme moyen* that can be described as laws. The whole of Quetelet's effort, indeed, may be seen as the devising of a hypothesis originally based on a few inductively arrived-at laws of phenomena and *successfully* extended to new classes of fact.

The relationship between Herschel and Whewell is complex. Herschel played the practicing scientist to Whewell's philosopher, a role which was congenial to Quetelet as well. Herschel shared Whewell's notions of the importance of prediction in verifying an induction, and the importance of "*extending* its application to cases not originally contemplated" (Herschel, 1830, p. 167, emphasis in original). Herschel distinguished such laws from those empirical laws which are derived "by the direct process of including in mathematical formulae the results of a greater or less number of measurements" (1830, p. 178).

A good example of such a law is that given by Dr. Young (Phil. Trans. 1826,) for the decrement of life, or the law of mortality. Empirical laws in this state are evidently *unverified inductions*, and are to be received and reasoned on with the utmost reserve. No confidence can ever be placed in them beyond the limits of the data from which they are derived (1830, p. 178, emphasis in original).

"Frequently," as in the case of Kepler's laws, these, "when afterwards verified theoretically by a deductive process, ... turn out to be rigorous laws of nature" (1830, p. 178). Herschel thought of laws of nature as *vera causa*, and took a scientist's delight in their discovery.

The discovery of a new law of nature, a new ultimate fact, or one that even temporarily puts on that appearance, is like the discovery of a new element in chemistry. Thus, selenium was hardly discovered by Berzelius in the vitriol works of Fahlun, when it presently made its appearance in the sublimates of Stromboli, and the rare and curious products of the Hungarian mines. And thus it is with every new law, or general fact. It is hardly announced before its traces are found every where, and every one is astonished at its having so long remained concealed (1830, p. 175).

Quetelet would have found this brand of astonishment congenial, for he thought that the concept of the *homme moyen*, once discovered, had led to new discoveries in one realm after another.

Herschel did Quetelet a great favor by his review, published as the lead article in the *Edinburgh Review*, a journal of enormous importance. The review agrees with Quetelet only in part. Herschel stated, more clearly than Quetelet did, that the problem of finding the value of a type as ascertained by the Gaussian sum of squares method "is, in effect identical with that of finding their centre of gravity" (Herschel, 1850, p. 10), underlining the hypothetical but 'precise' character of both problems. He ignored most of what Quetelet had to say about such things as partialling and handled the practical problem of statistical causes by the concept of "biassing causes" (1850, p. 15), thus assimilating the issue to the problem-structure of measurement error, the "*animus mensurandi*" (1850, p. 11). No inconsistency with other notions of cause, such as his own version of the concept of *vera causa*, is noticed. But he notices one important implication for the social sciences of the idea of biasing causes: "where the number of accidental causes of deviation is great, and the maximum effect of each separately minute in comparison of the result we seek to determine, – great total deviations can only arise from the conspiring of many of these small causes in one direction – the more that so conspire, the greater the deviation" (1850, p. 16). The argument undermines the Millian version of the idea that local causes can be ignored in the early stages of the development of a nomic structure for the social sciences. But it undermines more than Mill.

The recognition of the existence and effect of feeble causes which may, unbeknownst to us, bias our results, gives statistics

the true, and, we may add, the only office of this theory in the research of causes. Properly speaking, it discloses, not causes, but tendencies, working through opportunities, – which it is the business of an ulterior philosophy to connect with efficient or formal causes; and having disclosed them, it enables us to pronounce with decision, on the evidence of the numbers adduced, respecting the reliance to be placed on such indications, – the degree of assurance they afford us that we have come upon the traces of some deeply-seated cause, – and the precision with which the intensity of the tendency itself may be appreciated (Herschel, 1850, p. 17).

This led him to a rather different position than Quetelet's own. On the one hand, he accepted Quetelet's extension of *le Calcul* to the social realm.

What astronomical records or meterological registers are to a rational explanation of the movements of the planets or of the atmosphere, statistical returns are to social and political philosophy. They assign, at determinate intervals, the numerical values of the variables which form the subject matter of its reasonings, or at least of such 'functions' of them as are accessible to direct observation; which it is the business of sound theory so to analyse or to combine as to educe from them those deeper-seated elements which enter into the expression of general laws (1850, p. 22).

He also accepted Quetelet as having successfully disposed of free will.

Taken in the mass, and in reference both to the physical and moral laws of his existence, the boasted freedom of man disappears; and hardly an action of his life can be named which usages, conventions, and the stern necessities of his being, do not appear to enjoin on him as inevitable, rather than to leave to the free determination of his choice (1850, p. 22).

But he did not follow Quetelet's version of the ascent. "It must never be forgotten that tendencies only, not causes, emerge as the first product of statistical inquiry, – and this consideration, moreover, ought to make us extremely reserved in applying to any of the crude results of such inquiries the axioms or the language of direct unimpeded causation" (1850, p. 22). He rejected the "proportionality of cause to effect," remarking that it was "a principle, rather emphatically repudiated in the history of the correspondence of increase of imposts with increase of revenue, and of profits as compared with prices" (1850, p. 22), i.e. where many 'small' economic decisions have 'large' aggregate effects. He treated rates accordingly. National character, he suggested, is a matter of mixture. "The ratios of the helpless, the active, and the meditative elements of a population to the entire mass and to each other ... must necessarily give rise to corresponding features of national character" (1850, p. 23), a claim that is in conflict both with Mill's political ethology, which wished to explain national character by the composition of causes, and Quetelet's 'types'. This anticipates the more comprehensive and devastating criticisms formulated and published sixteen years later by John Venn.

A NOTE ON BUCKLE

Thomas Henry Buckle's *History of Civilization in England* of 1857–61 achieved an enormous readership throughout the world. In the English-speaking world, Buckle's formulations often were the focus of methodological discussions of the place of statistics in social science and in relation to the concept of law. Quetelet's central idea of the stability of rates was taken over by Buckle, and long quotations from Quetelet are found in the general introduction to Buckle's book. The stability of suicide and crime statistics fascinated him, and he reasoned, as had Quetelet, that

> suicide is merely the product of the general condition of society, and ... the individual felon only carries into effect what is a necessary consequence of preceding circumstances. In a given state of society, a certain number of persons must put an end to their own life. This is the general law; and the special questions as to who shall commit the crime depends of course upon special laws; which, however, in their total action, must obey the large social law to which they are all subordinate (Buckle, 1859, p. 20).

The last sentence contains the seeds of deep trouble, a trouble of which we see the beginning in Herschel's criticism of Quetelet. The flaw is evident if we compare this to tidology. Buckle's formulation seems to accept the premise held by Mill, that

> every human action, every murder for instance, is the concurrent result of two sets of causes. On the one part, the general circumstances of the country and its inhabitants; the moral, educational, economical, and other influences operating on the whole people, and constituting what we term the state of civilization. On the other part, the great variety of influences special to the individual (Mill, 1974, p. 933).

If the large causes are held to directly produce a specific number of suicides, the local causes only select who is to be called – a peculiar notion, quite unlike the notion of composition of causes and effects found in tidology. If the causes compose, and the total causal force impelling a person to suicide is a result of the additive effect of the larger law and the special laws, then the Queteletian concept of rates collapses, for the rates are not a direct reflection of a social law but a result of the composition of the social law with the special law. Buckle did not resolve the paradox by telling us how the special laws are made to 'obey the large social law'. The problem is found in Durkheim, and arises whenever the stability of rates is taken in the Queteletian sense of a fixed number or budget.

   The principle Buckle embraced is that the smaller the number of obser-vations, "the greater the chance of the operation of the larger laws being troubled by the operation of the smaller" (1859, p. 167), which is Quetelet's notion that disturbances 'equalize' and hence disappear at the level of stable regularities. Buckle left the paradoxes of composition aside, and used this reasoning only to claim that the highest-level universal historical laws possessed a kind of *de facto* autonomy from the explanation of particular individual actions. Buckle regarded 'removing disturbances' as the method of nomic science, and held that this 'removing' was the purpose of experiment. He argued that a similar 'removing' might, in those circumstances where it could not be done by experimental controls, be done by statistical means. This notion of law and disturbance goes back to the image of an orderly universe, the order of which was concealed and which man could, in a small way, disarrange – a theological image to which Buckle, whose mother was a strict Calvinist, came naturally. It fit with laissez-faire economics as well. Buckle regarded 'interferences', such as foreign interferences and government intervention in the economy, to be cases of disturbance or perturbation. This led him to argue that European history provided an *experimentum crucis* in which, by making suitable comparisons, we can strip off the effects of disturbances. England seemed to him to be a country which, because it was less under foreign influence, could be treated as a case where its development is "due to causes springing out of itself" (Buckle, 1859, p. 168), causes which "run their own course, and disclose the operation of their own law" (1859, p. 168). This is a teleological notion, and in the last analysis, Buckle was, at the level of universal history, a teleological intellectualist, who saw human development as driven primarily by intellectual development, a development that could be 'interfered with' by unfavorable conditions of climate, politics, religion, and the like: the notions of interference and disturbance, as he used them, are systematically ambiguous between teleological and nomic senses.

CHAPTER FIVE

THE INTERREGNUM

Robert Brown has recently argued that Mill

was the first person to bring the Enlightenment conception of the social sciences to a point sufficient for us fully to understand and appraise it. Subsequent elaboration has added nothing essential to his argument and removed nothing that makes a substantial difference. No one who either favours or opposes the basic claim – the claim that there are social laws just as there are physical laws, and that therefore the structure, procedure, and aims of the social sciences must resemble that of the physical sciences – is likely to have his opinion altered by considering conceptual developments after Mill. All the conceptual information necessary for concluding for, or against, the view which he advocates can be found in his writings (Brown, 1984, p. 5).

On a strict construction, emphasizing the phrase 'physical laws', this is perhaps true. Yet when Laplace characterized the method of the physical sciences as *le Calcul*, he stressed something different from law – and, as we have seen, Mill was far from having the last word on quantitative social science, precisely *because* the nomic conception of science fit so poorly with the developing statistical study of society. But one can give another sense to Brown's claim: a historical rupture followed Mill, and this made him the last great defender of this tradition.

By the middle of the 1850s there had been published a significant body of programmatic texts, which absorbed and explicated the achievements of the social science of the previous half-century. Comte's, Mill's, Quetelet's, and Buckle's were the most important of those texts, but not the only ones. The differences between these authors were real, but nevertheless limited. They shared, in different degrees, some basic ideas about causal law, about the implications of the extension of the methods of natural science to the realm of human action, on the complexity of the social body, on the character of human progress as intellectual progress, and so on. Although they differed on details, such as on the relevance and character of considerations of probability, they saw one another's views as alternatives. The friendship of Mill and Comte has already been mentioned. Buckle's book was carefully discussed in a later edition of *System of Logic*, just as Buckle had dealt with Quetelet, and had said of Comte's *Cours* that "there is much in the method and in the conclusions of this great work with which I cannot agree; but it would be unjust to deny its extraordinary merits" (Buckle, 1859, p.4n). The sense of intellectual community between these thinkers was sufficiently strong that Spencer, an early adherent who long outlived the others, felt wounded by Mill's criticisms on some relatively minor points of detail.

In the 1870s, this rough consensus was cut off. The main cause is easily identified – Darwinism, the influence of which was as enormous as it was obscure. The effects of Darwinism were evident to contemporaries. In the Darwin volume in the 'English worthies' series, we are told that "Buckle was exploded like an inflated wind-bag" by Darwinism (quoted in Robertson, 1895, p.23). The comment, as a later defender of Buckle remarked, "is sufficiently extravagant; but more remarkable than the mere terms of the judgment on Buckle, is the fact that it comes from a gentleman who had shortly before edited an issue in two volumes of the miscellaneous writings of the exploded wind-bag in question" (Robertson, 1895, p. 23). The reversal in fortunes was indeed sharp.

Horace Kallen, writing as an explicator of pragmatism in the nineteen thirties, suggests that the main

consequences of the impact of Darwinism upon the sciences of man and nature.... [were] to shift the conception of "scientific thinking" into a temporal perspective; to stress relations and activities as against terms and substances, genesis and development as against intrinsic character, transformation as against continuing form, dynamic pattern as against static organization, processes of conflict and integration as against formal composition out of unchanging elements. In short, the shift was from "structure" to "function" as the principal tool of scientific explanation and interpretation (Kallen, 1931, p. 523).

This was not all. Darwinism undermined the scientific pretensions of the intellectualist theory of human progress shared by all of the participants in the earlier conversation. Teleological intellectualism was shortly to reemerge, but when it did, it was on quite different bases.

Paradoxically, Darwinism was to indirectly aid this revival, for one effect of Darwinism was the reinvigoration of teleology as such. The term 'function', which Darwin used in 1862 in a paper on the fertility of orchids, goes back to older usages referring to the duties of an office or the consequences of a medicine. The usages are not themselves teleological. Yet none of them are inconsistent with teleology, either – indeed, they are readily subsumed under broader teleological hypotheses, and not so readily subsumed into a structure of causal laws. The teleological trend represented by Lamarckianism, rather than being defeated by Darwinism, was strengthened and legitimated by it in the eyes of many observers, a fact that requires some explanation. The conflict between the two accounts of evolution is best thought of as a twentieth-century realization. For contemporaries, Lamarckianism served as an interpretation of Darwinism, which supplied the principle of natural selection with the motive force or mechanism it so evidently lacked.

It is striking that Robertson's attempt at formulating a defense of Buckle discreetly dropped most of Buckle's talk about law. This is an important point in relation to what follows. The kind of reasoning Buckle engaged in by talking about interference with natural development seemed now to stand on its own, without any need for the complex nomic structures envisioned by these earlier writers. Spencer turned out to be the pivotal figure in this transformation, having retained the ideas of law and a kind of intellectualism, but arguing substantive cases in an 'evolutionary' way which was difficult to distinguish from Lamarckianism and which stressed the functional rather than the causal elements of the survival and development of ideas and social structures. *Qua* methodologists, Bacon, Comte, Mill, Quetelet, and Buckle were clearly against teleology, and were perceived as antiteleological by the writers of the period. Pasteur's attacks on positivism were motivated by this perception. Finch, in 1871, summarizing the earlier consensus in discussing Bacon and Comte, remarked that

it is noticeable that these profound and comprehensive thinkers agreed in rejecting the study or investigation of causes first and final, (regarding it as a theological invasion of scientific rights; for, in Bacon's witty conceit, "like a virgin consecrated to God, it bears nothing,") – in confining research to the invariable relations which constitute Natural Laws, and in limiting the range of their philosophical theories by the axioms, that observed facts are the only basis of sound speculation, and that no proposition that is not finally reducible to the enunciation of a fact, particular or general, can offer any real and intelligible meaning (Finch, 1872, pp. 39–40.)

In short, they were taken as denying both teleology and the speculative subsumption of history or nature under a teleological principle. The worm in this apple was visible to Finch, who concluded his lecture, which was a defense both of Bacon and Comte and of the achievements of the substantive social science represented by Farr, with a discussion of "the origin of man," which, he said, "is, at present, a great crux of science" (1872, p. 79).

Other Currents

So various and contradictory were the cross-currents that were set into motion by the doctrine of evolution that Spencerianism, its major beneficiary in the social sciences, was itself overwhelmed. A short list of some of the currents that temporarily combined with, or against, the general shift in perspective represented by Darwinism will suffice to indicate the extent of the chaos. The problem of free will gained a new lease on life, and it was widely argued in French intellectual circles that freedom of the will was assured by the existence of contingency in nature, an 'existence' which Darwinism seemed to confirm. Renouvier, who considered Spencer to be his primary target, argued that contingency existed in physical nature itself. He connected this argument for contingency with a defense of moral individualism which responded to what he saw as the moral fatalism implied by Spencerianism (Parodi, 1934, p. 288). The idea that sociology leads to fatalism was not solely a French perception. John Venn is also to be found arguing this (Venn, 1866, pp. 362–70). And the perceptions were not entirely wrong. A more consequential association was the Continental reading of Darwinism in terms of 'materialism'. In France, this represented a reinterpretation of, or variation on, the earlier dispute over determinism and free will, and gave rise to a series of new attempts to reconcile the trends of the day. Fouillée wished to synthesize racialism, socialism, and idealism in opposition to materialist determinism and gained a large audience.

In the United States, social Darwinism was used in defense of Buckle-like notions about 'intervention': William Graham Sumner decried "The Absurd Attempt to Make the World Over"; the geologist Joseph LeConte made a racialist argument to the effect that slavery was the social form evolutionarily necessitated by the evolutionary state of the Negro race. The premises for this reasoning included methodological arguments, or, more precisely, arguments about the deterministic nature of social evolution. The ideological associations of 'evolutionary' argument ultimately undermined the idea of an evolutionary social science. The reaction against the elaborate schemes of stages that Boas organized in the early years of the twentieth century relegated these schemes to the status of prescientific and ideological. So evolutionism came, at least temporarily, to a dead end, although it was a dead end to which it took a very long time to arrive. Part of what remained as the methodological heritage of this period was the idea of function, with all its ambiguities.

In Germany, for reasons intrinsic to the development of German Idealism, a reaction set in during the 1860s against Hegelianism, understood as a form of absolute idealism. The Kantian notion of the *a priori* premises for knowledge was reborn, with the important consequence that a response to empiricism, positivism, and causalism was constructed by way of the argument that the category of causality was itself a 'forming category'. This would have remained an esoteric point were it not for a related development, the rise of historical thinking, and the way in which

these neo-Kantian doctrines were made to bear on the problems of historiography.

The rise of historical thinking was a long-range movement. Jeffrey
Bergner has recently characterized it in terms of a "decisive change in what
is valued – what is unique, what is local, and what is temporal come to
assume a higher value than what is common or universal" (1981, p. 40). The
self-conscious recognition of the historicity of forms of thought arises both
as a consequence and as a critique of historical consciousness – as a
critique of the naive belief that knowledge of these newly valued historical
facts is knowledge of the most basic things, as a consequence, in that the
recognition of the historicity of forms of thought would have been incon-
ceivable without the change in valuation. Otherwise, the various forms of
thought found in history would have been treated simply as erroneous, or
barbaric.

The consciousness of other historical forms of thought had its most
dramatic manifestations in theology. The discipline of the history of religion, which emerged in the early part of the century, taught that the forms
and character of Christian belief had a history and had changed in various
ways. Thus, the comparative method was corrosive to religious belief. But
it was corrosive to Enlightenment notions of progress and the Whiggism
represented by Buckle as well. Applied to social and political institutions,
the 'comparative method' absorbed some of the challenge that Buckle and
Comte had presented by their insistence on the insufficiency and triviality
of a history composed largely of the records of political and military events.
In the early sixties, in France, Fustel de Coulanges published *The Ancient
City*, and in England, Maine published *Ancient Law* (Collini *et al.*, 1983,
pp. 145, 229). In Germany, the historical school in economics achieved an
extraordinary *succés d'éstime* by virtue of its development of a rigorous
history of economic institutions and by the unprecedented influence which
its followers came to have over the formation of public policy. Buckle, Mill,
and Spencer had been anti-interventionists: anti-interventionism was explicitly built into Buckle's methodology, and it entered into Mill's and
Spencer's sociological and economic doctrine. In the intervening years,
these positions became unfashionable. Richard T. Ely spread the gospel
that the state was an instrument delivered by God into the hands of man
for the purpose of human betterment to a generation of Americans, through
the first graduate program in social science in the United States, at Johns
Hopkins University, and through such popular means as Chatauqua reading
lists. Many American sociologists were inspired as youths by this message
and came to the study of social institutions with motivations that were

directly opposed to those of the earlier generation. They also followed Ely in the trek to German universities.

The rise of the comparative method had other consequences as well. In Anglo-Saxon countries, the long history of political institutions such as the moot court was seen as legitimating these traditions: traditions with such durability, it was presumed, were beneficial in ways that superficial considerations of utilitarian rationality failed to reveal. In the United States, where Spencer was influential, Lamarckian evolutionism provided a convenient vocabulary for discussing the 'deeper rationality' of these institutions. The concept of survivals and the contrast between the functional and the nonfunctional aspects of institutions were taken very seriously. In England, the 'theoretical' claims of Spencer were not taken as seriously, and the problem of a theoretical vocabulary was accordingly less central (Collini et al., 1983, p. 213). The English practitioners of the comparative method, indeed, saw the method as a means of refuting these theoretical schemes. Yet while the historical claims of Buckle, Comte, and Spencer were criticized as amateurish, the topics that the comparativists focused on were the topics that the earlier writers had, against their contemporaries, such as Macauley and Froude, asserted the centrality of: ideology, institutions, class, and political forms (Collini et al., 1983, pp. 209–46; esp. p. 220).

France was a consumer of philosophical ideas in the last half of the nineteenth century, and French philosophers saw themselves as such (Levy-Bruhl, 1924, p. 426). The official philosophy taught in the schools, Eclecticism, was congenial to consumption of past and foreign philosophy and regarded the task of present philosophy as critical connoisseurship. The generation of the 1870s and 1880s, which reacted against Eclecticism, including such figures as Renouvier and Durkheim's and Bergson's teacher, Boutroux, nevertheless shared much of this sense of philosophy as critical selection, which took the form of a "mania for synthesis," as Logue says of Fouillée (Logue, 1983, p. 132), and for synthetic constructions designed to reconcile disparate philosophical truths (Levy-Bruhl, 1924, p. 452), with science and morals, in a unified whole of some sort.[1] Characteristically, this was done by resolving conflicts at one level by some set of higher-level synthetic devices. Fouillée's synthetic effort, as Levy-Bruhl described it,

contains nearly every element of modern thought; the critical spirit which recognises no barriers and claims a right, despite the school of Criticisme, to test the very idea of duty; a tendency to adopt the historical and evolutionary point of view; respect for positive science; a taste for social problems; an effort to construct a positive psychology, and to found a science of metaphysics that shall sincerely take into account the modern theories of knowledge (Levy-Bruhl, 1924, p. 455).

The resolutions were in higher-level notions such as 'voluntaristic idealism' and 'positive metaphysics'. Among Fouillée's devices is the notion that ideas have objective reality in the sense of having causal force: *idées forces* affect individuals' minds and historical developments, and themselves have an evolutionary history. Boutroux reconciled teleology and cause by locating a teleological principle at the level of the evolution of the universe. As with Fouillée, the lists of components of these syntheses were often quite long. They usually included cause, materialism, determinism, and their teleological idealist and spiritualist counterparts. Probability concepts figured in many of these constructions. For example, Boutroux stressed contingency against determinism, as did Cournot (Levy-Bruhl, 1924, p. 458).

The figures of this generation left a peculiar legacy. These synthetic constructions gained readers, but did not produce 'schools', and generally were without much influence outside of France, save as handy sources of critical explication of contemporary philosophical currents. Students trained in French philosophy were thus likely to be well read, inclined toward idiosyncracy, and, compared to their German peers, unspecialized and 'literary' in their conception of their aims. The aftereffects of the German romanticism of the earlier half of the century had some analogous consequences. Teleology and organicism, in particular, had a central role in German political thought, as the creation of the German state itself was interpreted as the historical realization of a process of state formation, and in economic thought, where a form of teleological institutional historicism represented a 'German way' opposed to the economics of Mill and his 'Manchesterite' successors. German academic discourse, however, was not 'literary', and this was particularly true of philosophical writing. Neo-Kantianism, as practiced in the late nineteenth century, saw itself as rigorous and professional, as a form of *Forschung* rather than *pensée*. The professionalizers of English philosophy, such as T. H. Green, eagerly followed this German model. So the professionalization, academicization, and technicization of discourse in these countries separated philosophy from many of the concerns that had motivated Comte, Mill, and Buckle. Pride of place was given to the issues of concern to the audience of professional philosophers, especially technical issues of epistemology, to which cause and probability were usually seen as incidental.

As methodologists, Weber and Durkheim, writing in the wake of this welter of developments, were forced to select from a very wide range of possible modes of discourse, problems, and conceptual devices. Both returned to the key issues of the Mill-Quetelet era. But they reconstituted these problems in light of what intervened, and, not surprisingly, they selected differently – so differently that they ignored one another, in vivid contrast to the mutuality of the earlier generation.

PROBLEMS OF PROBABILITY

Within the narrow confines of the problem of probability, the period between Mill and Durkheim also saw some reversals in intellectual fortune. The 'astonishing' stability of rates suffered a consequential blow from a series of works on the interpretation of the concept of probability that appeared in the 1860s. The force behind much of this literature was derived from nonstatistical issues of the sort we have been describing. In Germany, Queteletism "met with very violent opposition, mainly on the part of German theologians, economists and statisticians, which was largely an expression of moral indignation against its extreme determinism" (Anderson, 1934, p. 366). By the 1870s Queteletism was defeated, and a new approach was developed, revolving in part around the problem of causality, by Rümelin (Anderson, 1934, p. 370) and von Kries. In England, there was a parallel development, exemplified by John Venn's *The Logic of Chance* (1866), which criticized Buckle and Quetelet at length, and raised objections to the traditional imagery of causality reproduced in the writings of Mill. Venn's statistical argument against Queteletism is similar to that given by Wilhelm Lexis in Germany (Anderson, 1934, p. 366), and we may take it as a strikingly clear representative of the objections of the new generation.[2]

Venn's book begins with a discussion of Quetelet's primary concern, the kind of series that "combines individual irregularity with aggregate regularity" (Venn, 1866, p. 4). The example of a probabilistic claim Venn analyzed, which has this property of aggregate stability, is "Some cows will not suckle their young" (Venn, 1866, p. 5), but the point holds generally:

If we are examining the length of human life, the different lives which fall under our notice compose a series presenting the same features. The length of a single life is proverbially uncertain, but the average duration of a batch of lives is becoming in an almost equal degree proverbially certain. The larger the number we take out of any mixed crowd, the clearer become the symptoms of order, the more nearly will the average length of each selected class be the same.... Fires, shipwrecks, yields of harvest, births, marriages, suicides; it scarcely seems to matter what feature we single out for observation. The irregularity of the single instances diminishes when we take a large number, and at last seems for all practical purposes to disappear (Venn, 1866, pp. 6–7).

The science of probability deals with series in which "occasional attributes, as distinguished from the permanent, are found on an extended exami-

nation to exist *in a certain definite proportion of the whole number of cases*"
(1866, p. 10, emphasis in original). The 'permanent attribute' in the claim
'some cows will not suckle their young' is that of belonging to the class of
cows, the 'occasional attribute' is unwillingness to suckle their young. If we
look at enough cows, it may be "that the proportion of instances in which
they are found to instances in which they are wanting, is gradually subject
to less and less variation, and approaches continually towards some
apparently fixed value" (1866, p. 11).

Then again, it may not: it is an empirical question as to whether in fact
this value holds up as the series continues. The value may be durable,
"though durable is not everlasting. Keep on watching it long enough, and
it will be found almost invariably to fluctuate, and in time may prove as
utterly irreducible to rule, and therefore as incapable of prediction, as the
individual cases themselves" (Venn, 1866, p. 14). The average length of
human life has changed – over time, for example – and this is characteristic
of ordinary empirical rates. "A type that is persistent and invariable is
scarcely to be found in nature" (1866, p. 16). Only observation can tell us
how far regularities apply: "our conclusions ultimately rest entirely on
experience, and are subject at any time to be tested and revised by specific
experience" (1866, p. 21).

Talk about 'penchants' and 'propensities' enabled Quetelet to overlook
this. Venn gave the example of the finding

that in the long run the male children are to the female in about the proportion of 106 to 100.
Now when we are told that there is nothing in this but the "development of their respective
probabilities," what is there in this sentence but a somewhat pretentious restatement of the
fact just asserted? The probability *is* nothing but that proportion, and is derived from the
statistics alone (Venn, 1866, p. 34).

Quetelet held that he was *investigating* the penchants or probabilities, as
though these were themselves things. Venn, who objected to any notion of
"objective probability" (1866, p. 35), called this the "realistic doctrine," and
addressed it in the form of Quetelet's distinction between averages and
means, found in his analogizing between such cases as the chest measurements of Scotch soldiers and different measurements of the same statue,
which was designed to suggest that there is a true value or true mean in
the case of Scotch soldiers, just as there is a determinate value to dimensions of the statue.

Venn denied that there is meaning in "asserting the real existence of the
type or mean" (Venn, 1866, p. 44). When comparative anatomists use the
term 'type', Venn argued, "it is nothing more ... than a statement of

resemblances which are actually found to subsist between different species" (1866, p. 44). Venn went on to give a *causal* interpretation of the concept of type. "If any additional hypothesis be intended, ... it would be one of a causal nature as to the process by which these species and their varieties had been produced. This is quite different from the existence of a real type in the sense which M. Quetelet seems to contemplate" (1866, p. 44). But there is a more serious error here as well. The arithmetic average, Venn pointed out, is a mathematical construction based on a specific set of cases (1866, p. 44). The leap from this construction to claims about real 'means' is only a leap (1866, p. 47). Quetelet attempted to support this leap by reference to the symmetry of the bell curve. But this curve is also an empirical construction, based on a specific set of cases. Venn also noted that the fit between the ideal and empirical is often not as good as Quetelet had pretended.

The puzzle is over what the patterns found in these sets warrant, and how they can be generalized. Quetelet generalized by making an inferential leap to real 'penchants' and means, and drew various conclusions about free will from their alleged existences. Buckle made a similar leap, from the same 'regularities' to the conclusion that it is the large-scale fact of the "general condition of society" which produces the result (Venn, 1866, p. 356). Both had taken the regularities to have quite direct implications about cause and the necessity of events. Quetelet had used the principle of proportionality of causes to direct the next Newton to very large causes of the regularities. Venn started with the point that individual events that compose averages, rates, and proportions are themselves caused; "take but one instance, – the observed fact that the number of misdirected letters remains about the same year by year." This might mean that "there is a tolerable regularity in the strength of ... [men's] memory." But in this case and in similar cases, "many external agencies ... produce the observed result." At most, statistics show "that these agencies themselves present a similar regularity" (Venn, 1866, p. 337).

But Venn was skeptical even of conclusions like this, for he believed that the evidence required to prove causation in any strong sense is not to be found in statistics. Actions like thefts, murders, and suicides

may have their causes and their effects, but before a sequence of any kind, whether complete or incomplete, near or remote, can be inferred from such statistical tables [as Quetelet's], we must have other tables before us which shall refer to the supposed regular antecedents and consequents alike (Venn, 1866 p. 333).

The *categories* used in statistical tables typically cannot serve this purpose.

"Statistics," he said, "from their nature, preclude any but a very slight degree of specialization" (1866, p. 332), and "at best are only concerned with the less intimate connection of the events, that is, with the looser sense of the term" (1866, p. 338).

CAUSE AND ITS PROBLEMS

Venn began his discussion of the problem of the relation between statistical constructions and causation with Mill's notion of cause as "invariable unconditional sequence," a usage "which is becoming almost universally adopted by scientific men" (Venn, 1866, p. 315). The concept of condition itself, and the relation between 'conditions' and causes, interested him most. Mill had suggested that cause be understood as "the sum total of the conditions, positive and negative, taken together; the whole of the contingencies of every description which being realized the consequent invariably follows" (quoted in Venn, 1866, p. 316). Venn pointed out that in the actual practice of causal reasoning, it is ordinarily assumed that the antecedent conditions in question are *immediately* antecedent, and that we are forced to work with a hypothetical formula that is necessarily selective of the conditions that actually obtain in the sort of cases one is making a causal rule about (Venn, 1866, p. 318). This necessity results from the fact that *exact* repetitions of conditions of which the effect 'invariably' is supposed to follow never, or only rarely, occur: in "cases of any degree of complexity, though there may be repetition of many of the separate elements, the precise combination is generally unique" (1866, p. 317). He gave the example of our bodies: "no man's constitution resembles exactly that of any one else" (1866, p. 317). This produces a dilemma:

If we adhere rigidly to the sense of the term which was laid down at first no use can be made of it, for repetition then is certainly rare, and perhaps is not to be looked for at all. If we are to make any use of the formula we are forced to omit some of the antecedents, and then it ceases to be conformable to fact. It appears that we are driven to make our election between the useless and the false (1866, p. 318).

Venn did not claim to have a solution to the dilemma. He used it in support of some skeptical reservations about some familiar notions and to drive a wedge between "the doctrine of Causation as it is practically made use of" and "the strict form in which it appears as the basis of a science of inference" (1866, pp. 318–19). His reservations pushed him away from Mill.

The first casualty of his skepticism was the contrast between 'accidental' laws and laws dependent on causation, a contrast that was central to the writings of Whewell and Mill and that had been "brought into notice in such recent disputes as those raised by the works of Mr. Buckle and others of the same school" (Venn, 1866, p. 319). Venn said that the contrast is an *idolum fori* (1866, p. 320), a case of using common language and commonplace examples in support of a distinction that has no place in the "strict form" of the doctrine of causation. A tolerably regular sequence in which the antecedent is not "immediate" "may generally be ultimately resolved into cases of causation by the discovery of intermediate links" (Venn, 1866, p. 319). This suggests that the familiar picture of the causal chain, which contains "determinate distinct links following one another in succession, of stages marked off from one another in nature as well as distinguished in language" (1866, p. 320), is a misleading abstraction when applied to the scientific study of nature:

what we really find in nature is an evolution rather than a succession; the stages when examined at a little distance from one another are tolerably distinct, but, when closely examined, each merges into the next and blends with it by insensible degrees. They are like the strands of a rope; at a little distance there may be what one might call successive patches or stages, but when we look closer we find that each strand continues without the slightest break of continuity. Instead of having links definitely marked out for us, the steps and stages have to be assigned by ourselves, and have a great deal of what is arbitrary in them (1866, p. 320).

"Even where the cause and effect seem most proximate, as for instance in an explosion giving rise to the sensation of sound, we might if we pleased interpolate any quantity more of what are called links" (1866, pp. 321–22). The distinction between accidental and causal laws, then, "vanishes, at least, as an accurate theoretical distinction, though it may be retained in a looser form for practical purposes" (1866, p. 322). Similarly for the causal notion of 'tendencies' found in Mill. Tendency statements are laws stated to exclude "the intrusion of some counteracting agency" (1866, p. 322). Venn asked:

By what right is the exclusion maintained, when the object is to prop up and insure from failure a law of causation, but refused when wanted to perform the same service for an empirical law? Only exclude counteracting agencies and any observed empirical uniformity will be as 'unconditional' and invariable as can be desired; suffer these agencies to enter and the laws of causation will cease to possess these characteristics (1866, p. 322).

One answer to this question might be to insist on 'immediacy' between alleged antecedent and consequence. But this, Venn said, "would at once make the formula of universal causation barren and impracticable" (1866, p. 323). The same difficulties exist in the concepts of 'chain', tendency, and immediacy. They are abstractions, or selected stopping points, which are arbitrary and unempirical.

Venn objected to several other kinds of 'idealization' that are part of the process of statistical inference. The standard case of tossing a penny involves such a step. Inferences about the series depend on "the sides themselves of the pence having been expressly idealized into absolute similarity" (Venn, 1866, p.216). This may be innocent enough. But other instances of idealization are not so innocent or clear. "We must also idealize the 'randomness' of the throwing of the penny, which is a process that one feels rather at a loss to know how to set about performing" (1866, p. 30). The implications of these idealizations are often obscured by the manner in which the reasoning is presented. Consider the example of inferring the joint occurrence of two kinds of events, "the chances of which are perfectly equal" (Venn, 1866, p. 225). Quetelet, who discussed this,

selects the example of births and deaths as found succeeding one another in a register. He assumes very justly (the number of males and females being equal) that the chance of any one entry being male is one half. Then follows the next step, that the chance of having two males succeeding is one fourth (Venn, 1866, p. 226).

As Venn pointed out, this step involves a distinct supposition of "independence," a word which, he noted "under an appearance of specious modesty ... really makes very extensive claims" (1866, p. 227).

In this case Quetelet did not even consider that independence may be an issue – it becomes an unstated assumption – and was high-handed about the question of the evidence that would bear on the calculation. "Thinking it possible that one might like to know 'how far experience justifies the calculation'," and, as Venn acidly remarked,

being a humourist as well as a mathematician, he remarks that the process of actually consulting the registers themselves would be "tedious," and that he will therefore resort to "experiments more expeditious and quite as conclusive." He therefore puts forty black and forty white balls into a bag, proceeds to draw them, and to note the successions of each colour that come out, and this is supposed to prove that men and women will die in certain proportions (1866, p. 226).

In fact, Venn pointed out, "on the rare occasions on which any large number of one sex did happen to die in succession it is quite possible that this might introduce a disturbance amongst the proportions of the deaths which succeeded such an occurrence" (1866, p. 227).

Idealization was generally taken to be the root of these difficulties, and this problem, as Venn saw, extended far beyond statistical practice. The themes were taken up by others, who agreed that the Millian notions of cause and tendencies themselves were open to extremely serious objections on the ground of the problem of idealization (cf. Passmore, 1967, p. 133). As we shall see in connection with Weber, German writers, notably von Kries, who were concerned with one specific form of the problem of practical causal reasoning, were to take these problems as a starting point.

PART II

DURKHEIM AS A METHODOLOGIST

CHAPTER SIX

REALISM, TELEOLOGY, AND ACTION

Durkheim's *The Rules of Sociological Method* does not begin with a dialogue with fashionable peers, nor, indeed, are Durkheim's philosophical peers seriously addressed in the text. He signals his aims by the striking assertion that methodology has been neglected in sociology. His audience might have thought of Spencer's *The Study of Sociology*, by then itself two decades old, as a methodology book. Durkheim pointed out, properly, that it was not, and suggested that to find a methodological work of importance one must go back to Mill and Comte. In 1895, when the *Rules* appeared, almost thirty years had passed since the end of Mill's productive scholarship, forty since the end of Comte's and Quetelet's.

The argument itself begins in a more distant philosophical past, with Bacon, a philosopher quite out of fashion in late nineteenth-century Paris. This signaled an intent to return to philosophical roots. It was a return to the problems that had been abandoned in the 1870s, an explicit rejection of the philosophy and sociology of the interregnum, and precisely the sort of radical step one might have expected from a philosopher whose dissertation examination had turned into a sparring match with two of the leading representatives of French philosophy, the Eclectic Paul Janet and Durkheim's own teacher, Emile Boutroux (Lukes, 1973, pp. 296–99). Both of these immediate predecessors had abandoned causality or subordinated it to teleology. The defense of causal law is the theme of Durkheim's book.

One cannot simply return to a dialogue that had effectively ceased long before, and Durkheim was necessarily faced with the task of selecting and critically revising in the light of the writing of the intervening years. As we have seen, this was a period marked, in France, by the revival of teleological concepts in the wake of Lamarckianism, Darwinism, and Spencerianism, and this revival was especially strong in France. This fact alone placed Durkheim in a radically different situation than the earlier writers. He was obliged to take teleology seriously and to reconcile his arguments with, or assimilate, the portions of this literature that had been legitimated by the scientific successes of Darwinism. The foe was much more formidable than it had been in Comte's time, the arguments improved and made more subtle in the course of the disputes over vitalism and evolution.

Durkheim's critical revision is not presented in the style of the time, as an exercise in eclectic synthesis, but takes the form of an original argument that begins with a novel definition of the object of sociology and proceeds through an examination of the methodological problems that arise in the course of its study. The argument is thus constructed to avoid what Durkheim took to be the errors of his predecessors. Yet the synthetic impulse is also to be found there: Durkheim was as concerned with capturing the truths contained in the works of his predecessors as he was in exposing their errors.

SOCIAL FACTS AS THINGS

The *Rules* begins with a short chapter defining the domain of sociology, which closes with a definition: "*A social fact is every way of acting, fixed or not, capable of exercising on the individual an external constraint*; or again, *every way of acting which is general throughout a given society, while at the same time existing in its own right independent of its individual manifestations*" (1964, p. 13; 1982, p. 59; 1937, p. 14, emphasis in original). The next chapter is prefaced with the slogan, "The first and most fundamental rule is: *consider social facts as things*" (1964 p. 14; 1982, p. 60; 1937, p. 15, emphasis in original), which is a virtual paraphrase of Quetelet's "*every thing which pertains to the human species considered as a whole, belongs to the order of physical facts*" (1842, p. 96, emphasis in original). The criterion of 'constraint' or 'generality'[1] is not Quetelet's, and it marks a fundamental difference between the two. The theory of the *homme moyen* provides an intellectual link by which rates may be connected to the individual agent: an agent acts in accordance with his type. Durkheim dispensed with this theory. But he retained the idea of rates as autonomous facts whose 'facticity' is proved by their stability. *Suicide* begins with the presentation of a long section of series of suicide rates that is designed to prove their 'stability'. Durkheim was faced with finding a substitute answer to the problem of the linkages between this fact and individual actions which the theory of the *homme moyen* answered. The notion of constraint was this alternative device. In the first long chapter in the *Rules*, 'Rules for the Observation of Social Facts', the novelty of his approach in relation to the earlier conversation becomes apparent.

Durkheim's style is itself part of the novelty. If one wished to divide philosophers into the categories of those who set up their problems in pictures and those who set them up in language, Durkheim would be a handy example of the first sort: to understand the *Rules* is to understand a picture of what sociological laws ought to be. The picture is easily misunderstood unless we take care to see what Durkheim committed himself to by each addition to it. The first step in the picture creating of the *Rules* was to cast doubt on the adequacy of the language employed by ordinary persons in speaking of social life, and therefore on previous theories that in one fashion or another assume this language, such as those theories of society Comte would have called theological or metaphysical. This account of the language of action explanation took him out of the line of development – best represented by Mill – in which ordinary explanations of actions in terms of motives and reasons are taken to be closely correlative to the language in which the causal regularities of social science can be expected to be formulated. Bacon supplied Durkheim with a vocabulary for this argument, which turns the 'realist' elements of Bacon against the empiricist elements that are continued in Mill. Durkheim charged his predecessors with using what he called the 'ideological method'. The examples he gave of the ideological method are various: Spencerianism, Mill's economics, and Catholic Natural Law. As Durkheim described these bodies of thought, they proceed by following out the implications of received ideas, rather than dealing with reality. The term '*idola*' is used, in the sense of ideas which cloak and obscure realities (to which they are only imperfectly connected), in order to characterize the ideas – such as the idea of 'value', studied by economics – from which these approaches proceed (1964, p. 17; 1982, p. 62; 1937, p. 18). Venn, of course, also used Baconian terminology, as did many other nineteenth-century methodologists. Durkheim's use had an obvious rhetorical point – to dramatize the depth to which he wished to push his rejection of his predecessors – but it was more than a literary conceit. He went on to make the Baconian point that access to the realities of the realm of social fact must be made "where it offers the easiest access to scientific investigation" (1964, p. 46; 1982, p. 83; 1937, p. 46). Shortly before the chapter of the *Rules*, which is devoted primarily to the question of the applicability of Mill's methods to the study of social facts, Durkheim made the famous but puzzling remark, "Even one well-made observation will be enough in many cases, just as one well-constructed experiment often suffices for the establishment of a law" (1964, p. 80; 1982, p. 111; 1937, p. 80). Of course this is Bacon's theory of "the prerogative instance," the theory that certain cases can show "the true difference, ... the operative nature, the law of the phenomenon" (Fischer, 1857, p. 122), and it is Bacon as a realist, rather than an inductivist or empiricist. Thus Durkheim's use of Baconian language signals both a commitment to a realist, or 'substantialist', conception of social reality and a causal conception of the structure of social reality.

Being a substantialist or realist in this Baconian sense is not the same as being a 'social realist' in the sense of a believer in the 'reality of society'. To be sure, a long tradition of Durkheim criticism has taken the latter question for the former and dealt with Durkheim as a teleologist whose conception of the reality of 'society' was metaphysical, or which involved an "illegitimate teleology" (Turner and Maryanski, 1979, p. 119). Talcott Parsons, in *The Structure of Social Action*, suggested that Durkheim failed to avoid a "metaphysical" conception of the reality of society (1968, p. 357). This kind of interpretation goes back to the time of the publication of the books, when his critics accused him of replacing science with ontology and claimed that he had revived Scholasticism, i.e., the teleological realism of the classics and Aquinas (Lukes, 1973, p. 306). The persistence of these interpretations is not surprising, for it has a solid textual basis in Durkheim's writings, particularly in his continuation of Mill's, Comte's, Quetelet's, and Spencer's usages of the terms 'social organism' and 'social body', in his fondness for the analogy between sociology and biology, in particular usages such as his concepts of normalcy and pathology, and in his 'functionalist' substantive explanations, for example in *The Division of Labor in Society*.

As we have seen, the dispute over cause and teleology ran through the nineteenth century and had reached a confused peak shortly before Durkheim wrote. Recognizing the salience of these issues at the time is a first step in sorting out the usages, and answering the question of what Durkheim himself meant by them. Durkheim continued to write actively on philosophical topics throughout his life and was certainly aware of the issues, so he cannot be regarded as though he were a *naive* borrower of vague 'organic' analogies and usages. His own self-characterizations underline this: he denied that he was influenced by the unambiguously organicist Schäffle, as one of his contemporary interpreters had claimed (Durkheim, 1982, p. 259), and the poses he struck generally placed him on the side of the antiteleologists. In his thesis defense (of The Division of Labor), he denied that he had departed from an absolute "mechanicism" (Lukes, 1973, p. 297): "I am a scientist: I study motion" (quoted in Lukes, 1973, p. 298).

Many usages that are superficially 'teleological', such as 'normalcy' and 'equilibrium', have a prior history. Such writers as Quetelet used them in nonteleological ways and as part of a causalist, 'physical science model', sociology. Thus, to assess Durkheim's uses of the concepts, it is essential to see how they figure in the strict development of his technical methodological argument. As it happens, Durkheim took care to address the logical issues surrounding each usage.

The problem of distinguishing the normal and the pathological, perhaps the most delicate of these issues, is handled in Chapter Three of the *Rules*. Durkheim's approach is characteristic of his other discussions of usages that can be given teleological interpretations: the issues raised in the preceding thirty years, from evolution to the revival of vitalism, are touched on, but lightly, and only to make a highly specific point in connection with his own argument. In this case, the point is to show the dependence of the distinction between normal and pathological on causal analysis, i.e., to analyze a teleological notion causally. The role of the concept in his account may be seen by a comparison to Quetelet, who had suggested that the physician's concept of health "is only a similar estimate to that which" Quetelet wished "to make on a greater scale and with more accuracy" by the calculation of precise statistical limits (Quetelet, 1842, p. 99).

Durkheim gave two basic arguments on this topic, one that relies on Quetelet's point about the *de facto* relationship between normalcy or averageness and health, another that turns it upside down. The first is a conceptual argument. Following Quetelet, he defined the "average type" as "the hypothetical being which might be constituted by assembling in one entity, as a kind of individual abstraction, the most frequently occurring characteristics of the species in their most frequent forms" (1982, pp. 91–92; cf. 1964, p. 56; 1937, p. 56). The remaining characteristics are, by definition, exceptional: they may occur infrequently in the life of an individual, as sicknesses do, or in a minority of cases. Durkheim here was forced to resort to legerdemain. He *defined* characteristics with these distributions of occurrence as pathological. "We may then say," he concluded, "that the normal type merges into the average type and that any deviation from that standard of healthiness is a morbid phenomenon" (1982, pp. 91–92; cf. 1964, p. 56; 1937, p. 56).

Durkheim's second argument is that the characteristics that form the normal type must have 'adaptive value' (1964, p. 50; 1982, pp. 87–88; 1937, p. 50). In the muddle of contemporary biology, this concept was little more than a muddle itself. Rather than base anything on these biological doctrines, Durkheim's discussion relies on the notion of probabilities of survival, again borrowed from Quetelet. But he gave this concept a 'causal' twist. If the distribution from which one plots statistical 'norms' can itself be explained causally, it can be explained without recourse to such devices as the theory of the *homme moyen*. And these causal explanations suggest a notion of normalcy more fundamental than 'averageness'. The need for some more fundamental notion was evident to Durkheim from the first. In his thesis, he had characterized the current forms of the division of labor as abnormal – so this use of 'abnormal' conflicts with the actual distributions of present forms of the division of labor. This mode of social criticism, especially in the form of the claim that particular institutions or practices were suited to earlier historical periods, and irrational or unjustified in the present, was characteristic of post-Enlightenment thought. This suggests that if a feature of society is found universally within a social species, it may nevertheless not be an adaptation. It may, for example, be a throwback, which persists only as a consequence of blind force of habit.

If a distribution has been causally explained by way of explanations that appeal to a "mechanically necessary effect of these conditions" of existence (1964, p. 60; 1982, p. 94; 1937, p. 60), one can ask whether the feature is an effect of current conditions or merely of conditions that no longer hold. By this reasoning, Durkheim demystified Quetelet's averages: "the general distribution of normal phenomena" is, he argued, "itself an explainable phenomenon," and "after it has been definitely established by observation it should be explained" (1964, p. 59; 1982, p. 94; 1937, p. 59). He avoided any commitment to an explanatory use of the term 'normal': the *causes* do the explaining. Normalcy vanishes under this analysis: the normalcy of a social fact is no more than its presence in the average society of a particular species of society at the corresponding stage of its development – when its general presence "*is bound up with the general conditions of collective life of the social type considered*" (1964, p. 64; 1982, p. 97; 1937, p. 64, emphasis in original).

In practice, causal sociological explanations of adaptation will often resemble the reasoning about adaptation characteristic of teleological utilitarianism, because "showing that the trait is useful to the organism" will often be a part of the total causal explanation of a social fact. But "it can also happen ... that a situation is normal without being at all useful, simply because it is necessarily implied in the nature of the being" (1964, p. 59; 1982, p. 94; 1937, p. 59), or, as in the case of survivals, phenomena are explainable but are neither 'useful' nor connected with the *current* constitution of the social organism (1964, pp. 60–61; 1982, pp. 94–95; 1937, pp. 60–61). So the fact that something is normal does not imply it is useful (1964, p. 63; 1982, p. 96; 1937, p. 63). Consequently, teleological utilitarianism cannot be a substitute for a full causal sociology.

CLASSIFICATION AND SPECIES

Understood in a causal way, Durkheim suggested, 'normal' means consistent with the law of development for the particular type of society, a law which is determinable only at a fairly "advanced stage of science" (1964, pp. 54–55; 1982, p. 91; 1937, p. 55). "Each species has a health of its own, because it has an average type of its own. Hence, there exists a state of health for the lowest species as well as for the highest. The same principle applies to sociology, although it is often misunderstood here" (1964, p. 56; 1982, p. 92; 1937, p. 56). One motivation for this claim is evident enough: the standards of health in the simpler societies can obviously not be applied to modern societies. But to the extent that the notions of social species and 'social organism' are themselves teleological or 'metaphysically realist' Durkheim has gone from the frying pan into the fire. The same questions about teleology need to be asked about his concept of social species, which is developed in Chapter Four of the *Rules*.

The chapter begins by giving some methodological guidelines for classifying societies into species. The guidelines amount to the admonition that the classification be inductive rather than 'ideological'. He suggested a classification on the basis of structural simplicity and complexity, based on the idea of social segmentation. His argument for this classification is that the undifferentiated horde, i.e., one without any segmentation, is the logical limit of the concept of segmentation. Paul Hirst, in his account of Durkheim's view of the origin of society, has argued that this is an illicit move, since the

whole discussion ... is based upon a play on the word 'element'. In the beginning of the discussion he treats the social whole as a simple unity without social parts whose 'elements' consist of 'things and persons'. But when he comes to discuss the different effects of the forms of association, combination and juxtaposition, he is discussing what he previously called 'complex' wholes, and the 'elements' of those wholes are not 'things and persons' but simpler societies (1975, p. 168).

If this is illicit, it is a flaw in a central place in Durkheim's argument, for it is here that the level of social fact which Durkheim's explanations involve first emerges.

The term 'element' has a considerable prehistory in the methodological literature. It is found in both Quetelet and Buckle. In Quetelet it referred to what would now be called 'variables' (1842, pp. 79, 96, 106–107). In Buckle it was a term for basic building blocks of society, such as "the mental element," religion, literature, and government (1859, p. 183). To show that the classifications Durkheim spoke of involve 'elements' of this kind does not involve him in the contradiction Hirst has in mind: societies may well be 'made of men' without this meaning that they must be classified in terms of units that refer to individual persons. Nevertheless, the term 'element' does suggest that new ontological commitments are being made. Durkheim recognized that his readers, like Hirst, would suspect he had put something over on them, and he responded to the question which "the reader has perhaps put to himself as he has followed this discussion: How can we deal with social species as if there were such things without having directly established their existence?" (1964, p. 86; 1982, p. 116; 1937, p. 86).

"We have seen," he said, "that societies are only different combinations of one and the same original society" (1964, p. 86; 1982, p. 116; 1937, p. 86). By this he meant that the type which he took to be the logical limit of the concept of society, the undifferentiated horde, may be combined with other units in various ways. Historical societies, which are differentiated, pre-sumably derived from earlier, undifferentiated hordes. Durkheim had in mind that the social idea that defines membership of a given horde persists after 'combination' with other societies: the new 'society' created by this combination retains an 'element' – the collectively held social or legal distinctions – of the precombination situation. The simplest case of this is found at the first step above the horde, a society made of 'clans', which originally were no more than juxtaposed hordes: the recognition by the members of one group of the categories of the other group is a kind of symbolic change which creates a 'union' between two separate units.

The 'elements' which Durkheim chose when he suggested segmentation as a basis of a system of classification are defined by the collective represen-tations of the actors in the social aggregate itself. Thus the 'reality' of 'society' so classified derives from the reality of the collective represen-tations themselves. These representations have already been admitted, provisionally, to the status of 'fact' by Durkheim's original definition of social fact, for they are among the things that have the constraining charac-ter that distinguishes the category of social fact. The concept of 'morphol-ogy' has a distinct history in Durkheim's own writing. Throughout his work, the constitutive classifying and organizing features of society, what he called "collective ways of being," play a central explanatory role. In the early writings, these ways of being are put into the category of morphologi-cal facts (1982, pp. 57–58; 1964, pp. 11–12; 1937, pp. 12–14). Later the term fades – the 'segments' discussed in such essays as 'Primitive Classifi-cation' (Durkheim and Mauss, 1963) are treated as representations.[2]

Thus Durkheim was careful to add no ontological implications by his discussion of social species to what had already been admitted by his discussion of social fact. He was not forced to claim that 'society' is 'real' in any sense beyond that in which the various collective representations are 'real'. The reality of 'society', as it is spoken of here, is derivative from these collective representations in that one identifies 'a society' and its state of organization by first identifying the collective representations by which individuals define themselves and one another. The concept of representations permits the use of the concept 'society', but there is no additional explanatory need to claim *metaphysical* reality for 'society'. This explains why Durkheim described his notion of social species as a middle ground between the 'realist' conception of society, which he attributed to philosophers, and the nominalist conception (1964, p. 76; 1982, p. 108; 1937, p. 76). It differs from the nominalist conception in that his classification is derived from facts which are themselves 'real'. However, it may be recalled that, on Durkheim's own definition, social facts, including such collective representations as '*la France*', are real or exist only insofar as they constrain individuals, a 'reality' that 'realism' would regard as nominalistic in contradistinction to the reality it would claim for its own concepts of 'humanity', 'community', or the *polis*.

THE CRITIQUE OF TELEOLOGY

A metaphysical theory of society would base its explanations on its definition of society: this is the 'ideological method'. Teleological evolutionism does this in a subtle way, by means of classifications that define 'advanced' in a way that confirms the explanation. Spencer's evolutionism falls into the error of substituting a teleological classification for an explanation, and Comte too, Durkheim suggested, was a teleologist, tracing "the entire progressive force of the human species to ... [a] fundamental tendency 'which directly impels man constantly to ameliorate his condition, whatever it may be, under all circumstances'" (quoted in Durkheim, 1964, p. 89; 1982, p. 119; 1937, p. 89). Durkheim was careful to claim that his own concept of social species is not explanatory. Chapter Five, 'Rules for the Explanation of Social Facts', begins with the assertion that "social morphology is only one step towards the truly explanatory part of the science" (1982, p. 119; cf. 1964, p. 89; 1937, p. 89).

We have noted that Durkheim himself frequently used teleological utilitarian arguments. Nevertheless, he denied that this kind of explanation was sufficient for the explanation of social facts. In this chapter, Durkheim mounted a more aggressive attack against teleology. He pointed out that utility cannot by itself explain why a thing comes into being in the first place, nor can it explain the specific nature of a thing. To explain the creation of a thing one would show how it was created, and this explanation would appeal to efficient causes or antecedent forces (1964, p. 90; 1982, pp. 119–20; 1937, p. 90). It might seem that *actions* could be explained by their utility, and that therefore social facts that have been produced by actions resulting from individual desires and needs can be explained by appeal to some principle of utility. Durkheim argued that they cannot: a "*tendance*," an impulse, need, or desire, "is itself ... objectively real; it can, then, neither be created nor modified by the mere fact that we judge it useful. It is a force having a nature of its own," which must be produced or changed by other prior forces (1964, p. 92; 1982, p. 121; 1937, p. 92).

Durkheim questioned the application of teleology to social life more generally when he pointed out that "where purpose reigns, there reigns also a more or less wide contingency," for many different ways can be taken to arrive at the same goal (1964, p. 94; 1982, p. 122; 1937, p. 94). By identifying an end one does not determine which of a wide range of means must be selected. Therefore, it is especially weak as a mode of theorizing. 'Cause', on the other hand, is a mode that may be refined to the ultimate in determinateness. And this fits the explanatory needs of sociology. When we look at social facts, Durkheim pointed out, we see evidence of an orderliness that goes far beyond the orderliness of 'purpose'. We see "astonishing regularity" in such "trivial practices" as the nuptial practice of carrying off the betrothed, which "is to be found wherever a certain family type exists" (1964, p. 94; cf. 1982, p. 123; 1937, p. 94).[3] These regularities would remain forever inexplicable if sociology restricted itself to teleology.

In these discussions of causal explanation, Durkheim seems to identify it with explanation *tout court*, and there is to be found in his writings no further discussion of functional explanation as an additional special type of explanation. Yet Durkheim nevertheless spoke of functions, and some of his explanations have been taken by later writers to be the paradigm of 'functionalism'. One may wonder whether there is an implicit theory of functional explanation in Durkheim that nullifies all his explicit methodological claims about explanation. Parsons, who turned away Durkheim's criticisms of teleology by such remarks as "A repudiation of teleology in this simple sense does not force one to accept naturalistic causation as the only alternative" (1968, p. 406), would have answered 'yes', and the answer has its attractions: it resolves the apparent conflict between Durkheim's strictures in the *Rules* and his more casual and lavish uses of functional analyses in the sociological writings. One form of this resolution is given by Nisbet, who distinguishes between 'functional' and 'teleological' reasoning by characterizing teleology as the argument "that all social behavior must be seen in terms of a design formed by certain ends which are antecedent to the behavior, thus making for the kind of symmetry much prized by 17th-century rationalists" (Nisbet, 1974, p. 68). Some textual warrant for thinking that Durkheim himself identified 'teleology' with this argument may indeed be found in the methodological writings, as when he spoke of teleology as the view that "society is only a system of means instituted by men to attain certain ends" (1964, p. 97; 1982, p. 125; 1937, p. 97). But this is not the only context in which he used the term 'teleology', and therefore the net effect of this line of interpretation is to point up these variations in usage and to create a new puzzle over the conflict between Durkheim's methodological claims and his practice.

'FUNCTION' AND 'MAINTENANCE'

One can scarcely read too much into Durkheim's comments on cause and teleology, for at the time Durkheim wrote no issue so dominated French philosophy. Boutroux and Paul Janet had made these issues a focus of their work: Boutroux in *The Contingency of the Laws of Nature* (1916), first published in 1874, and *Natural Law in Science and Philosophy* (1914), first published in 1895, Janet in *Final Causes* (1878), first published in 1876. Boutroux attempted to salvage teleology at the cosmological level. Janet sought to show that final causes are not inconsistent with physical causation, and that physical causation is not sufficient. Durkheim's argument is a mirror image of this.

Much of Janet's book is a detailed analysis of the distinctions made by various physiologists in support of specific biological doctrines, for, as he put it, the "battlefield of the two theories [mechanism and finality] is the domain of the organism" (1878, p. 155). It is difficult to recapture his dialectical style without explaining a great deal of the local intellectual context. Much of the discussion consists in showing how teleological interpretations of various scientific concepts may be made consistent with the 'facts' of science, and the analyses often amount to teleological reinterpretations of terms that scientists had originally devised to avoid teleology. A fair sample of this is Janet's discussion of instinctual action in animals:

What characterises the actions of man is to act knowingly for an end. As to the actions of which we are speaking, everything leads to the belief that they are not done knowingly. But apart from this difference, the similarity is entire. It therefore remains to be said that, without knowing it, these animals act for an end. Thus the end which we had already recognised in the intelligent actions of animals cannot disappear merely because we here meet with a new and unexpected condition, namely unconsciousness. Instinct, then, will reveal to us an unconscious finality, but still a finality (1878, p. 95).

To Janet, the preference for nonteleological language in this case is simply unwarranted. "Why should the same fact, exactly the same, produced by means strictly similar (although the operation be instinctive, in place of being voluntary), be called in this case an *end*, in that a *result*? Why should the web of the workman be an end, the web of the spider a result?" (1878, p. 96, emphasis in original). Indeed, he went on to argue, "what instinctive motions have in common with voluntary" is that they *have* an end, such as a web (1878, pp. 96–97). The same point holds for an animal's "internal operations, which are called its functions" (1878, p. 97). These "are equally directed towards an end" (1878, p. 102).

The fact that Janet treated function as a notion that needs *analysis* in order to be made teleological shows that, like instinct, the term was understood to be *nonteleological* or neutral. Other usages, such as 'organization' and the 'harmony' of 'parts and wholes', are given the same treatment (1878, pp. 126, 143). Janet recognized that "often ... after having nominally excluded final causes, one resumes them without perceiving it, by attributing to living nature a spontaneous property of accommodation and adaptation, which is nothing else than finality itself under another name" (1878, p. 144). However, he did not attempt to give a conceptual argument to the effect that this is necessary. He was content to show that the teleological vocabulary is equally applicable in the biological contexts in which these various nonteleological concepts are used, i.e., to treat mechanism and teleology as rival hypotheses, because he believed that an *exclusively* 'mechanical' interpretation of reality is impossible or insufficient, and that this suffices to legitimate teleology. In a curious passage on Bacon, Janet remarked:

When Bacon removed final causes from physics, in order to remit them to metaphysics, it was no vain subterfuge, but a distinction as solid as profound. The physicist seeks for the physical and concrete conditions of phenomena; the metaphysician seeks their intellectual signification. But the second of these points of view is in no way excluded by the first; and after having explained how things happen, it is still competent to ask why they happen thus. The question of the how does not exclude that of the why, and leaves it entirely open (1878, p. 181).

This is what Janet wished to leave open: the possibility of this second line of defense, which had, by this time, become the inner perimeter of teleologism.

Durkheim, one may suppose, knew all of these philosophical arguments and was very far from unwitting in his choice of language. When he used the term 'function', it was in place of 'end' or 'purpose', and was used in order to avoid the criticism that he was really offering teleological arguments. The way in which he introduced the term 'function', by defining it in *causal* terms, also suggests that his aim was to avoid these criticisms. He nevertheless, on occasion, used such notions as "the general needs of the social organism," which suggest teleology. The short resolution to this puzzle is that Durkheim did not think of such phrases as 'needs of the organism' as teleological, and that this was not so much a result of error on his part as a result of a subsequent shift in the use of the term 'teleology'.

The shift is evident in Ernest Nagel's *The Structure of Science*, where he distinguishes between teleological and nonteleological statements in a way that assumes that function is a *teleological* term.

Consider, for example, the teleological statement 'The function of the leucocytes in human blood is to defend the body against foreign micro-organisms'. Now whatever may be the evidence that warrants this statement, that evidence also confirms the nonteleological statement 'Unless human blood contains a sufficient number of leucocytes, certain normal activities of the body are impaired', and conversely (1961, p. 405).

One may question whether this analysis is any better as a response to the claims of teleology than Durkheim's. Victor Gourevitch, commenting on Nagel, asks:

In what possible sense are such terms as 'sufficient', 'normal activities', and 'impaired' less teleological than the terms 'function' and 'defend' which they replace? Taken in and by itself alone a blood-count is a mere number. As such, it is wholly meaningless and uninformative. It yields information only when it is compared to a normal blood-count, that is to say to the blood-count of persons who are known to be healthy and whose bodies are *therefore* said to exhibit 'normal activities'. The knowledge that someone is healthy precedes and is independent of our taking their blood-count as a standard. It is pre-scientific, or first for us (Gourevitch, 1968, p. 293, emphasin in original).

"The only real difference between Nagel's two statements," Gourevitch concludes, "is that the so-called nonteleological statement takes for granted what the teleological statement renders explicit" (1968, p. 293). Durkheim, as we have seen, would have rejected as 'teleological' Gourevitch's idea that our knowledge of 'health' 'precedes and is independent of' our causal understanding of normalcy. But he would have considered Nagel's 'teleological statement' to be 'nonteleological'. *How* he would have interpreted it is best seen in his own uses in the *Rules*.

These uses need a bit of disentangling. Durkheim's primary use of 'function' is in the context of advice about the conduct of inquiries. He advised that problems of function and cause be separated, and that questions about cause be treated first, questions about function second: "This order of precedence corresponds to that of the facts. It is natural to seek the cause of a phenomenon before attempting to determine its effects" (1982, pp. 123–24; cf. 1964, p. 95; 1937, p. 95). This implies that a 'function' for Durkheim is a kind of effect. He said that "social phenomena generally do not exist for the usefulness of the results they produce." 'Function', then, does not mean 'useful effects' (1982, p. 123; 1964, p. 95; 1937, p. 95). But he also said, in the next sentence, that "we must determine whether there is a correspondence between the fact under consideration and the general needs of the social organism." This makes sense only if one usually expects to find some connection between functions and 'needs of the organism' – an expectation that seems to amount to teleological utilitarianism.

A few pages before, Durkheim had expressed strong objections to both teleological utilitarianism and the notion of adaptation, characterizing them as hopelessly vague and imprecise. How, one might ask, can any explanatory use of function in relation to 'needs' escape these devastating objections? Durkheim's general account of complex systems is itself an answer to this question. He observed that the relation of cause to effect is to some extent reciprocal. An effect cannot exist without its cause. But often the cause cannot exist without its effect, since the effect often "restores" the "energy" of the cause (1964, p. 95; 1982, p. 124; 1937, p. 95). The effects, in other words, may include some of the preconditions for the fact that is the cause. This consideration is the key to Durkheim's own analysis.

'Maintenance' might be explicated either teleologically or entirely in terms of cause and effect. Durkheim said that it is generally necessary that a social fact be useful in order for it to maintain itself (1964, p. 97; 1982, p. 124; 1937, p. 96). But the reason for this is not that there is a true teleological principle, such as 'all social facts are useful to the social organism'. On the contrary, some social facts, such as survivals, are simply not useful (1964, p. 91; 1982, p. 120; 1937, p. 91). So whether a fact is useful is contingent, not necessary. The reason *most* social facts are useful is that the maintenance of a social fact requires effort. If most social facts were parasitic in character, i.e., made no contribution to social life, "the budget of the organism would have a deficit" (1964, p. 97; 1982, p. 124; 1937, p. 97). These are puzzling passages. But they can be understood in a causalist way, and this fits best with Durkheim's general views.

Durkheim's intention was to give a causalist analysis of 'maintenance' in terms of reciprocity, and he was so pleased with his results that he remarked, in a note, that "if more profoundly analyzed, this reciprocity of cause and effect might furnish a means of reconciling scientific mechanism with the teleology which the existence, and especially the persistence, of life implies" (1964, p. 96n; 1982, p. 144n; 1937, pp. 95–96n). He seems to have been oblivious to the 'teleological' implications of the language of effort, budget, and vital force which the analysis employs. Part of the explanation for this obliviousness is historical. The latter two usages are each to be found in Quetelet (1842, pp. 102, 5), who seemed not to consider them to carry any teleological implications. Among the most stunning scientific achievements of the nineteenth century was Carnot's theory of the transformation of forces, and this theory and its successors were the source of much of Durkheim's vocabulary – including his pet term 'current' and, for that matter, the term 'vital power'. J. P. Joule, who was the first person to grasp the significance of Carnot's work, entitled a key work 'Matter, Living Force, and Heat' (Joule, 1963). This paper has been called "the first full and clear exposition of that principle now called *energy*" (Singer, 1959, p. 376, emphasis in original). By Durkheim's time the applications of the related concept of reservoir had become a commonplace in psychology.[4] None of these usages were understood to be 'teleological' in their original scientific contexts.

It is reasonable to think that a social fact that maintains itself over a long period of time has a cause to which its own effects somehow contribute. Thus, seeking the functions of a fact in order to see how it maintains itself amounts to seeking this reciprocal relationship between cause and effect and identifying the particular links in the causal chain, or net of causal links, that make up this reciprocal relationship. Notice that there is no *necessity* here apart from the necessary relationship between each cause and each effect. The *existence* of such a reciprocal relationship itself is not necessitated by anything at all. It is *merely contingent* that a fact is part of a net – that the effect of a given fact contributes to the maintenance of this fact.

This suggests that Durkheim was merely offering prudential advice when he suggested that one should seek 'functions' as well as causes. His intention is clear from the way the concluding sentence of the section on functions is formulated: "Thus to explain a fact which is vital, it is not enough to show the cause on which it depends. We must also – at least in most cases – discover the part that it plays in the establishment of that general harmony" (1982, p. 125; 1964, p. 97; 1937, p. 97).[5] We can take this 'harmony' to be a contingent, causal result – and Durkheim has given us good reasons to think that this is the only useful way it can be spoken of. The reason we must seek functions in *most* cases rather than *all* cases is that all social facts do not depend on a reciprocal relation in which their effects are conditions for their causes. Moreover, there is no necessity that even those facts that maintain themselves depend on such reciprocal relations. 'Survivals', to choose Durkheim's own example, do not.

The meaning of 'function' for Durkheim, then, was not 'effects that are useful to the social organism'. It was 'effects that are conditions for the cause of the fact', i.e., effects that are part of this kind of reciprocal relationship. Even Durkheim's reference to 'the establishment of harmony' in the concluding sentence of the section must be understood not as a reference to a teleological 'need for order' in the 'social organism'. The 'harmony of the organism' that is explained by the tracing of causal relationships is no more or less than the maintenance of particular social facts in a kind of 'system of reciprocities'. The maintenance of the 'system' is itself a kind of precondition for the existence of the particular social facts that compose the system. But these reciprocities are entirely causal, and the 'system' may be explained entirely through causal explanations. The facts that are maintained by these causes are, from the point of view of the causes, the 'ends' which the causes 'function' to produce.

Durkheim's point in this section, then, is that teleological explanations are not necessary to account for the phenomenon of the 'maintenance' of social facts. He was thus not smuggling teleology back in with the concept of function, but banishing teleology more effectively by showing that the facts which the teleologists attempt to explain may be explained, and explained better, by causal explanations. If Durkheim had intended to propound a teleological functionalism, it would have been necessary for him to identify a kind of fixed 'end' toward which society is oriented. It is not surprising that he did not. Instead his argument is that the maintenance of a particular social fact is causally explainable, as is the maintenance of a set of social facts that are related through causal reciprocities, and that not only do these explanations not require any *telos*, they render entirely superfluous explanations offered in a less satisfactory, less precise form by teleologists, such as Spencer.

Durkheim's self-consciousness about the eliminability of teleological arguments is most visible in the *Rules*. In the earlier *The Division of Labor*, he, to use his own words, "explained the constant development of the division of labour by showing that it is necessary in order that man may maintain himself in the new conditions of existence as he advances in history" (1964, p. 92; 1982, p. 121; 1937, p. 92). The need of man to 'maintain himself' perhaps sounds like a teleological principle, indeed the very teleological principle that figured in the writings of some of his predecessors – Spencer again comes to mind. In the *Rules*, Durkheim denied that this explanation even partially reverts to teleology. His reasoning is that the so-called 'instinct of self-preservation' does not in itself account for any facts about the division of labor. The work of the explanation is done by the appeal to various specific causal conditions plus 'impulses.'

Impulse is a term to which we will return in connection with Durkheim's model of individual action. For the moment it will suffice to notice that impulse is a paradigmatically causal notion, as is 'condition'. The effect of the conditions was that the particular direction that attempts at self-preservation took were constrained. Individuals pursuing unspecialized tasks found survival more difficult, so they were constrained to specialize. The individual's alternatives to specializing were emigration, suicide, or crime. But these paths are blocked, by the constraints: his ties to his country, his sympathy for his fellows, and the like. In the average case, specialization is the path of least resistance. The habits that prevent narrower specialization "had inevitably to yield to each impulse that arose" (1964, p. 93; 1982, p. 122; 1937, p. 93).

The phenomenon of social development that would be explained by the teleological principle of self-preservation, then, may be explained in causal terms, and teleology in this particular case serves no explanatory role.[6] This analysis of a teleological principle into causal components carries out one of the basic intentions of the *Rules*: to show the gratuitousness, on the one hand, and inferiority, on the other, of teleological explanations of social facts. This is the animus behind his argument that his approach can best handle the facts that the teleological approach had traditionally handled, the fact of the maintenance of beneficial institutions, and his desire in his discussions of such characteristically teleological notions as 'normalcy' and 'pathology' to show that they can be given a causalist, nonteleological interpretation, and also to show that his realism is not the realism appropriate to the teleological tradition, but is Baconian substantialism. His defense of cause is a mirror of the kind of defense of teleology mounted by Janet and Boutroux: their argument that causal analysis alone is 'insufficient' is countered by his argument that teleology is eliminable.

CHAPTER SEVEN

COLLECTIVE FORCES, CAUSATION, AND PROBABILITY

THE CASE FOR COLLECTIVE FORCES

Morals is the paradigmatic area for which the case for Durkheim's account of the reality of social facts is articulated (Giddens, 1971, p. 218). The thrust of Durkheim's argument is that obligation cannot be understood without some notion of causally compelling social facts. This is a puzzling argument, in part because of its structure. As we have seen, the *Rules* begins with a definition of social facts that defines these facts in terms of 'generality', and identifies generality with the possession of an obligatory character – this last left only vaguely specified (1964, p. 9; 1982, p. 56; 1937, p. 10). By the point in the text that it is claimed that 'social facts' are *necessary* to explain obligation (e.g., 1964, pp. 121–24; 1982, pp. 142–44; 1937, pp. 120–23), a great many things other than obligations have been included in the category, and the argument begins to seem to be little more than a tautology, whose tautologous structure is concealed by the strange variousness of the things that fall into the category of social facts, a diversity that many commentators have complained about (e.g. Giddens, 1971, p. 218; Lukes, 1971, pp. 190–93).

Durkheim had a response to the apparent peculiarities of placing these things into the same category. He argued that there is a common feature to all of the things in the category, a 'collective aspect' which he construed in each case as involving 'consciousness'. In *Suicide*, a work that appeared between the two editions of the *Rules*, he said that "it is clear that essentially social life is made up of representations" (1951, p. 312; 1930, p. 352). This slogan puts the point the other way around – but hardly resolves the puzzle.

One of Durkheim's motivations for classing social facts in the category of facts of consciousness is obvious. Doing so avoids a painful set of difficulties over causality. Conceiving of social facts as facts of consciousness avoids well-known Cartesian difficulties (which Eclecticism, and writers such as Fouillée, with his *idées forces*, had preserved as part of Durkheim's philosophical present) over the question of how a *direct* causal connection could exist between, e.g., a material fact and a command, or between a material fact and a fact of consciousness. The notion of causal

124

relations between various facts of consciousness is itself problematic, but from one point of view it is less problematic than the notion of causal relations between material facts and facts of consciousness.

Facts such as population density or the laws of a nation are not in any simple sense facts of consciousness, as Durkheim was aware. Density, a favorite explanatory fact in Spencer and Sumner as well, is more like a material or environmental fact. Legal codes are more frequently understood as having the character of commands of the sovereign or agreements of the legislature than as facts of 'consciousness'. So these facts would not ordinarily be thought of as being governed by 'laws of consciousness', collective or otherwise, and Durkheim needed to make an effort to construe them as such.

If one is to claim that the legal code is properly understood as a fact of the collective consciousness, it is useful to have already argued, as Durkheim had, that the prescientific understanding of social and political things is defective, or potentially defective, for it takes something of a suspension of our ordinary understanding of these things to claim that the fundamental character of these facts is their character as 'facts of consciousness'. And this is precisely what must be claimed. If we are to say that the laws governing the collective consciousness explain the fact that a particular legal code exists in a particular society, the fact of consciousness cannot simply be a consequence of the fact that the sovereign commanded or the legislature agreed to the legal code. Yet that is how we ordinarily would reason – that we become 'collectively aware' of a new law *because* it has been adopted. Durkheim must argue the other way around. He must say that the law is a manifestation of a collective sentiment, and serves as an index of this fact of collective consciousness. This is by no means an incomprehensible argument. One could hardly understand the changes in obscenity law or the disuse of the death penalty in recent years merely as 'commands of the sovereign' or 'agreements of the legislature'. It would be necessary to understand the changes in the common conceptions of sexuality and human life as well. And these conceptions more readily answer to the name 'collective consciousness'.

'Density' becomes a fact of consciousness by a similar transformation. Density, if it is understood purely as a physical fact, "can have no effect if the individuals, or rather the groups of individuals, remain separated by social distance" (1964, pp. 113–14; 1982, p. 136; 1937, p. 112). Durkheim defined 'dynamic density' in terms of the numbers of individuals actually having social relations. He confessed, "We made the mistake, in our

Division du travail, of presenting material density too much as the exact expression of dynamic density" (1964, p. 115n; 1982, p. 146n; 1937, p. 113n). In the *Rules* he was clear that the best expression of the dynamic density was "le degré de coalescence des segments sociaux" (1937, p. 113; 1964, p. 114; 1982, p. 137), a notion that appeared in the chapter on classification, in connection with the binding together of the segments of segmentary societies. Here the notion is generalized to modern societies. The existence of roads and railroads, which we might think of as the cause of an increase in the number of social relations, is understood by Durkheim as an "imperfect index" of the "fusion of populations," which he treated as a fact of consciousness. Durkheim's example is the difference between France and England. In England, Durkheim said, "local spirit" persists to a greater extent than in France, meaning that the *coalescence* is less complete, and therefore the "dynamic density" is not as great (1964, p. 115; 1982, p. 137; 1937, p. 114).

The conclusion of these conceptually high-handed discussions of density and legal regulations is that these facts *can* be conceived of as facts of consciousness. But the arguments establish no more than the *possibility* of conceiving of them in this way. They show that there is an aspect of each of these facts that may be understood as a fact of consciousness. They are not, however, philosophical or conceptual arguments to the effect that this aspect is fundamental. Indeed, the entire notion that there are 'social facts', facts beyond the order of our ordinary understanding of social and political things, was treated by Durkheim as a kind of large hypothesis. No logical or conceptual necessity attaches to it. In order to treat them as facts at all, facts that explain individual human action scientifically, they must themselves be shown to be within the realm of scientific law and the order this implies. To do this, Durkheim must produce some indication of the existence of systematic regular relations between the facts of social life conceived as 'social facts'. Put differently, a case for treating the 'consciousness' aspect of these facts as fundamental must rest on the discovery of causal laws that systematically govern relations between these facts. If he fails to discover such laws, the whole notion of 'social facts' and 'laws of the collective consciousness' must be dismissed as a possible but unsupported hypothesis.

Yet – and this is really the key to Durkheim – if he had succeeded in generating a significant set of strict regularities between 'social facts', we would find no special difficulty in accepting that the relevant feature of an institution is its ideational aspect. In the face of many regularities of this sort, a complaint like Lukes's remark that there is an "ambiguity" in

Durkheim's category of social facts between things that are "imposed" by means of sanctions and things that are imposed by means of internalization (1971, p. 193), or Giddens's complaint that "moral sanction is not intrinsic to the act which is sanctioned" (1971, p. 218), would gradually come to carry no more weight than the complaint of a Schoolman to Newton that his category of 'motion' failed to differentiate between motions that were essentially 'natural' and those that were essentially 'violent'. In contexts where there are laws, what counts for us as natural or 'intrinsic' is insepara- ble from the laws themselves, as in the case of natural motion, and not a criterion for the acceptability of the laws. The issue here may be put another way. For Durkheim, our phenomenological sense of the difference between moral sanction and 'internalized' constraints, to which Lukes appeals, is spurious, a Baconian *idola*. The reality of a social fact and its causal force is a matter of what are, in principle, calculable relations between this fact and other facts, particularly such outcomes as acts in violation of the law. Lukes's contrast between 'imposed' and 'internalized' social facts, Durkheim would say, is formulable only in the epistemologically dubious terminology of phenomenological experience or introspection.

TECHNICAL ASPECTS OF THE PROBLEM OF CAUSE

For the methodologist, as distinct from the metaphysician, choosing sides in the quarrel over cause and teleology is just a beginning. To make good on his picture of a causal, nomic sociology, Durkheim must not only show that causal laws govern social facts, but prior to doing so he must settle, or at least take sides on, the various issues about causality and the form of causal explanation in the human sciences that could be taken to vitiate any claim that a particular pattern he was to discover was really a law. To produce an instance of a law, in short, he must first give an intelligible account of that kind of thing as a law.

In this, the weight of the tradition of Comte, Mill, and Quetelet was a hindrance as well as a help. Their sociology, and specifically the intellec- tualism that had provided them with a mode of organizing historical development, was discredited. Comte's account of causality was not directed to the task of providing a framework for explanatory practice. The methodological discussions in the previous forty years of Mill's Canons had resulted in the erosion of their intellectual authority, especially to the extent that they were understood as an inductivist program. The tension, evident to Mill, between the quest for laws, hitherto barren, and the proliferation of statistical information of all sorts, was, if anything, more apparent in Durkheim's time than it had been in Mill's. Yet the combined legacy of Comte, Mill, and Quetelet, with all its tensions, provided a structured framework of problems which Durkheim could take as given.

The chapter on 'The Explanation of Social Facts' and the penultimate chapter, 'Establishing Sociological Proofs', are Durkheim's attempts to resolve these problems and define himself in relation to this heritage. His critique of Comte begins with a criticism of his implicitly teleological scheme of classification of societies (1964, p. 89; 1982, p. 119; 1937, p. 89), continues with an attack on his teleological psychology (1964, p. 98; 1982, p. 126; 1937, p. 98), and concludes with a rejection of his notion of sociological law. As Durkheim characterized it, Comte's view of law was that the laws of sociology "reveal not definite relations of causality but the direction which human evolution in general takes" (1964, p. 125; 1982, p. 147; 1937, pp. 124–25). The 'historical method' of Comte he considered manifestly circular. Its aim is simply to confirm the developmental law: Comte attempted "to reunite in a single view the successive states of humanity in such a way as to perceive 'the continued growth of each human trait, physical, intellectual, moral, and political'." The method is "stripped of all purpose as soon as one has rejected the fundamental conception of Comtist sociology" (1964, p. 126; 1982, p. 148; 1937, p. 125). The law itself, Durkheim argued, "if it is true, ... is, and can be, only empirical. It is a bird's-eye view of the elapsed history of the human species" (1964, p. 119; 1982, p. 140; 1937, p. 117). The phrase, 'bird's-eye view', curiously, is drawn from the opening of Quetelet's *Social Physics* (1842, p. 5), against which Durkheim will turn an analogous argument.

Durkheim's discussions of Mill and Quetelet are more complex, for he wished to use technical elements supplied by each writer in his own solution to the problem of identifying particular intellectual constructions as causal laws. To understand his approach to these problems, it is necessary to see the underlying consistency in the way he dealt with four basic problems:

> eliminative arguments;
> the plurality of causes;
> probability;
> the composition of forces.

Durkheim's commitments on these issues are closely connected to his practice in *Suicide*, his primary exemplification of a sociological 'law', so it is essential to show how he applied the reasoning.

Durkheim's crucial disagreement with Mill on cause is over the doctrine of the plurality of causes, which is discussed at length in the *Rules*. Durkheim's argument is a conventional one, that the doctrine that different causes can have the same effect depends on a confusion over the concept of 'same effect'. "For common sense, the word 'fever' designates one single morbid condition; for science, there are many fevers, specifically different, and the causes are as numerous as are the effects" (1964, p. 128; 1982, p. 149; 1937, p. 127). The usual way of formulating this point is to observe that a description like 'fever' is incomplete. When the physician makes a diagnosis, the effect that is of interest is the syndrome or bundle of symptoms for which a cause may be assigned. 'Fever' is *part* of the description of the effect, but the causal relation holds under a description of the *total* effect. Durkheim made a somewhat different point,[1] by arguing that to observe a case of plurality of causes one must "have established beforehand either that this plurality is not simply apparent" or that the apparent "*unity* of the effect does not conceal a real *plurality* of effects" (1964, pp. 127–28; 1982, p. 149; cf.1937, pp. 126–27).[2] The centrality to science of the process of identifying real underlying structures is what ultimately tells against the assumption of plurality. "How many times has it has happened that science has reduced to unity causes whose diversity, at first sight, appeared irreducible!" (1982, p. 149; 1964, p. 128; 1937, p. 127). Mill's own observation that the theory of the production of heat took this course – a revealing example – is cited in support of this. In Durkheim's characterization of the lessons of thermodynamics, realism takes the form of skepticism about the adequacy of descriptions of causes. "The production of heat by friction, percussion, chemical action, etc., is in reality only a product from the same single cause" (1964, p. 128; 1982, p. 149; 1937, p. 127).

In the case of various fevers, science shows that the effects are different. "If, among all these different kinds of diseases [i.e., as science describes them] there is, however, something all have in common," the causes of these effects will be found, in the various other cases, to be mingled with other causes (1982, p. 149; 1964, p. 128; 1937, p. 127). If there is nothing in common, we have different effects, and different causes. Where alternative causal explanations of the same effect seem equally plausible, as in the case of punishment, it is a sign that "we have not perceived the common element to be found in all its antecedents, by virtue of which they produce their common effect" (1982, p. 150; 1964, p. 129; 1937, p. 128). The methodological force of this reasoning is regulative. The rule it assumes is: "*To the same effect there always corresponds the same cause*" (1982, p. 150; 1964, p. 128; 1937, p. 127, emphasis in original).

One consequence of this principle is that the eliminative methods which Mill included in the Canons can have, at best, a provisional status, always ready to be overturned by a new advance in science in which a real unity is found below the apparent plurality of causes. Durkheim made the case against these methods on grounds of complexity as well. The sheer number of putative causes in the social sciences in itself makes eliminative arguments futile.

Owing to the too great complexity of the phenomena and the impossibility of all artificial experiments.... the chances of allowing a phenomenon to escape are far greater than those of observing all. Consequently, such a method of demonstration can yield only conjectures which, when considered by themselves, are almost devoid of all scientific value (1964, p. 130; 1982, p. 151; 1937, p. 129).

As a practical matter, then, Mill's Methods of Residues, Agreement, and Difference are useless for the social sciences.

Durkheim's positive picture of causal law also derived from Mill, from his account of the Method of Concomitant Variation. Mill had rejected the application of this method to social science. From Durkheim's point of view, it is an attractive method because it is not subject to the logical problems of the plurality of causes. Since it involves showing that when the property of the cause waxes, the property of the effect waxes and when the cause wanes, the effect wanes, there would be no need for the impractical eliminative arguments countenanced earlier.

What defeats the method in the social sciences, according to Mill, is the fact that

every attribute of the social body is influenced by innumerable causes; and such is the mutual action of the coexisting elements of society that whatever affects any one of the more important of them, will by that alone, if it does not affect the others directly, affect them indirectly (Mill, 1974, p. 884).

Since the method is concerned entirely with quantitative and not qualitative differences, we are powerless to disentangle these effects. If the effect we were concerned with was national wealth, for example, we would always find, together with the effect of national wealth, a great variety of facts, such as the causes that make a people virtuous, or peaceful, or intelligent, which contribute to the effect. The effect is the mixed quantitative result of all the causes, and the total effect "cannot bear any uniform proportion to those of any one of its component parts" (Mill, 1974, p. 884).

Mill's argument is interesting because its conclusion is somewhat weaker than those he mounted against other methods of causal analysis. It asserted a practical methodological difficulty that is very much on a par with the difficulties in explaining a murder rate, not a fundamental logical problem, such as the need to have properly 'decomposed' facts in advance of using the methods. Even where experiment is impossible, we can aim at the discovery of concepts with which we can frame concomitant variations. These conceptualizations might not answer the questions Mill took as paradigmatic, such as, 'What is the cause of national wealth?' (Mill, 1974, pp. 883–84). But they would rightfully answer to the name 'laws of social science'.

Although the discovery of nomic categories is a task of science itself, not an *a priori* task, we may nevertheless ask some extra-scientific questions about it. Why did Durkheim suppose it could be performed? How did he propose to perform it? In searching for the quantitative parallelisms that make up a concomitant variation we are not, Durkheim told us, looking for patterns that are actually universal. Laws, he suggested, following Mill, are tendencies – where B follows A if nothing prevents it from doing so – rather than uniformities, where B *invariably* follows A (1964, p. 131; 1982, p. 152; 1937, p. 130. Cf. Ryan, 1970). He went beyond Mill to say that there must be some sort of connection between cause and effect beyond that which is merely coincidental or external. This is an important requirement for Durkheim to add. Since he has conceded the impossibility of experimental manipulation in sociology, he must find some means to distinguish 'accidental' parallelism between two facts and 'law-governed' connections.

He treated this distinction as a difference in the way in which the links are 'mentally elaborated', a notion in the line of descent of Whewell and of an idea that was later to become part of the Positivist canon, the requirement that an explanatory connection be governed by a hypothesis that is deduced from known laws or from 'theoretical' generalizations. Durkheim suggested that if we happen to stumble on a parallelism in the course of our empirical inquiries without the aid of a theory, we must define a mechanism consistent with known laws and then test it out with new comparisons of series of values before we can accept it as an explanation. Prudence suggests that in such a case our first step should be to look for a third cause "on which the other two depend equally or which have served as an intermediary between them" (1964, p. 132; 1982, p. 152; 1937, p. 131).

Durkheim's reason for supposing that concomitant variations can be found in sociology is that society is the one domain of phenomena in which variations are ubiquitous, and occur over wide ranges. This is a lesson learned from Quetelet, and Durkheim's list of variations (1964, p. 135; 1982, p. 154; 1937, p. 133) is very similar to the list given by Quetelet. Some of the substantive ideas of the two are similar as well. Beyond his interest in quantitative measures, Quetelet was interested in "the influence of religious ideas" and held that:

A very useful addition to moral statistics, would be to point out the dates at which certain practices and customs existed, and also the time when they commenced, and when they ceased. For example, at what period prosecutions for witchcraft were most numerous, when they began to take place, and when they were discontinued (1842, pp. 79–80).

Durkheim could himself have written this passage.

Durkheim makes the broader point that the specific nature of social life is that it "is an uninterrupted series of transformations, parallel to other transformations in the conditions of collective existence" (1964, pp. 134–35; 1982, p. 154; 1937, p. 133). These transformations were understood by Durkheim to include not only the parallelisms that occur within a given society over short ranges of time, but also the parallelisms that occur through the whole range of the history of humanity and for all peoples. Social life is in sharp contrast to biological life in respect of the sheer number and extent of variation. The changes that take place in the course of the life of an organism, Durkheim said, "are few in number and very restricted" (1964, p. 134; 1982, p. 154; 1937, p. 133). So the feature that permits causal explanation in sociology is also the feature that distinguishes sociological causal explanation from biological causal explanation.

PROBABILITY AND CONCOMITANT VARIATION

If we apply Durkheim's arguments, against the plurality of causes and for concomitant variation, to his own texts and treat them as an explanation of his own practice, we get a new sense of his argument in *Suicide* and the *Rules*. His case against eliminative arguments can be made consistent with his own practice by supposing that Durkheim simply did not regard the arguments as strong eliminations, but merely as a means of provisionally eliminating possible causes in the course of searching for true sociological parallelisms. Once identified, true parallelisms would stand convincingly as laws in their own right, apart from any eliminative arguments. Construed as a kind of sieve, eliminative arguments prepare us for the acceptance of the new type of explanation, but nothing ultimately rests on them.

There is some textual evidence that this is how Durkheim regarded them. For example, in his 'eliminative' discussion of 'neurasthenia' as a cause of suicide he showed that there is no precise causal parallelism. He kept in mind such possibilities as the composition of causes, however, and conceded that the lack of parallelism can only establish that neurasthenia is itself not the *primary* cause. So he conceded that the argument leaves untouched such questions as the extent and nature of the significance of neurasthenia as a general predisposition exerting influence as a contributing or secondary cause. It is plausible to suppose that the reason he considered himself in a position to make such concessions was that he believed he could demonstrate the appropriate kind of parallelism.

The particular notion of causality Durkheim took from Mill, concomitant variation, is the notion that survives the nineteenth century to become standard in the twentieth, as 'functional dependence' in the mathematical sense of 'function', or more simply, curve fitting. The 'method' thus coincides with the sorts of 'laws' found in Quetelet and Farr, and the moral statisticians supplied Durkheim with methods of tabular presentation, methods of presenting maps (Quetelet, 1842, pp. 86–87), a body of well-established statistical relationships on a large variety of topics, and, in the course of 'statistical commentary' on these relationships, a great many suggestive observations and commonsense explanations. The suicide rate was of course a major topic for moral statistics, and most of the specific empirical issues dealt with by Durkheim had been identified by his predecessors. The relation between suicide and bachelorhood (Quetelet, 1842, p. 82), the irrelevance of the poverty of a region to its rates of immorality (1842, pp. 95–96), and the injuriousness of knowledge (1842, p. 84) are all discussed by Quetelet. The sociological novelty of Durkheim's approach is in the way in which he went beneath these surface relationships – beyond statistical commentary – to identify the more basic forces that produce the rates. The methodological novelty of his approach is in the way he dealt with causality and probability in relation to curve fitting.

As Selvin has correctly pointed out, the eliminative arguments Durkheim presented in *Suicide* would not work if he allowed for the possibility of probabilistic causal sequences (1976, p. 41). This should be no surprise, since many of the arguments he 'eliminated' were the work of the nineteenth century's great quantifiers of man, and involved rather strong statistical relations. But Durkheim's point in each eliminative argument is that no *regular*, or generalizable, pattern exists connecting a given variable with the suicide rate. Thus if a probabilistic relation between a given variable and a suicide rate existed, and if the actual probabilities were not extremely high, the variable would be eliminated by such arguments. Selvin concludes from this that Durkheim's statistical methods were insufficiently sophisticated, for he failed to notice the relationships that existed.

One notices, however, that Durkheim was not inconsistent in rejecting the arguments he eliminated and accepting his own sociological arguments. The significant presentations of evidence in *Suicide* are designed to support the generalizations just as he stated them, i.e., nonprobabilistically. His tables on suicides per confession show that, as he himself said, "everywhere without exception, Protestants show far more suicide," and his tables on family density and political disturbances likewise show *perfect* regularity, in these cases inverse rankings (1951, pp. 154, 199, 203–05; 1930, pp. 152, 209, 216–18).

Probability enters into the picture, but at a different level. One may think of a probability as a magnitude, that is governed, in its relations with other magnitudes, by nonprobabilistic laws. Quetelet did this when he presented tables of ratios, which he described as 'propensities', in which the values of the ratios are ordered, e.g. by age, and he called such a function a 'law'. Quetelet also discussed parallelisms between ordered sets of ratios, such as between rates of alienation and crime rates (1842, p. 90). A concomitant variation between propensities or between a propensity and some other magnitude can be understood as a causal relation. The difficulty in conceiving of the probabilities of moral statistics in this way is that the probabilities are not considered as magnitudes that are properties *of* anything.[3] With Quetelet's usages of penchant one wonders *what* has the penchant? Quetelet answered the question by attributing it to the *homme moyen*, i.e., to a type. We shall see that Durkheim made some salient objections to this. One alternative would be to say that the rates are relative frequencies composed of individual occurrences. In the case of a suicide rate, for example, the probability of suicide is the relative frequency of suicide in a population. The rate is composed of individuals and individual events of suicide.

Durkheim supplied us with something else for the rate to be a measure of, namely properties of the collective consciousness. Thus for Durkheim the suicide rate is, on the one hand, a measure of the magnitude of the suicidal current in the collective consciousness, and on the other hand, by the definition of 'social fact', a 'constraint' on the individual consciousness of this magnitude. For Durkheim, the place of probability is strictly limited to this role as a measure of a social fact. The social fact of the suicidal current is a fixed force that impinges on the individual. The strength of this force and its variations in strength between various social groups – as represented by the distribution of suicides – are themselves explained nonprobabilistically: the laws of the collective consciousness themselves, which apply only to facts that are attributes of social groupings, involve perfect, not 'probable', parallelisms.

The assumption that Durkheim was concerned with the sorts of probabilistic relations between sociological variables that standard statistical measures of association bear on is the basis of the 'ecological fallacy' critique of *Suicide* advanced by Selvin. The critique depends on the argument that it is wrong to assume "that associations computed from group means or group proportions are valid estimates of the associations that would be obtained from individual data" (1965, p. 125). Durkheim, Selvin says, "reports that the rate of suicide in departments of France varies according to the proportion of 'persons of independent means'" (1965, p. 126; Durkheim, 1951, p. 245; 1930, p. 269). This is a valid procedure, Selvin concedes, "when the unit of analysis is a group rather than the individuals in it. However," Selvin goes on,

Durkheim never theorizes about wealthy and poor departments, only about wealthy and poor individuals. And if he were interested in group characteristics – at the level, say, of departments or provinces – why would he replicate for successively finer subdivisions within these groups, in two cases carrying the replications down to individuals. It is clear that Durkheim was guilty of the ecological fallacy (1965, p. 126).

The proper response to this is to point out that Durkheim 'replicates for successively finer subdivisions' only when he is *not* interested in group characteristics. But this can be seen only after we establish, on the one hand, what he did about probabilistic causes, and, on the other, what he took as a 'group'.

The primary source of misinterpretations of Durkheim's position is the failure to recognize the implications of his commitment to a concomitant variation view of causality. One crucial implication is as follows: if cause is conceived of as concomitant variation, for any case, absent interference, if the cause occurs, the effect will occur. Therefore for any set of cases, if the cause occurs in x% of the cases, the effect will occur in x% of the cases. If only persons exposed to radiation get bone cancer, and the relation between exposure and cancer is not itself distorted by interfering other causes, the proportion of persons getting bone cancer will rise and fall parallel to the proportion of persons exposed, regardless of how the 'groups' are selected. If we replace exposure with a social cause, subject to the same restrictions, the same principle holds: if membership in a particular group produces a particular 'current' which leads to a particular action, as long as one uses categories that do not subdivide the group, the parallelism between the relative size of the group and the rate of occurrence of that action within the category should hold. This is the basis of Durkheim's practice.

Two basic kinds of categorizations figure in Durkheim's tabular analyses. Besides facts about social categories that are facts about social
groups, Durkheim also dealt with facts about social categories that are not
understood as facts about groups, but merely as averages of individual facts
about persons falling into the category, and with facts about persons falling
into psychological categories. The tables use *social* categories in the
chapters on the types of suicide and *psychological* categories in the chapters
on psychological explanations. In the tables designed to eliminate the
'social' explanations he rejected, the social categories are selected to fit the
causal factors of the opposed explanation, and, accordingly, they do not
always represent social groupings. The category may simply represent a set
of persons in a similar situation. One such table is designed to disconfirm
the notion that disgust with military life is a cause of military suicide (1951,
p. 232; 1930, p. 251). If one assumes with Durkheim that 'disgust' must be
stronger at the beginning of a military career and decrease as the soldier
becomes accustomed to military life (1951, p. 231; 1930, p. 251), we can use
the categories of 'first year in service', 'second year in service', and so forth
to indicate disgust. 'Disgust' is, however, a fact that acts on individuals and
presumably arises through the individual consciousness. When we say 'The
whole troop was disgusted', we mean, 'Every member of the troop was
individually disgusted'. 'Disgust' is not an attribute of a social grouping.

Selvin's example, of rich and poor departments of France, works in a
similar way. If one was to claim that there was in fact a concomitant
variation between poverty and suicide, i.e., a causal relation on the
individual level, one would, absent other causes, find a perfect parallelism
– the more poor, the higher the rate of suicide. Durkheim showed that not
only is this not the case, there is a probabilistic relationship that goes in
the other direction (1951, p. 245; 1930, p. 269). But he did not claim that
it is a perfect relationship, nor did he use it to warrant anything but the
negative conclusion that poverty is not a cause of suicide. And this is
perfectly appropriate, for if it were a genuine cause in Durkheim's sense,
at the individual level, then the more poor individuals there are in a
department the more suicides there would be. To be sure, one might change
the hypothesis in such a way that Durkheim's evidence would not constitute disconfirmation, by saying, e.g., that poverty is a cause of suicide in
the face of relative deprivation, or that poor people in rich departments are
more likely to commit suicide. But Durkheim was not considering such
hypotheses.

When we turn to Durkheim's positive arguments, i.e., his use of data to support his own explanations, we find a consistent usage as well. A social cause can arise from any social grouping. The nation is a social grouping and native citizenship is a category that corresponds to a social grouping that is defined by a particular collective representation, 'the nation'. The suicide rate for France can be regarded as an attribute of a social group because there is a collective representation 'France' to which Frenchmen adhere. But the nation is only one among many groups. When Durkheim spoke of the collective consciousness and causes whose substratum "can be no other than society, either the political society as a whole or some one of the partial groups it includes, such as religious denominations, political, literary, and occupational associations, etc." (1964, p. 3; 1982, p. 52; 1937, p. 5), he echoed Rousseau's view that a new moral being is created by and with every form of association (of which the nation is the highest or sovereign form), Aristotle's beautiful phrase 'friendship is one soul in two bodies', and Comte's notion that the family is the basic element of society. For Durkheim, each social grouping embodied in a representation (such as the idea of France or the rite of marriage) to which a person is party may be a source of 'social' causal forces. Thus, when he used the categories of 'married' and 'unmarried', these categories did not represent categories of persons operating under similar *individual* causes, but categories that distinguish a) persons under the influence of the particular social causes arising from each distinct marriage understood as a distinct marital association, from b) persons not under the influence of *any* such association.

This way of thinking of the cases has a straightforward implication for data analysis. It makes sense to divide the category of 'married' into various subcategories within the nation, such as the married in each region, and to determine whether there is a regular relationship between some social fact represented by its rate in a region and the regional rate of family density, because if the relation is indeed invariant, the relationship between the two rates should be regular. However, categorizing by region is not the ideal set of categories for proving the regularity. The ideal set of categories would be categories that correspond to the social group from which the cause arises. In this case, the ideal set would be derived from a categorization of families themselves in terms of family 'density', and if a categorization directly in terms of density failed to exhibit the parallelism, this would be disconfirming evidence. In practice, this is not an attainable ideal, for we have no direct measure of degree of "common life" – and an ersatz measure of density is used (Durkheim, 1951, p. 202; 1930, p. 214).

The rule that governs Durkheim's use of rates, then, is this: never categorize a putative cause into categories that are not inclusive of the social group from which the putative cause arises. Thus one may categorize 'region' causes by 'nation', but not vice versa (because to say the suicide rate in France varies with political integration is not to say that the suicide rate in Provence does). This rule, however, only *excludes* certain categorizations. The arbitrariness of Durkheim's data analysis results from the necessity to use ersatz measures in which the categories do not directly correspond to the collectivities that produce the causes. He selected the particular categorization, in accordance with this rule, that enabled him to find a perfect parallelism. Such a procedure may appear procrustean, yet one must consider the difficulty Durkheim faced of being unable to measure the 'collective consciousness' directly. The observable manifestations (especially actions) of these 'collective consciousness' regularities are often affected by various interfering causes. Although his selection of categories may produce a parallelism whose perfection is simply an artifact of the categorization, it is nevertheless also true that in a situation where various other causes may interfere, the nonexistence of a parallelism under any given categorization does not disconfirm the law.

'MECHANICAL' COMPOSITION

The individual act of suicide does not take on a range of values: an act either is or is not suicide. So a difference in strengths of two suicidogenic currents can only be expressed as a difference in the probability of such an act and measured by a difference in a rate. If we follow the principle 'similar causes, similar effects', everyone in the group would have the same response – either to commit or not to commit suicide – and thus there would be no rate of suicide corresponding to different strengths of the suicidal current. In view of this, it is significant that Durkheim did not identify 'the suicidal current' as a force arising out of family life, religious life, or political life, but spoke of the family, the religious collectivity, and political passions as forces *preserving* members from suicide. So the three propositions Durkheim explicitly stated as concomitant variations,

> Suicide varies inversely with the degree of integration of religious society.
> Suicide varies inversely with the degree of integration of domestic society.
> Suicide varies inversely with the degree of integration of political society. (1951, p. 208; 1930, p. 222),

are not meant to be causal propositions about the causes of *suicide*, strictly speaking. They are propositions about *preservation* against a force. This means that suicide is a result of the composition of forces.

Two types of 'composition' figure in Durkheim's methodological argument. In connection with the explanation of suicide, the relevant type is what Mill called 'mechanical composition', a type familiar from Quetelet as well. 'Mechanical' composition of forces in physics can be additive, as in the example of computing the trajectory of a cannonball, or it can produce an equilibrium between forces, as in the case of the orbit of the moon. Both of these subtypes of mechanical composition figure in the explanation in *Suicide*. The total suicide rate of the society is a result of the equilibrium-producing composition that occurs between 'opposed' forces that produce suicide. Anomy, egoism, and altruism are universal collective currents: "There is no people among whom these three currents of opinion do not co-exist," we are told.

Where they offset one another, the moral agent is in a state of equilibrium which shelters him against any thought of suicide. But let one of them exceed a certain strength to the detriment of the others, and as it becomes individualized, it also becomes suicidogenetic (1951, p. 321; 1930, p. 363).

The point of Durkheim's conceiving these various social currents as *opposed* forces and not merely *different* forces is that only 'opposed' forces could intelligibly be claimed to be 'in equilibrium' or to 'offset' one another.

The equilibrating variety of composition works in an extraordinarily complex way, because of the fact that the sources of collective currents include not only society as a whole, as we can see in connection with two of the propositions governing preservation against the suicidal current, but various subsocietal associations as well, such as religious society and domestic society, whose causal influence composes with the causal influence of societal-level collective currents. In discussing marriage, Durkheim considered both aggravating and preservative effects of this particular subsocietal association on suicide. These effects compose with the current arising from the larger collectivity to produce a total collective influence that impels the given individual to act.

There are some interesting technical advantages to formulating these relations in terms of composition. Durkheim knew that there are different rates for different categories in the population. One might explain these rates by an antecedent cause governed by some principle that accounted for variations between groups, or one might seek a mechanism intrinsic to each grouping that could plausibly be claimed to produce the 'suicidal current' for that grouping. Durkheim's solution is different. First, he distinguished between such causes as egoism, which he said "not only frees man's inclination to do away with himself from a protective obstacle, but creates this inclination out of whole cloth and thus gives birth to a special suicide which bears its mark," and those that only result "in favoring the action of suicidogenic currents" (1951, p. 210; 1930, p. 224). The basic causes can then be left at the original three: egoism, anomia, and altruism.[4] The factors that merely favor or inhibit, 'aggravate' or 'preserve', these causes are many, since the rates vary with each new association to which the individual is party, as it aggravates or preserves against the basic causes.

Thus Durkheim need only identify the suicidogenic mechanism of the basic causes; he need not account for such a thing as 'the suicidogenic current arising from the family'. He need only account for the preserving or aggravating influence of these other associations, which, once the basic mechanisms are identified, is not particularly difficult, in that the mechanisms involve the same types of force. It should be noted that this distinction with respect to basic and secondary influences does not correspond to the distinction between societal and subsocietal associations, for in the case of altruism it is clear that one association that is a basic source is the military, a subsocietal association. Which associations are sources and which merely aggravate or preserve depends on the nature of the cause. For egoism and anomia, which involve a lack, there is no single association that is the source, and the influence of any given association can only be to aggravate or preserve.

The technical advantages are balanced by some disadvantages. One question that arises in connection with these applications is: Where does the composition occur? It may seem odd to speak of composition as occurring spatially, but for Durkheim, who often spoke of the 'substratum' of a cause, it is an important question. Do collective causes compose while hovered over the individual's head, like the soul of Mercutio? Or does the composition occur within the individual, under the regulation of the mechanisms of individual psychology? This is an issue that will be taken up shortly. Here it will suffice to make two points. In the chapter on individual forms of suicide, Durkheim described three types of 'mixed' cases, all of which are the result of composition or convergence of causes. So Durkheim clearly had in mind that the 'composition' is not merely a matter of adding up the individual cases that compose a rate, each with its distinct, single 'cause', but that it will be reflected in specific properties of the act itself, in accordance with the principle he endorsed in his critique of the doctrine of plurality of causes.

Of the types of suicide he described, one is composed of *opposite* causes. If we are to think of these forces as 'equilibrating', this is paradoxical: ego-altruistic suicide should be a nonstarter. Durkheim resolved this apparent contradiction and preserved his argument by saying that the two causes arise from different sources, one from the general condition of egoism, the other from distinct supraindividual representations, and compose only under a specific condition, the decadence of a society. Since egoism drives a person from society, a situation that occurs widely in the state of decadence, the person is open to the influence of certain representations with altruistic effects. But these can only be 'imaginary' objects, for attachments to 'real' collective goals would be precluded by the egoism the person is in the grip of. So what occurs here is not so much the composition as the succession of suicidogenic conditions.

All these rather abstract arguments and considerations may be usefully clarified and tied together by applying them to an ordinary example of a fact of concern to sociologists, the criminal act of a juvenile gang member. In constructing such an explanation one might begin with the most substantial collective cause, the probability of criminal activity in the society at large. One would find that the rate of criminal activity varies with age, and there may be a mechanism and a provable law governing this and other relations at the societal level. One would then consider the aggravating or diminishing effects of the various subsocietal associations to which the child was party, such as religious associations, family associations, and membership in the gang itself. All of the causes would *compose* to produce the 'collective' component of the explanation of the act. Of course, the effects of these associations may be subject to many conditions. The contact of the child with these associations may, for example, be intermittent, or there may be other conditions that interfere with these associations' production of effects. The mechanical composition of these effects will produce a collective quantity of impelling force that is the probability that the individual will commit the act.

The Problem of Origins

In his discussion of the origins of society and of particular collective representations, Durkheim used another compositional device discussed by Mill, the 'chemical' type of composition. In the mechanical type, Mill said, the "effects of the separate causes do not terminate and give place to others ... but are intermingled with, and disguised by, the homogenous and closely allied effects of other causes" (1973, p. 443). In the chemical type the effects are not merely 'intermingled' with allied effects, but have new properties or effects. Mill's rejection of the chemical method in social science follows from his inductivist aims: he supposed that the practical impossibility of experiment makes the notion of 'chemical' composition irrelevant. The attraction of the concept of chemical composition is that it fits with the problem of accounting for the fact of obligation, which could not arise from the mere mechanical composition of individual causes. Durkheim used a distinctive phrase, 'analysis and synthesis', in describing the explanation of an institution's origin. The phrase is originally Euclidean, and refers to a particular form of metamathematical argument (cf. Lakatos, 1978, pp. 70–103), and is used by Hobbes in taking over and explaining the Galilean notions of resolution and composition (Peters, 1967, p. 64). For Galileo, resolution and composition is the reconstruction of a physical situation in mathematical terms by formulating the situation in terms of known laws and the initial conditions appropriate to the production of the outcomes of the situation.

Durkheim said that the method he would employ to explain the development of an institution from its earliest form, which he called the 'genetic' method, "would give at once the analysis and synthesis of the phenomenon" (1964, p. 138; 1982, p. 157; 1937, p. 137). He explained that the method would both show the elements composing the phenomena and enable us to find the conditions on which their formation depends. In short, then, this moment of origin is analogous to the moment in which a chemical experiment in a laboratory yields a new compound. So the 'analysis and synthesis' reconstructs the process and conditions on which the phenomena depend, and in so doing reveals the true character of the phenomena. This foreshadows Durkheim's later study of primitive classification and the elementary forms of religious life.

Durkheim's account of the two methods of composition, taken together with his general account of the nature of causal laws in sociology and the character of 'social facts', suggest a picture of the logical structure of what Durkheim would have regarded as a developed scientific sociology. If we begin with variations on which we have extensive statistical information within one society, such as information on suicide, we may establish striking parallelisms that can be accounted for by identifying underlying, 'internal' causal mechanisms. This evidence may be a prerogative instance, and may demonstrate a law. But to demonstrate the law conclusively,

Durkheim said, it is preferable to confirm results by showing that they hold up for other peoples of the same social species.

If the fact to be explained is an institution, it becomes absolutely necessary to deal with more extended comparisons, since the 'waxing and waning' of these institutions, to use Mill's phrase, varies with so many other institutions within the same society that it is impossible to disentangle their relations. In such cases, one must first make comparisons with other societies of the same type, which provide new series of variations to deal with. Yet even this method will not suffice for the full explanation of institutions, such as the family, which originated in preceding societies. And the more developed a society is, the more frequent and significant are such elements.

Each form of association, from the largest collective unit to the smallest, has its own explanation of its origin and of its 'waxing and waning'. One might find, for example, a law governing the rate of occurrence of gangs of a particular type, marriage rates, or rates of association with a particular type of religious collectivity. One will also be able to trace the largest collectivity back to its origin in the chemical composition of prior collectivities, and discover the conditions and 'chemical' structure of the origin of all the collectivities or species of this type. The same thing may be done for all the remaining collectivities that influence the act, collectivities whose origin may extend far beyond and before those of the larger collectivity, and which may be subject to discoverable laws governing their waxing and waning. A *full* explanation requires all of these forces and relations to be taken into account.

CHAPTER EIGHT

DURKHEIM'S INDIVIDUAL

Puzzles over the nature of the individual mount, unanswered, in the course of the *Rules* and *Suicide*. The Baconian doctrine of *idola* supplies us with a picture of the nature of falsity in thinking about individual action, and of the inadequacies of intentional language. 'Currents', impulses, and the rest are the 'scientific' terms Durkheim himself used in action explanations, and these suggest a picture of the individual. His comments in the preface to the second edition of the *Rules* on the analogies between the psychological laws governing the combination of and "the manner in which social representations adhere to and repel one another, how they fuse or separate from one another, etc." (1964, p. 1i; 1982, pp. 41–42; 1937, p. xix) and the laws of sociology governing collective representations are suggestive. But how do they fit together, and how do they fit into the logic of his argument and his practice? Other questions, of where the composition of causes occurs, and about the details of the causal mechanisms involved, of the relation between 'impulses', individual predispositions, and various social facts, arise from Durkheim's own usages. His technical usages, particularly his statistical methods, also raise questions about his individual as a real, causal structure.

With questions like these we gradually move to less solid ground, where the texts are less and less helpful. Two bodies of text bear on the questions: the larger and more diffuse body of text is the material on the relations of psychology and sociology, the boundaries of the individual, the reliability of our introspective knowledge, and the degree to which common parlance mirrors the causal reality of the person; the smaller body is the discussion of the character of the forces that correspond to statistical rates, carried on as a dialogue with Quetelet. Reconciling these bodies of text with one another answers some of the questions. Reconciling them with Durkheim's causal imagery answers others.

PHENOMENOLOGY, CAUSE, AND THE PERSON

For the Introspectionist, the limits of mind are the limits of the power of introspection; for the empiricist, one's knowledge of the limits of one's own person is built up from experienced associations, paradigmatically by the experienced association between an intention and an action. Durkheim denied the possibility of drawing a line around the individual mind on the basis of introspection when he argued for the "incompetence of consciousness" in the matter of assessing causes of action (1974, p. 21n). Where James argued that "If I imagine that I hate or am indifferent when in fact I am in love, I have merely misnamed a condition of which I am fully conscious" (paraphrased by Durkheim in 1974, p. 21n.). Against this, Durkheim remarked that "If I misname a condition, it is because my consciousness of it also is false and does not express all the characteristics of this condition" (1974, p. 21n). Durkheim's reasoning is that such a misnamed 'condition' still is part of a causal structure and has consequences. "My feelings have all the constituent traits of love since they affect my conduct; but I do not recognize them, so that in a sense my passions direct me one way and the knowledge which I have of them, another" (1974, p. 21n). Thus it is possible for the causal processes that go on in the mind to be inscrutable to the actor himself.

Yet Durkheim frequently used traditional psychological language in the context of 'causal' questions: in *Suicide*, for example, he even spoke of reasons as causes (1951, p. 128; 1930, p. 114), and appealed to reports of the phenomenological experiences of the suicidal agent in explicating his views on the types of suicide. The way in which he did this seems rather to invite misunderstanding. Is there an inconsistency between Durkheim's Baconian distrust of the senses, especially his argument on the incompetence of consciousness, and his repeated uses of phenomenological data?

Conflicts appear, particularly in places where Durkheim attempted to show that certain distinctively 'psychological' facts, such as habit and inhibition, are separable from yet compatible with the characteristics of 'social fact' which attach to the same phenomena at the same time, as with duties that are habitually performed. These arguments are designed primarily to show the social character of putatively psychological concepts, and they suggest the degree to which the territory of psychology is to be claimed for sociology. The arguments are also 'contextually' salient. His analysis of crowd sentiment dealt with a crucial issue between his doctrines and those of his contemporaries LeBon and Tarde. "Great movements of enthusiasm" are less clearly "outside" the individual (1964, p. 2; 1982, p. 51; 1937, p. 4) than are such "crystallized" facts as moral regulations and financial systems (1964, p. 4; 1982, pp. 52–53; 1937, p. 6). In part this is because the influence of the crowd is not expressed with the aid of outward

forms, such as regulations, but more directly. To argue that this influence
nevertheless amounts to 'collective constraint', in spite of the lack of
'external' manifestations like written laws, and in spite of the fact that the
constraint is not directly felt or seen as a constraint, requires him to use
introspective evidence and to analyze the phenomenological experience of
the individual in the crowd.

He distinguished between two kinds of experience, of those persons who
give themselves up to the enthusiasm and therefore feel no pressure, and
of those persons who oppose the social current. The experience of the
person who tries to stand against the influence of the crowd is revealing.
"The emotions [of the crowd] that he denies will turn against him" (1964,
p. 5; 1982, p. 53; 1937, p. 6). So for this person the 'external' influence of
the crowd is experienced phenomenologically as inner conflict. The picture
this suggests is that the individual harbors sources of opposition to collective emotions, and these various forces fight it out for control of the
individual's actions.

In such a situation, the mind is in some sense divided against itself,
divided between the various social forces represented in the mind or
between these forces and those which originate in himself. The picture, of
course, does not directly correspond with one's phenomenological experience. Similarly for a person who has been in the grip of crowd emotions
and has not 'resisted'. In their grip, he is not cognizant of their externality.
Yet after these crowd emotions have, so to speak, 'passed through the
mind' and are no longer influencing our action, or are no longer felt other
than as a memory, we can recognize their externality and can even be
horrified by them.

The apparent inconsistency of Durkheim's reliance in some contexts on
phenomenological experience and denial of its credibility in others shows
clearly here: a great deal seems to be based on these presumably defective
or bracketed experiences. This is so not only in marginal contexts, but at
the core of Durkheim's methodological doctrine: in describing "the distinctive characteristics" of a social fact, we are told that "the most important
characteristic of a 'thing' is the impossibility of its modification by a simple
effort of the will" (1964, p. 28; 1982, p. 70; 1937, pp. 28–29).

The realist resolution to the conflict is to insist that the phenomenological experiences one has of the world are, as Durkheim also insisted,
unreliable – but to claim as well that they are experiences, in the large, *of*
something. To be sure, one cannot draw a line around the reliable experiences, nor can one guarantee the veridical character of *any* particular
experience, including the introspective 'experience' of the contents of one's

own mind. Nevertheless, one's experiences may point, for the reflective thinker, to the deeper contours of the real which are only indicated by the surface we 'experience'. Thus one can be mistaken about the limits of one's will, but the fact that one experiences such limits suggests something, a 'something' that can only be properly articulated in causal, scientific terms.

When we observe ourselves responding to the crowd, we are nascent sociologists, not mere introspectors. We observe a causal regularity in the reaction of the crowd, which we ourselves instantiate, and in this way realize, as we would not realize by introspection alone, that we are in the grip of a collective force. Yet rarely are we in the position of being able to directly observe the causal consequences of the collective current, since we are ordinarily in and a part of society, just as we never feel atmospheric pressure. So there is no handy everyday experience that will give us any reliable insight into the limits of the collective current, and therefore of the location of the line between our individual consciousness and the collective consciousness.

The underlying consistency in these claims is thus to be found in Durkheim's realism. Durkheim did not want to place us in the position of denying the validity of all our experiences, for this would include the data of sociology as well. What he wished to do was to show that we are in the same position in relation to our own psychology as we are with any fact of nature. Our phenomenological experience is a ladder to be kicked away once we arrive at more reliable data. But the process of ascent to reliable data necessarily consists in building on one part of our experience, its most 'objective' part, to replace the less reliable parts of our experience. If we take the *idola* imagery seriously, as Durkheim certainly did (1964, p. 17; 1982, pp. 82–83; 1937, p. 18), the problem of the explanation of action changes. All the usual terms for describing action and the social world are bracketed. Some parts of this terminology will fit through the needle's eye of this standard; most will not. If the experience of physics is any guide, very little of our ordinary conceptual or descriptive armamentary will survive.

Where Durkheim differs from predecessors like Hobbes and Mill is in the directions and degree to which he pushed his critique of concepts. The usual bias is to regard social concepts as more suspect, more open to revision or analysis than 'individual' concepts. A term like 'custom' or 'law', for example, is analyzable in individual terms, such as 'the commands of the sovereign' or in psychological terms, such as 'habituation'. Durkheim rejected this bias toward accepting the individualist forms of concepts, and denied that psychological terminology has any better claim to mirroring reality than terms like 'law' or 'custom' (1964, pp. 44–46; 1982, pp. 81–83; 1937, pp. 43–46). This is an argument that, conjoined with realism, has a variety of novel consequences for our conception of the individual. Once one concedes the possibility of the causal reality of such things as moral obligations, the realm of the psychological begins to look very different, and we get a quite different picture of action.

The novelty can be seen in an example familiar from Aristotelean psychology, deliberation. The Hobbesian deliberating person is a 'causal' person: the sense of control this person has is merely a phenomenological manifestation of the fact of competing impulses. Durkheim's man who acts morally is one in whom the causal forces arising from collective, obligation-producing facts dominate his other impulses, and in whom the deliberations are themselves experienced as though they are the causes of action, but, as in Hobbes, they are not.

Deliberations, in fact, so far as reflective consciousness affects them are often only purely formal, with no object but confirmation of a resolve previously formed for reasons unknown to consciousness (1951, p. 297; 1930, p. 334).

'Resolve' is a characteristically psychological notion. Durkheim's use of it in this context is meant to suggest that the outcome is causally fixed, as a result of the relative strength of the impulses, by the time the 'deliberations' occur.

THE REALIST PERSON

The novelty of Durkheim's revision of the concept of deliberation is thus in its 'social' direction. But there is also novelty in the contrast or distance Durkheim envisioned between our concepts and the concepts appropriate to science. Hobbes wrote as though one could take the usual terminology of action explanation and simply translate this language into the language of 'motions', and Mill supposed that the relevant language for the causal analysis of action was very close to the language of ordinary usage. The difficulties in this supposition became evident in several ways, the most familiar of which is in attempts to resolve issues over the logical form of explanation. Popper's account of 'logic of the situation' explanations was an attempt to explicate historical explanation, which relies largely on agents' terminology, by showing precisely where 'generalizations' were required (Popper, 1964, pp. 143–52). Hempel's classic paper, 'The Function of General Laws in History' (1959), attempted to show that proper historical explanations could be analyzed to show the essential role of generalizations. At the end of this long road it became evident that the laws of psychology, whatever these might be, would have little to do with agents' terminology. So one establishes the relevance of generalization to ordinary action explanation at the expense of the close connection to a causalist psychology which Hobbes and Mill assumed.

Durkheim arrived at a similar result by another, more direct, road. When he rejected the language of consciousness and intention – represented for him by the Introspectionist psychology of Wundt and James – as *idola*, he rejected, as a matter of realist principle, the whole body of ordinary language with which introspective experience was described. In practice, Durkheim was less draconian. He qualified his usages of such terms as suicide by giving them a slightly different definition than ordinary usage, but treated the ordinary descriptions as *de facto* equivalents of the 'scientific' descriptions. This was done without elaborate justification. Justification, however, is not needed, for this reason: a concept proves its suitability to the task of forming nomic generalizations by actually figuring in a true causal generalization, not by any *a priori* reasoning.

To accept what "has been commonly accepted, even by those generally sympathetic to Durkheim's viewpoint, that his stress on the constraining nature of social facts leaves no place for the social actor as a conscious willing agent" (Giddens, 1971, p. 218), is to accept the idea that there is a line between the psychological and the sociological which corresponds to the boundary marked by one's phenomenological sense of what is and what is not subject to one's will. When Giddens criticizes Durkheim for his failure to leave a 'place', he does so by using and appealing to the vocabulary that Durkheim had rejected, or bracketed. Durkheim's strategy was more radical, at least at the level of principle, than Giddens has given him credit for: the problem of the conscious willing agent and the vocabulary of 'will' would have been bracketed as *idola*.

What makes it plausible to accuse Durkheim of leaving no place for the conscious willing agent is that he wished to push the boundaries of the collective consciousness very far indeed into the territory of what has traditionally been conceived as 'individual consciousness'. When he described the causal psychological sequence that leads to anomic suicide, he was careful to emphasize just how little control the individual as a rational agent has. A man who loses status "cannot avoid exasperation" and "naturally revolts against the cause, whether real or imaginary, to which he attributes his ruin." If he blames himself, he commits suicide. If he blames another person, suicide may be preceded by homicide. The "reversal of all his habits reduces him to a state of acute over-excitation, which necessarily tends to seek solace in acts of destruction" (1951, p. 285; 1930, p. 322). In this state, the object of the passions is "of secondary importance" determined by "the accident of circumstances" (1951, p. 285; 1930, p. 322). In short, the individual is not in control of his impulses – they are in control of him, and he cannot avoid their taking their course. In these cases, the causally determinative source of control is the external social facts.

'External', though it is a term Durkheim used, is misleading, if it is taken to correspond to the 'externality' of the person as it is prescientifically conceived. Durkheim himself did a great deal to efface the prescientific concept of the self. Part of this discussion is itself sociological. Durkheim described the forces of altruism and egoism as 'excessive' and 'insufficient individuation', respectively. The latter, he said, is manifested in "the idea that what reality there is in the individual is foreign to his nature, that the soul which animates him is not his own, and that consequently he has no personal existence" (1951, p. 226; 1930, p. 244). This theme was extended by Levy-Bruhl, in *The 'Soul' of the Primitive*, where he argued that "in the representations of the primitives, each man's individuality does not stop short at his personal exterior. The limits which surround it are indecisive, ill-defined, and even variable according to the amount of mystic force or *mana* which an individual may possess" (1966, p. 115). 'Primitives', of course, are not alone in these confusions – the wrath of Achilles was divine, Jesus cast out demons, and so on. Personhood is thus socially variable.

Casting doubt on commonsense concepts of personhood is part of the strategy of treating them as *idola*. Durkheim's skepticism about the concept went beyond this, however. He went so far as to deny that a line can be drawn at all: "We do not admit that there is a precise point at which the individual comes to an end and the social realm commences" (1951, p. 313n; 1930, p. 353n). The reasoning in support of this claim is revealing, for the point is argued not from an account of the nature of the individual, but from an account of the nature of the social. He remarked that "association is not established and does not produce its effects all at once; it requires time and there are consequently moments at which the reality is indeterminate" (1951, p. 313n; 1930, p. 353n). This 'indeterminacy' results from the fact that when new forms of association produce collective currents (and a new *substratum* for ideas) there is no decisive mark that distinguishes when the point at which (causally effective) individual representations held in common by a few individuals become 'collective' (and, therefore, 'collective' causes). One can only discover the causal consequences of the new collective representations *ex post facto*, and there is no quantitative point at which the change of quality from individual idea to collective idea occurs.

One may also notice that new forms of association produce new causes *ad infinitum* – as, for example, new chemicals with new pharmacological properties may be invented *ad infinitum*. The task of completing the nomological structure of sociology, at least with respect to the laws governing the influence of these new social facts on individuals, which is prior to the task of definitively drawing the boundary line, is thus not a completable task. And this would be so even if all the 'laws of association' of collective representations were in our grasp (just as knowledge about the laws of chemical bonding would not tell us everything about the pharmacology of the new chemicals). So the drawing of the line between individual and collective is not finally possible, although the recognition of a distinction is essential.

Durkheim used the term 'constraint' in his definition of social fact, and it is this term that most commentators have taken to be the key to Durkheim's individual. Giddens, for example, asks, "In what sense ... are social facts 'constraining'," and tries to answer the question by identifying various ordinary uses of 'constraint' in connection with action and seeing which of those fit Durkheim's usage (Giddens, 1971, p. 218). This way of approaching the usage presupposes that Durkheim was doing something that he denied he was doing, and ignores the whole picture of the relationship between ordinary concepts and the real structure of the world which he had been arguing for.

According to a realist, causalist view of social life, sociology is concerned with real causal relations. It is idle to ask such questions as 'How do social facts constrain?', because these questions ask that the regularities be somehow 'cashed in' in a language alien to them. In speaking of the *real* causal structure of the world, in terms of his picture of causal relations between social facts and between social facts and individual actions, 'constraint' signifies no more and no less than the existence of a law-governed relationship. To restate this law-governed relationship in some other terminology, such as the vocabulary of 'individual will', is potentially to misstate it, for the terminology in which one wants 'constraint' explained is *idola* terminology. The question 'How do they constrain?' is thus akin to 'How does gravity really pull?', asked as though there would be an answer like 'By a string'. The only answer to a question like 'How do gravitational force fields constrain?' is to show the interlocutor the quantitative law relating the facts. Other answers are superfluous, and, in the case of sociology, detrimental, for they demand that these 'real' relations be restated in the *idola* of ordinary action explanations, thus contributing to the illusions about action contained in ordinary action terminology. The *circularity* in Durkheim's definition of social fact as 'something that constrains' exists only from a nonrealist perspective on these facts.

RATES AND INDIVIDUALS

Quetelet's concept of the *homme moyen* is a device by which the individual is related, in an explanatory way, to a rate: the explanatory force of the rate rests on the idea that the rates describe a type; to be a case of the type is similar to being an instance of a law. To be sure, this makes for an odd combination: the *homme moyen* is a fictive being, in Whewell's sense, but its *explanatory* force is that of a 'real type'. Causal questions about the properties of the type were relegated by Quetelet to a higher level. The properties of *hommes moyens* are determined by constant causes, just as the planetary paths are determined by constant causes. When Durkheim borrowed from Quetelet, he radically reconstructed Quetelet's argument on the lines of his own causal realism, and the reconstruction has direct implications for the concept of the individual. Durkheim's primary borrowing is the concept of stability of rates. His demurrer is over the explanatory use of the concept of type.

One technical borrowing is particularly striking, and also particularly revealing of the way in which Durkheim reconstructed Quetelet. Durkheim asserted – without argument – that since rates contain all of the individual cases indiscriminately, the special individual circumstances are 'neutralized' and do not contribute to the determination or fixing of the rate. The point that in stable rates accidental causes are canceled out is taken over from Quetelet. But Quetelet, as we have seen, arrived at the conclusion that accidental causes were canceled out in stable rates through several questionable steps. Stability was taken by Quetelet as an ersatz proof for the existence of a bell curve. He took the curve, in turn, as evidence that accidental causes have canceled one another out. Neither step was warranted.

Durkheim ignored the statistical background to Quetelet's account of accidental cause and proceeded to construct a new argument for his own use of rates. Quetelet had concluded that individual acts of *free will* disappear in the rates. Statistically, they behave like accidental causes which 'cancel one another out'. Durkheim assimilated this attack on free will to his own attack on psychological explanations. To the extent that a rate is stable, Durkheim reasoned, the effects of individual circumstances also disappear in the rates. What remains, Durkheim presumed, is a filtrate of pure 'social fact'. His argumentative strategy is to defend this presumption against rival accounts of the stability of rates.

The defense is thus not, as it was for Quetelet, a general argument for a particular interpretation of rates, but a context-specific argument that depends on an examination of particular causal alternatives. In *Suicide*, this takes the form of a consideration of two classes of 'individual' explanations of suicide, those giving reasons that involve individual external circumstances, such as bankruptcy (1951, p. 297; 1930, p. 333) and those that appeal to "the intrinsic nature of the person," i.e., to psychological types (1951, p. 298; 1930, p. 335). Having in mind arguments like Venn's remark on the stability of the annual numbers of lost letters, he argued that "these individual peculiarities could not explain the social suicide-rate; for the latter varies in considerable proportions, whereas the different combinations of circumstances which constitute the immediate antecedents of individual cases of suicide retain approximately the same relative frequency" (1951, p. 297; 1930, p. 333). The response to Venn-like critiques, then, is that there is stability in proportions of individual circumstances and events – but that the suicide rate varies *socially*.

Against explanations involving psychological types, Durkheim pointed to the failure of his psychological competitors to show empirical relationships between their *explanans* and the *explanandum* of the suicide rate (1951, p. 298; 1930, pp. 334–35). It should be noted that in his discussions of these rival hypotheses, Durkheim made no attempt to give statistical arguments. He ignored the various statistical associations which supported these hypotheses, for he assumed that a 'primary' cause would exhibit an "immediate and regular relationship" (1951, p. 298; 1930, p. 335). The failures of these explanations to produce any such relations contrast to

the results we obtained when we forgot the individual and sought the causes of the suicidal aptitude of each society in the nature of the societies themselves. The relations of suicide to certain states of social environment are as direct and constant as its relations to facts of a biological and physical character were seen to be uncertain and ambiguous (1951, p. 299; 1930, p. 335).

"Here at last," Durkheim said, "we are face to face with real laws" (1951, p. 299; 1930, p. 335).

The negative argument Durkheim mounted against Venn-like critiques, his social variation argument, is obviously congenial to Quetelet. Indeed, the theory of the *homme moyen* may be regarded as a rival hypothesis which happens to fit with the kind of stability Durkheim claimed for suicide statistics. Durkheim's argument against the theory as an account of suicide is based on a critique of the concept of type. To treat the relation between type and instance as explanatory, Durkheim argued, one needs to be able to show that the type is "to some extent independent of" the instances (and not merely their mathematical consequence), and *also* to give some sort of account of the causal mechanism by which the type insinuates itself into the instances (1951, p. 301; 1930, p. 339). If we take the *homme moyen* to be equivalent to the racial or ethnic type, the problem is apparently solved. But when we consider *explananda* such as suicide, it turns out that the notion that the tendency to suicide depends strictly on race is unsupported (1951, p. 302; 1930, p. 339). Beyond this, it is obscure what sort of *causal* mechanism one might conceive to connect 'averageness' and suicide. Suicide, after all, is a rarity. To the extent that the inclination to suicide is part of the 'average' type, it must be extremely weak – too weak to determine, by itself, a single suicide (1951, p. 303; 1930, p. 341).

Durkheim's reasoning here is striking for its absolute commitment to a nonprobabilistic notion of the causal bond itself. He did not deny that there are statistical associations between race and suicide – only that the associations do not amount to a proper causal relation. Quetelet's results are "simply the probability that a single man belonging to a definite social group will kill himself during the year" (1951, p. 304; 1930, p. 342). In itself, such a result is causally opaque:

This probability in no sense gives us a measure of the average inclination to suicide, or helps prove the existence of such an inclination. The fact that so many individuals out of 100 kill themselves does not imply that the others are exposed to any degree and can teach us nothing concerning the nature and intensity of the causes leading to suicide (1951, p. 304; 1930, p. 342).

Yet this is itself mysterious, for this probability is precisely what Durkheim's own curve fitting is designed to explain. Durkheim's own idea is that there is a collective force that produces these suicides so that "everything takes place as if they were obeying a single order" (1951, p. 305; 1930, p. 343). We know the force is 'collective' because of the way in which the rates vary between societies.

This regular recurrence of identical events in proportions constant within the same population but very inconstant from one population to another would be inexplicable had not each society definite currents impelling its inhabitants with a definite force to commercial and industrial ventures, to behaviour of every sort likely to involve families in trouble, etc. (1951, p. 306; 1930, p. 344).

Thus turning the rate into a measure of a 'collective force' makes the rate into a cause rather than a type. But it is of course a cause of a peculiar sort.

The language of 'inclination', 'force', and the like, together with Durkheim's discussion, in the *Rules*, of mechanical composition, would lead one to expect that Durkheim considered the collective force for suicide to compose with individual causes, including the incidents that occasion suicide (such as bankruptcy) and the psychological traits that predispose a person to suicide (such as neurasthenia), to determine that act of suicide. The problem Durkheim would have with this is that one might very well expect that the distributions of neurasthenia, bankruptcy, and the like were *not* statistically independent of suicide, and therefore would not disappear in the rate in the same way that individual circumstances would. Durkheim, indeed, considered it likely that there would be some relationship. However, he had no vocabulary for discussing the possibilities of relationships other than causal relationships, and in the absence of quantitative laws for their causal effects, no means for dealing with the problem of subtracting the compositional 'contribution' made by neurasthenia, bankruptcy, and the like from the total rate.

Once he had borrowed Quetelet's *conclusion*, that accidental causes disappear in stable rates, and reconstrued the rates as manifestations of a special realm of social fact, he was pushed away from these questions and forced to come up with some line of reasoning that preserved the independent 'facticity' and causal power of the rate. He did this by *denying* that the individual causes compose with the collective causes, and this denial was the source of the most striking and peculiar claims in the text, claims that echo Quetelet's most lachrymose talk about the 'budget' which had to be paid on the gallows, in prison, and so on. The terminology Durkheim used is different. The causal forces originating in society, such as altruism and egoism, are 'currents'. These currents *"cause a definite number to kill themselves in each society in a definite period of time"* (1951, p. 324; 1930, p. 366, emphasis in original). Individual circumstances determine *where* the toll is exacted. If

certain individuals are affected and certain others not, this is undoubtedly, in great part, because the formers' mental constitution, as elaborated by nature and events, offers less resistance to the suicidogenetic current. But though these conditions may share in determining the particular persons in whom this current becomes embodied, neither the special qualities nor the intensity of the current depend on these conditions (1951, p. 323; 1930, p. 366).

Thus, while neuropathic conditions, for example, dispose the individual to suicide, they "only cause the suicides to succumb with greater readiness" (1951, p. 323; 1930, p. 366).

Durkheim conceded that "it seems certain that no collective sentiment can affect individuals when they are absolutely indisposed to it" (1951, p. 222; 1930, p. 365). Nevertheless, a "harmony" must be achieved between collective forces and individual dispositions such that the numbers of persons predisposed to the current must match the toll to be exacted (1951, p. 323; 1930, p. 365). In the case of suicide, the explanation of this harmony is a "natural affinity": "the causes determining the social currents affect individuals simultaneously and predispose them to receive the collective influences." "The hypercivilization which breeds the anomic tendency and the egoistic tendency also refines nervous systems, making them excessively delicate" (1951, p. 323; 1930, pp. 365–66). The "crude, rough culture implicit in the excessive altruism of primitive man develops a lack of sensitivity which favors renunciation" (1951, p. 323; 1930, p. 366). Consequently, society "cannot lack the material for its needs, for it has, so to speak, kneaded it with its own hands" (1951, p. 323; 1930, p. 366).

Durkheim seemed to sense the implausibility of this, and went on to argue that "no society exists in which the various forms of nervous degeneration do not provide suicide with more than the necessary number of candidates" (1951, p. 324; 1930, p. 367). It may be noted that these narrow escapes are entirely *ad hoc*. The whole process of determining the appropriate natural affinities between currents and predispositions needs to be repeated for each current, at least to the extent that the individual offers 'resistance' to the act. The logical problem these 'affinities' solve flows directly from treating rates as indices of the strength of social causes. The problem is that if a given social cause can compose mechanically with biasing individual causes, these causes would perhaps bias the rate, raising or lowering it to a *de facto* undeterminable extent. Yet to claim that the cause behind the rate always exacts its toll depends on the even more astonishing idea that there is no mechanical composition between individual and social forces.

CURRENTS AND RESISTANCE

In his essays in the *Hermes* volumes, Michael Serres returns repeatedly to the theme of the centrality of the images of thermodynamic systems to the nineteenth century. "The notion of system," he says, may be mathematical, as in Euclid's elements. It "may also be mechanical: a set which remains stable throughout variations of objects which are either in movement or relatively stationary. Laplace speaks in this sense of the solar system."

In another essay I have called mechanical systems 'statues' or *stateurs*: they are based on a fixity or an equilibrium. After Carnot they become motors. They create movement, they go beyond the simple relation of forces, they create them by energy or power. They produce circulation by means of reservoirs and differences of temperature (Serres, 1982, p. 71).

The "three types all have closure in common" (1982, p. 72).

What Comte called 'electrology', the science that "deals with the circulation of electrical flux between terminals, beginning at centers with a fixed difference in potential" (1982, p. 33), as Serres remarks, continues the series of images of the world as an engine. "First it is a static, then a dynamic machine; now it is an electrical one" (1982, p. 33). The fundamental 'engine' in this system of concepts is thermodynamic, Carnot's engine.[1] This engine supplies the key concepts of 'reservoir' and 'circulation', and these concepts become an interpretive grid which can be widely applied:

the reservoir is capital, the quantity of energy, the constancy of force, the libidinal reservoir, and so forth; what can be applied to the pattern of general circulation or the circle of circles is language, speech, words, vocabulary, values, money, desire. Here are some examples of related questions: What blocks circulation? What stimulates it? Who or what governs or forms the reservoir? And so on. With these questions and these answers, varied and multiplied into several voices, you will reconstruct the entire set of interpretative organons formed in the nineteenth century (Serres, 1982, p. 37).

And so Durkheim: the images are from the same family of concepts. Although Durkheim was far from mechanical in his borrowings from natural science vocabulary, using terms from a wide range of scientific domains, affinities between Durkheim's concepts and those of electricity and thermodynamics are evident everywhere. In the preface to the second edition of the *Rules*, it is suggested that psychology and sociology may share some formal laws. Social and individual representations may resemble one another, and "in consequence of these resemblances, certain abstract laws" governing the ways in which representations "attract and repel each other, unite or separate," may exist which apply to both kinds of representation (1964, p. 1; 1982, p. 41; 1937, p. xviii). Repulsion is an electromagnetic phenomenon central to the development of the nineteenth-century concept of forces and their transformation. When Durkheim described individual actions, as we have seen, he treated 'impulses' as the more or less direct causes of action. Durkheim spoke of the effect of a collective current on the individual as an "external impulse" (1964, p. 101; 1982, p. 128; 1937, p. 101) and of what he called "prolongations of [collective] causes inside of individuals" (1951, p. 287; 1930, p. 324) as a "spark" of the collective current (1951, p. 316; 1930, p. 357); the individual, as we have seen, can have 'resistance' to this current and can come into contact with it frequently, or intermittently.

The attractions of the imagery are evident in a famous story from the history of French science. In a monastery in Paris, Abbé Jean-Antoine Nollet, in the presence of members of the court of Louis XV, had seven hundred monks join hands: the monk at one end of the line held one terminal of a Leyden jar. When the monk at the other end was connected to the other terminal, all seven hundred jumped into the air. Durkheim's crowds could not have behaved more congenially. In *Suicide*, the current is sometimes spoken of as a fluid (1951, pp. 366, 369; 1930, pp. 419, 423), a usage consistent with the theory developed in the 1820s by Ampere (who performed experiments on repulsion between charged wires) of electrical charge as fluid flowing around the charged particle. These affinities form enough of a pattern to give a new sense to other usages which may be made to fit into this system of ideas, such as 'vital power' – Joule's language.

Affinities, showy as they sometimes are, usually do little interpretive work, and the diversity of Durkheim's borrowings make it difficult to add much coherence simply through identifying affinities. In this case, the language of currents can do a bit more than usual. The technical problem of rates, as we have seen, ends in a puzzle. Durkheim treated the demands of society for victims of suicide like the fixed appetite of a pride of lions, which ordinarily preys only on sick and weak animals, but which will attack the healthy and strong if there is an insufficient supply of the sick and the weak. The imagery of thermodynamics and electricity fits this, in one crucial way. The key to Carnot's engine is the conservation of force, the idea that forces may be (reversibly) transformed from one kind of force to another, so that work may be defined in terms of heat (or electrical charge in terms of work), and that nothing is 'lost' in the transformations. The energy of the suicidal current, similarly, cannot be destroyed. If it meets 'resistance' from the individual,[2] it expresses itself elsewhere in the system, which is closed and complete. If it does not meet resistance, it is nevertheless exhausted, in the sense of being "reduced by all its losses through individuation" (1951, p. 319; 1930, p. 361). To square this language with the claim that the suicidal force takes a fixed number, it is not enough to point to the conservation of force. Suicide does not admit of degrees. With a distribution of persons whose mental constitution makes them resist the current equally, there presumably would be no suicides, for the suicidal current could not individuate, just as switches with a particular resistance would not respond to a current of low intensity. When he discussed the individual, Durkheim tried to respond to this kind of criticism by way of auxiliary arguments that clarify the relation between forces and rates.

In contrast to the *Rules*, where the canceling of accidental causes is asserted as a premise, *Suicide* contains an argument that comes curiously close to Quetelet's distinction between constant, accidental, and variable causes. Durkheim's argument is that the sort of example envisioned here, where there was no outlet for the force, could not occur. He held that general human dispositions are constant causes, that the distribution of such strictly personal qualities is therefore fixed, and that only the social element may vary (1951, pp. 321–22; 1930, pp. 363–64). The point of this particular argument is to show that individual circumstances, to the extent that they affect rates, themselves *ultimately* vary only as the result of social causes (and thus independently of psychological causes). In contrast, in, e.g. tidology, the independence assumption does not hold. Durkheim's argument here gives causal grounds for believing that it does in the case of suicide.[3]

The 'exhaustion' of a collective current occurs when it is passed into the realm of individual action. The realm of the individual mind is of course the ultimate source of collective force, and the force that attaches to particular representations. In describing the 'losses through individuation' of the collective current which result in action, we are, so to say, describing one cycle in a Carnot engine. When we show the origin of primitive social bonds in 'collective effervesence' we identify a primal source for the reservoir of collective force (cf. 1951, pp. 126–27; 1930, pp. 111–12).[4]

If we again ask the question of the location of the composition of various forces or 'impulses' of particular intensities in terms of this family of images, the texts yield some answers. Durkheim's root image is of *homo duplex*, an individuality composed of basic, but plastic, predispositions, private impulses, unshared representations, and the like, and a social side, the collective element, with its sparks, impulses, and currents. Within this mind, the collective and individual forces "confront each other." "To be sure, the former is much stronger than the latter, since it is made of a combination of all the individual forces" (1951, p. 319; 1930, pp. 360–61), but these forces are weakened in their effect on the individual in various ways: by resistance, by intermittent contact, and, most importantly, by counteracting collective forces, such as those which preserve the individual against suicide. The question of where the composition occurs is a non-starter. When the collective forces offset one another, they do not become individualized; when they do not offset one another, they do become individualized, precisely where there is the least resistance, or the least countervailing force.

The Aftermath

Durkheim was able to perform the analytic magic of *Suicide* just once. The structure of laws he envisioned in the *Rules* was never filled in with other, related laws, so the promise of showing an underlying orderliness to social reality was never fulfilled. This is the decisive blow against Durkheim's position. But Durkheim did not abandon the program, and the 'Durkheimians' he schooled followed it through an incredible range of studies. They increasingly became concerned with the problem of origins, which is only briefly discussed in the *Rules*, and, following Durkheim's own lead in this redirection of interest, became less and less concerned with the causal principles that subsequent sociology would also seek. When his student Maurice Halbwachs returned to questions like the social causes of suicide after his death, the logical machinery Durkheim constructed was discreetly abandoned. In the introduction to his own book, Halbwachs remarked that Durkheim's "dialectic was more persuasive than the facts" (1978, p. 4). Halbwach's own approach was to use "calculations of deviations, indices of correlation, dispersion, etc." (1978, p. 5).

Halbwachs thought of this as 'modern'. From the point of view of explanatory structure, however, it was a return to an older tradition of statistical commentary, in which causes were thought of more loosely. The book *Suicide* itself, as Phillipe Besnard has shown, went into a "purgatory" soon after its publication, and was largely ignored until the fifties, when the concept of anomy was reborn as a part of American sociology (Besnard, 1983, p. 605, 1984).

PART III

WEBER ON ACTION

CHAPTER NINE

OBJECTIVE POSSIBILITY AND ADEQUATE CAUSE

John Venn is traditionally regarded as the founder of the relative frequency interpretation of probability, but this tradition is misleading, both historically and textually. In *The Logic of Chance*, Venn was skeptical about such concepts as propensities, which he regarded as unmeaning restatements of descriptive statements of empirical relative frequencies. But while he often said that particular relations described by probabilities or rates are 'nothing but' expressions of the relative frequency of occurrences within a class (1866, p. 34) – a literally true characterization of such things as crime rates – he did not elevate this into a 'theory' of distinct probability, as writers such as Richard von Mises were to do in the period after the First World War. The German probability writing that arose out of the reaction to Quetelet was based on a kind of skepticism as well.

If we are to go beyond the sort of skepticism that says that probability is *nothing but* a relative frequency within a reference class and treat probability claims as 'analyzable' as relative frequency claims, the concept of class becomes a keystone. A relative frequency is relative *within* a class; without an applicable concept of class, there is no means of determining a probability. If there is a conceptual feature of a given class – such as vagueness of extension – that blocks the application of the sorts of precise limits necessary for counting, the concept of probability itself is conceptually inapplicable. If it turns out that the limits of classes cannot in general be adequately conceptualized or empirically applied, the idea of a determinate probability is itself threatened.

The early relative frequentists accepted this. Von Mises's response to the contemporary charge that

it is easy to formulate a self-consistent theory based on exactly defined artificial concepts, but in the practical applications of the theory we always have to deal with vague processes which can only be adequately described in terms of correspondingly vague concepts which have evolved in a natural way (1957, p. 7)

was to say that this was a "deficiency which is to be found in any theoretical treatment of reality" (1957, p. 7). With this, frequentism turned to the concerns of the logical foundations of probability and rejected the task of clarifying the informal use of probabilistic notions in such nonscientific contexts as jurisprudence, where an extensive German literature on probability had developed from the 1870s to the First World War.

Weber published a closely related set of methodological essays in the middle of the first decade of the twentieth century: 'Roscher and Knies' (in 1903), 'Objectivity in Social Science' (in 1904), 'The Logic of the Cultural Sciences' (in 1906), and the 'Critique of Stammler' (in 1907). Two of these papers were published in the *Archiv für Sozialwissenschaft und Sozialpolitik* (in 1904 and 1906), as was 'The Protestant Ethic' (in 1905). All of the methodological papers of this period appeal to a particular doctrine of probabilistic causation which figured heavily in the jurisprudential literature on probability: they use the technical terms of this doctrine and draw conclusions about the character of historical knowledge on the basis of the technical features of the doctrine. Probabilistic concepts play large roles in other, later texts as well. Weber's views in these essays were derived from the work of Johannes von Kries, Weber's contemporary at Freiburg in the nineties. Weber's younger friend, the attorney (and later minister of justice), Gustav Radbruch, wrote an extensive study of the technical problems of cause, probability, and jurisprudence.

Weber's own testimony on his indebtedness to these writings was unambiguous.

I find the extent to which, here as in many previous discussions, I have 'plundered' von Kries' ideas almost embarrassing, especially since the formulation must often fall short in precision of von Kries' (1978b, p. 128n; 1949, p. 186n; 1922, p. 288n).

This statement, in 'The Logic of the Cultural Sciences', is not an expression of false modesty. Weber did not develop, but rather relied on, the extant technical literature on probability and probabilistic cause. Moreover, he spent little effort at directly working out the implications of the use of von Kriesian causality for the explanation of human action. He took it that the issues have already been dealt with by jurists:

... the question of penal guilt, insofar as it involves the problem: under what circumstances can it be asserted that someone through his action has 'caused' a certain external effect, is purely a question of causation. And, indeed, this problem obviously has *exactly the same logical structure* as the problem of historical 'causality' (1949, p. 168; 1922, p. 270, emphasis supplied).

Weber's 'plundering' did not consist of his simply repeating von Kries. When Weber wrote on historical subjects, he used the ideas on cause and probability as part of arguments and polemics that typically had different targets, and the conclusions were often considerably broader in their implications: the arguments are made to bear on all our knowledge of the historical world, and to mark the limits of our causal knowledge of this world.

Probabilistic ideas are usually submerged in these methodological arguments, and the precise relation between the problem-structure that derives
from the probability literature and problem-structures that derive from
other literatures – contemporary historiography and contemporary neo-
Kantian epistemology, for example – is often unclear. The relation between
the methodological texts and the substantive texts is extremely ambiguous
and obscure. Most interpreters of Weber have, as we shall see, simply
imposed an explanatory structure on the substantive texts – usually one
that is in conflict with Weber's own methodological assertions. Yet probability concepts are to be found in the substantive writings as well, often
conspicuously.

In this section of the book, I will discuss three topics: the jurisprudential
theories that were the source of Weber's probability usages, the changing
concepts of the explanation and interpretation of individual action that
develop in the course of his methodological reflections, and his application
of causal reasoning to the problem of capitalism. The last of these topics
opens into the wider literature on Weber's intentions as a historical thinker.
In discussing this topic there can be no pretense of comprehensiveness.
Instead, I have chosen to concentrate on two well-known and much-dis-
cussed problem cases: *The Protestant Ethic and the Spirit of Capitalism*, his
most famous work, and his final explanation of capitalism, which was the
theme of his last lectures.

To surface the probability arguments in these texts and come to terms
with the question of their relation to the whole, it will be necessary first to
make sense of the literature that Weber 'plundered'. It will then be
necessary to show how the probability notions were made to fit into the
various polemics and methodological arguments Weber developed. These
arguments cross the borders of epistemology, ontology, hermeneutics, and
decision theory, and the thread of the reasoning is easily lost. In the course
of this discussion it will turn out that some light can be shed on a number
of traditional problems of Weber interpretation, primarily as a result of
showing a different kind of coherence in the oeuvre.

CAUSE AND JURISPRUDENCE

Where common-law jurisdictions rely on juries, precedent, and notions of
what a reasonable man would do, continental law was, and is, more formal
and 'scientific'. The continental alternative to the ramshackle structure of
practices that makes up the common-law 'system' for answering questions

about causal responsibility was to develop an academic theory of causality which rationalized judicial decision making for both criminal and civil liability. Mill's methods are, with the exception of the Method of Concomitant Variations, methods of dealing with conditions, and for this reason they were particularly useful for the German academic legal theorists who were concerned with, questions of the attribution of causal responsibility. In curious contrast to contemporary German academic philosophy, the intellectual authority of *A System of Logic* among legal theorists was enormous, and Millian concepts were basic to the traditions that developed in response to the problem of liability.

The dominant jurisprudential theory of cause, the von Buri–von Bar theory, held that responsibility attached to actions that constituted necessary conditions of a harmful result. The difficulty with this theory was that it extended liability too broadly, and the various *ad hoc* restrictions of this extension that were proposed seemed unsatisfactory. The alternative theory, the adequate cause theory, was designed to overcome the difficulties by a change in the structure of the concept of cause, a change toward a probabilistic theory of cause. The major exponent of the theory was von Kries, who had played a role in the reaction against Quetelet, although others, notably Leipmann and Rümelin, wrote extensively on these topics.

The cases in which the original von Buri–von Bar doctrine ran into trouble were those in which an actor did something that was a necessary condition for the result but which would not ordinarily be regarded as a 'cause'. Suppose a shirt salesman sold a victim a red shirt, and the victim went to Spain and was gored by a bull while wearing the shirt during the running of the bulls. In a criminal context, if the act of the sale *also* met the requirement of intent, i.e. if he sold the shirt in order to procure the death, he would be liable for the killing, since his conduct was a necessary condition of the killing. In a civil context, where intent is not a test, this extends liability too far: the salesman would be liable, under von Buri–von Bar's theory, merely if the red shirt was a necessary condition for the harm. The adequacy theory says that liability depends on the probability that action would result in the harm. Since in this case the probability would be small, it is possible to say that the salesman is not liable. More generally, one may say that a certain degree of probability must be reached before a judgment of liability is possible (Radbruch, 1902, pp. 17–18).

Radbruch made the point (against von Kries, who wished to apply the adequacy theory in both criminal and civil contexts) that the adequacy theory alone does not account for ordinary legal practice in cases of criminal liability. Weber endorsed this point but suggested that it is irrelevant to the purposes of the historian, who is not concerned with cause in the sense of criminal liability but in the sense of civil liability. The criminal law, as Radbruch and Weber agreed, is concerned to punish the actor with 'the bad will' (or criminal intent) who acts with this will (Radbruch, 1902, p. 30; Weber, 1949, p. 169; 1922, p. 271). Civil liability does not involve the question of bad will, which is, one may say, a normative question, but is nevertheless concerned with responsibility and degree of responsibility. The central distinction within the law of liability, between intended and unintended damages, is analogous to the historian's concern with responsibility: subjective *guilt* is not an issue for the historian or the civil lawyer, but the *fact* of intent *is* an issue, especially in connection with the distinction between actually foreseen and unforeseen consequences of an action: a judgment of intent depends in part on whether or not the actor did in fact foresee a particular consequence. This fact is, however, a 'subjective fact', in the sense that it is an assertion about the subjective standpoint of the actor.

The alternative theory shared many features of the original, nonprobabilistic, theory. As Radbruch explained, the two theories share the assumption that all the necessary conditions are 'equivalent' in the sense that they are all equally necessary for the production of the act. The theories also share the principle that the combination of conditions is the 'cause' of the result (Radbruch, 1902, p. 9). The novelty of the theory derived from the identification of 'adequate' causal contribution with the quantitative increase in the probability of an outcome which is attributable to the presence of a given necessary condition.

From the point of view of jurisprudence, this definition has some serious difficulties. One is that if probability is defined in a subjectivist fashion, i.e., in terms of 'expectation', the probability judgment becomes 'subjective', and therefore not suitable for a court. Von Kries attempted to avoid this by defining it in terms of 'objective possibility', which he formulated in a way that is designed to contrast to subjective notions of 'probability', or estimates. Von Kries's point can be seen if one contrasts ordinary relative-frequency estimates, which are necessarily based on a reference class within which a probability is calculated, to what might be described as a 'reference-class-free' notion of probability. One may say, for example, that the chance of an American dying of cancer is X, where X is a percentage of Americans. The chance of a smoker dying of cancer, or a person with a history of cancer, is of course higher. Each category, 'American', 'smoker', 'person with a history of cancer', is a reference class for which statistics can be gathered. Von Kries wished to contrast such probabilities to the absolute probability of George Smith's getting cancer given the unstatable myriad of conditions which actually are statistically relevant to the outcome. This notion makes some intuitive sense – if George has a probability of getting cancer as an American, a smoker, and as a person with a history of previous cancer, it seems plausible to say that he has a determinate chance of getting cancer as a particular individual, given the actual conditions of his life. Von Kries traded on this by focusing on the peculiarity of holding that a single event can have a variety of true but different probabilities, and concluded from the fact that different reference classes produced different 'probabilities' for the same event that these reference-class-based probabilities cannot be the 'true' probability. The true probability of an event, its 'objective possibility', was the only objective probabilistic fact about a given event. Relative frequencies within classes, he suggested, are 'probabilities', but only in a figurative sense (cf. Radbruch, 1902, p. 10).[1] The probabilities within a given reference class are no more than 'signs' of the true probability of cancer, which inheres in the individual case. Indeed, because 'relative frequency' probabilities vary with the reference class that is selected, and the selection of a reference class is not governed by any clear rule, these probabilities seem arbitrary or subjective, in contrast to the 'objective' fact of the inherent or absolute probability of George's getting cancer.[2]

Von Kries's theory developed and was elaborated on the intuitive basis of this concept of 'objective possibility' as the inherent or absolute probability of an individual event given the infinity of actual past conditions. The peculiarity of single event 'objective possibilities' was that they could not be calculated. No one could fully state the enormous, perhaps infinite, number of events that are conditional to the outcome events of interest – to stop short of this would be to select a reference class arbitrarily.

Heuristic value in clarifying the concept of cause aside, the nonempirical or hypothetical or heuristic character of the notion of 'objective possibility' would seem to make it irrelevant to factual determinations, such as those made by a court of law or a historian. Yet the common property of historical and legal inquiry is that the 'possibilities' of historians and the legal system are possibilities that have already been realized. So the determination of a numerical probability for an event is going to have a hypothetical character anyway. The same point holds for the problem of determinations of the necessity of conditions that the adequacy theory shares with the von

Buri–von Bar theory. Determinations of 'necessity', i.e., of which past facts are the 'conditions' of an event, were always handled in these theories by rather vague appeals to 'thought' or 'past experience'. But there is no easy alternative to these vague appeals, for one cannot, as in an experiment, 'remove' the conditions of a past event. 'Sufficiency' is, superficially, less problematic. In law and history there is no question that some combination of the conditions that actually obtained prior to a past event were in fact sufficient for the result. As Weber put it, "historical exposition undoubtedly is governed by the assumption that the 'causes' to which the 'effect' is imputed have to be regarded as unqualifiedly the sufficient conditions for its occurrence" (1949, p. 168n; 1922, p. 270n).

Describing this combination of conditions *in toto* is not the aim either of historians or lawyers, who acknowledge that "an infinity of conditions which are only summarily referred to as scientifically 'without interest' are associated with the causes which are deemed the sufficient conditions of the effect" (Weber, 1949, p. 168n; 1922, p. 170n). What is interesting to historians and lawyers is making determinations of responsibility or the *extent* of the contribution of particular acts to the outcome. The Millian notions of sufficiency and necessity are not of much help here, except as a starting point, because of the assumption of the equivalence of necessary conditions. The adequacy theory purports to provide a means of 'weighing' causal contributions to a given result that does not contradict the principle of equality of necessary conditions (Weber, 1949, p. 164; 1922, p. 266). By starting with the recognition that a combination of conditions sufficient for outcome events of interest has in fact occurred, we can proceed by 'sub-tracting' conditions from hypothetical 'condition complexes', i.e., sets of conditions, and measuring the contribution by showing the effect of the 'subtraction' on the probabilities of given outcomes. The concept this yields is quite simple: the 'objective possibility' is the degree to which particular necessary conditions, in combination with some set of other necessary conditions, tend to occur with particular results. The degrees range from zero to one: 'zero' objective possibility would be a case where, under condition A, in combination with a given set of conditions, the outcome never occurs; 'one', or invariant succession, would mean that this condition A, in combination with the given set of other conditions, was sufficient.

Von Kries developed this notion of quantifying the degree of causal contribution in contrast to Mill's picture of the composition of a rate. Mill – in one of his concessions to common usage – said that for any outcome, various conditions exist which either increase the likelihood of or 'thwart' the outcome. The probability of an outcome that one calculates for a class of cases is a direct reflection of the 'balance' between 'thwarting' and 'increasing' conditions that act on this outcome. In *A System of Logic*, Mill told us that

> If the actuary of an insurance office infers from his tables that among a hundred persons now living, of a particular age, five on the average will attain the age of seventy, his inference is legitimate, not for the simple reason that this is the proportion who have lived till seventy in times past, but because the fact of their having so lived shows that this is the proportion existing, at that place and time, between the causes which prolong life to the age of seventy and those tending to bring it to an earlier close (1973, p. 542).

Von Kries objected to this way of talking about probability on the ground that one can never simply divide the 'hindering' and 'prolonging' causes (1888, pp. 396–99; 1927, pp. 283–84). What is ordinarily a 'prolonging' cause may, in combination with some other condition, turn out to 'hinder'. In the usual cases one is concerned with conditions that act in concert with other conditions, and it is these combinations of conditions which, over the long run, turn out to have determinable statistical relations to the outcome and which are of interest.

Weber agreed with von Kries on this point, and criticized Mill for his 'anthropomorphic' way of speaking about prolonging and hindering (1949, p. 186; 1922, p. 288). Instead of classifying causes as positive or negative, the adequacy theorists considered the probability of an outcome in terms of, as Radbruch put it, "concrete condition complexes," each of which produces an outcome with a particular degree of probability. A total rate, such as the actuary's, is a result not of a balance of prolonging and hindering causes, as for Mill, but of the empirical mix of occurrences of various types of condition complexes, with their different degrees of dependent probability.

PROBLEMS OF 'ABSTRACTION'

The specification of the intuitive notion of 'degree of causal contribution' of a condition as the difference between the probability of an outcome on a condition complex and the probability of the same outcome on this condition complex with the condition of interest removed is undeniably appealing. One may question whether these attractions remain once one faces the difficulties that become apparent when one considers the problem of numerically determining these probabilities.

The way in which the problem of determining the degree of association enters the legal literature is in connection with the problem of defining 'adequacy'. Recall that the point of the appeal to probability is to distinguish mere necessary conditions from adequate causes. If one defines 'objective possibility' as the degree of probability of an outcome on a given necessary condition, all necessary conditions will have *some* such probability. So the distinction between an adequate cause and a mere condition must be in the *degree* of possibility. The standard needs to be set high enough that the sale of the red shirt that catches the eye of the bull is not held to be a 'cause' of the goring, but should also be low enough that a dangerous act, such as giving a lunatic a gun, would be an adequate cause.

The problem of setting the minimal level of increase to call a necessary condition an 'adequate cause' was never settled, for it became evident that difficulties with the necessary steps of abstraction precluded any simple solution to the problem of numerically specifying probabilities. Rümelin argued that the

fundamental peculiarity of the statistical search for causal associations arises from the fact that it relates cause universes to effect universes, both of which include in addition to cause elements and effect elements other components having no bearing upon the cause and effect relationship. Moreover, since it is of the very essence of the statistical method that separate elements or individual units in the universes are disregarded, interest is centered entirely upon their common, or 'average', interactions. These considerations account for the fact that statistical inferences as to causal associations belong to the realm of probability and lack the incisiveness of classical induction (Anderson, 1934, pp. 370–71).

The 'lack of incisiveness' which derives from the necessity of 'disregarding' elements was understood not, as it was in later statistical writing, as a matter of the necessity of making 'assumptions', but in terms of the concept of abstraction.

To get an estimate of the dependent probability of an event on a given prior event or set of prior conditions, one must 'abstract' in two major ways, by 'isolating' and 'generalizing', to use the terms used by Weber (1949, p. 175; 1922, p. 277). To isolate is to consider a causal relation in terms of some particular set of conditions, thus isolating these conditions from the remaining 'infinity of conditions' which must be left unstated. To generalize is to describe in general terms. Both types of abstraction are required in making judgments of objective possibility. One must consider the relation as an element in a class of factually equivalent cases in order to calculate the dependent probability, and one's estimate of the dependent probability will be equivalent to the relative frequency of the outcome event in the class of events with equivalent conditions.

In the first place, given the fact that each event, considered in its full particularity, has an infinity of 'necessary conditions', one can select a reference class of 'same' conditions only by considering a relatively small set of conditions, and by ignoring or leaving unstated a great many conditions. To apply the probabilities one derives in the reference class to a relationship between a particular set of conditions and a particular outcome event (for which the conditions are independently known to be 'necessary'), one must assume the factual equivalency of unstated conditions between the events one is considering as a class for the purpose of calculating dependent probabilities, i.e., the reference class. If relevant unstated conditions vary, one will have the wrong estimate of the dependent probability for the particular case (Radbruch, 1902, pp. 11–14). The assumption that there are no such relevant conditions is usually false. In a causal universe as complex as the social world, one can usually show that some of the unstated conditions have some degree of association – perhaps small – with the outcome events. Hence there can be no illusions about these estimates being 'true values' or 'real' probabilities.

The problem of 'generalization' or description is just as intractable as the problem of unstated conditions. Events may be described in different ways: described in one way, they will be part of one class; described in another way, they will be part of another. If one is considering the liability of a person who strikes another person, and describes his action as 'striking another person', and then calculates the probability of the outcome of death, one will get a relatively low probability, perhaps one below the threshold of adequacy. However, if one describes the same act as 'a 250-pound man striking a 95-pound man in the windpipe with full force', one will calculate a far higher probability of death as an outcome. Yet both descriptions may be 'true' of the event (Radbruch, 1902, pp. 13–26).

It would extend liability too far if one adopted the rule of always using the fullest, or most detailed, description. The relative frequency probability in the class equivalent to the event in its fullest description would be very high in cases where the person is not usually considered liable, such as cases where the actor did not intend or could not foresee outcomes that had been rendered more probable by conditions that obtained unbeknownst to him. If a person struck a fly on a curtain with full force, not knowing that someone was behind the curtain facing out, and hit that person in the windpipe, killing the person, we would in ordinary usage call this a 'freak' occurrence. From the omniscient point of view, however, and under suitably detailed descriptions (e.g., striking a man behind a curtain in the throat with full force, etc.), the act would have increased the probability of the outcome considerably, making it an adequate cause. The ultimate detailed descriptions are those envisioned by Mill's atomism. If Mill were right and if there were an 'atomic' level of description at which everything is governed by deterministic laws, the outcome would be a matter of fate, determined from the beginning of time (cf. Weber, 1949, p. 164; 1922, p. 266).

Yet both in the law and in history it is important to speak of cause. So the concept of adequate cause serves primarily in contexts where nomological principles do not directly apply, but where causal explanations are nevertheless important. In these contexts one's choice of descriptions does not and cannot depend on the task of refining concepts to the point where one can frame true deterministic laws with them. But the question arises as to what does and should determine selections of descriptive categories. In legal contexts, there is a tradition and a traditional set of problems and distinctions which the descriptive terminology must serve. So in these contexts, one can identify constraints on the choice of a terminology. Nevertheless, these constraints do not diminish the enormous arbitrariness by enough to make the quantitative notion of 'objective possibility' a useful tool for the purposes of either historians or judges.

Rules for selecting descriptions prove to be similarly unsatisfactory. Radbruch described the problem of 'generalization' or description in terms of the 'degree' of generalization, noticing that when a condition was described in its full particulars, the probability of its producing a given result described generally would be higher than the probability if the condition were described generally, and also that when a result was described in its full particulars, its dependent probability on a given condition described 'generally' would be low. The probability of a 'blow' producing a 'contusion of the right parietal during a Sunday afternoon in the park' would be low, while if the result is described more generally, e.g., as an 'injury', the probability would be higher (Radbruch, 1902, p. 15). But this is too simple, for descriptions vary not only in the 'degree' to which they are generalized but in the way in which they are generalized. The same event may be truly described in a variety of distinct ways at any given degree of 'generalization', yielding different numerical estimates. So Radbruch's rule does not hold universally, and the notion of 'degree of generalization' proves of little relevance. No general rule using it, such as 'Generalize only as much as necessary to satisfy the requirements of legal classification', can yield consistent numerical results. In every case one will be faced with a set of different, equally general, descriptions, each yielding different numerical 'objective possibilities'.[3]

Hart and Honoré remark that von Kries's belief that the "bare relationship signified by *sine qua non* or necessary condition ... can be established
... by attending solely to the particular case" (1959, p. 415) is "mistaken,
since generalizations are needed in order to establish the existence of the
relationship of necessary condition" (1959, p. 415n). This is perhaps not
quite to the point. The reason von Kries could not concede this is that his
whole approach depends on it. His reliance on this peculiar notion of
necessary condition enabled him to avoid the problem of 'accidental' relationships, for the conditions the technique measures are, by definition,
necessary, hence 'causal'. If he could not claim to make this determination
directly, he would be forced to produce some sort of grounds for considering something a cause, such as the 'generalizations' mentioned by Hart
and Honoré, and this necessity would place him directly into one of the
central muddles of probabilistic theories of causation.

To establish such generalizations, he would need either to establish the
relations experimentally or in some other fashion that is *independent* of the
statistical evidence on which the adequate cause analysis is to be performed. Ordinarily, experiment is either impossible or the conditions under
which experiments can be performed so little resemble the conditions
under which the outcome is to be explained that inferences from the
experimental situation to the natural setting are highly questionable. If
experiment is impossible, the statistician is forced to rely on some form of
evidence showing the empirical probabilities of some outcome within a
given reference class, such as the class defined by a von Kriesian 'condition
complex'. These calculations are, as Mill would say, no more than an
application of the Method of Agreement, and do not establish cause. In
particular, they leave open the possibility that the relationship is 'accidental' – rather a compelling consideration when, as in the cases of concern
to historians and lawyers, the probabilities in question are not very high,
and alternative 'condition complexes' can be identified that also are statistically relevant to the outcome. To establish a given relationship as causal
– which is what Hart and Honoré ask – requires some method of
distinguishing between those relationships that are accidental or spurious
and those that are genuinely causal. If cause can be distinguished from
'coincidence' on *a priori* grounds, the problem does not arise. If it cannot,
none of the causal analyses envisioned by von Kries can be freed from the
possibility that the relations are spurious or accidental.

For many familiar empirical situations, 'complete' spuriousness, the case
where every outcome in a reference class is caused by conditions other than
those in the 'condition complex', is perhaps *a priori* sufficiently unlikely that

we can accept, as a practical expedient, *a priori* determinations that a relation is to some extent 'causal'. Unfortunately, to the extent that the concept of a condition as *sine qua non* in relation to an event comes to be confused with the different commonsense notion of 'abetting' a course of events, this practice runs into serious difficulties. Presumably, a condition that is not strictly *necessary* for an outcome (that is, an outcome described generally) can abet it, i.e., increase the probability of the outcome. Von Kries perhaps failed to recognize this, because he considered individual outcomes described 'generally' to be 'abstractions', and held that the relationship of the necessary conditionality properly holds only between individual cases in their full particulars. In estimating probabilities, which necessarily involves 'general' descriptions, the distinction between necessary conditions and coincidences is not sufficient, for a large part of the effect – the probability within the reference class – may be the result of one or more 'abetting' causes: smoking may not be a necessary condition for lung cancer, but if it is excluded from the condition complex on this ground, the observed probabilities of cancer will be largely spurious, because they would be higher than they would have been had smoking not been a condition. Thus, although this kind of 'causation' has a large impact on the numerical probabilities, von Kries had no conceptual category to place it in.

Suffice to say this is not a problem only for von Kries: it is questionable whether any adequate account has been given of, for example, the causal force of statistical analyses of the relation between smoking and cancer. Often the problem of defining a distinct concept of probabilistic causation is avoided by treating the causal element of the explanation in nonprobabilistic terms – in this case, in terms of biological mechanisms. But this does not solve the general problem of distinguishing probabilistic relations that are causal from those that are coincidental.

TWO KINDS OF DESCRIPTION

In legal contexts, 'abstraction' or redescription in the abstract vocabulary of the law is done as a matter of course and necessity. Weber accepted this, and accepted that this meant that legal descriptions do not directly correspond to 'reality'. As we have seen, Weber considered the logical structure of historical and legal causal explanations to be identical. To generalize these lessons to history, one needs to show that historians also abstract as a matter of necessity, and, in particular, "that the formulation of propositions about historical causal connections ... makes use of both types of

abstraction" characteristic of 'adequate cause' reasoning, "namely, isolation and generalization" (1949, p. 175; 1922, p. 277).

The two texts in which Weber formulated these arguments, 'Objectivity'
and 'The Logic of the Cultural Sciences', are methodological polemics. In
'Objectivity', one of Weber's antagonists, who is unnamed,[4]

claims that the task of psychology is to play a role comparable to mathematics for the
Geisteswissenschaften in the sense that it analyzes the complicated phenomena of social life into
their psychic conditions and effects, reduces them to their most elementary possible psychic
factors and then analyzes their functional interdependencies (1949, pp. 74–75; 1922, p. 173),

and wishes to create "thereby, a sort of 'chemistry' if not 'mechanics' of the
psychic foundations of social life" (1949, p. 75; 1922, p. 173). The epistemological premise of this conception of social science, according to Weber, was
the possibility of analyzing "all the observed and imaginable relationships
of social phenomena into some ultimate elementary 'factors'," so that one
can make "an exhaustive analysis and classification of them," and then
formulate "rigorously exact laws covering their behavior" (1949, p. 75;
1922, p. 174).

Weber presented his own views in the course of a critique of this strategy.
He proceeded by asking what would happen were this methodological
advice successfully followed and what sense we would be able to make of
the explanations we would get. He concluded that there would be a gap
between the historical facts we would *like* to have explained, which come
in a vocabulary that cannot be readily dispensed with, and the atomistically
described facts which the laws would explain. One might deal with this gap
by arguing that the historian's vocabulary is scientifically inadequate, and
that the replacement of questions framed in this vocabulary by questions
framed in 'atomic' descriptions is, after all, a routine part of scientific
progress. Venn, it may be recalled, pointed out the irrelevance of the sorts
of categories for which statistics are usually collected to the categories in
which genuine causal explanations are framed, and suggested that causal
explanations are properly sought by examining intermediate links. Weber
took a different approach. The historian's interest, he claimed, necessitates
the framing of questions in the particular concepts and terminology of the
historian's own historical and cultural world, i.e., in terms meaningful to
us.

Weber's point here is essentially that of Donald Davidson, who much
later was to argue, in such essays as 'Action, Reasons, and Causes', 'Psychology as Philosophy', 'Mental Events', and 'Hempel on Explaining
Action' (Davidson, 1982), that we have no means of translating mental

descriptions into physical language – that the two sets of terms simply do not correspond. As Davidson formulates 'the problem of many descriptions', the terms of ordinary 'reasons' explanations of action are related to the terms of the nomic explanations as the term 'clear cool day' is related to the terms under which physical laws explain: one would not find a law of physics that contained terms such as 'cool cloudy day with rain in the afternoon', but this is not to say that the laws of physics and chemistry do not cover the event; it is only to say that "the descriptions under which the event interests us ... have only remote connections with the concepts employed by the more precise known laws" (1982, p. 17). One might regard these different descriptions as equally valid – denying that any has any claim to any special status (e.g., 'atomic'). Or one might say that the descriptions suited to physical explanation are, in some sense, the 'basic' descriptions, the historian's vocabulary existing only, so to say, on the sufferance of the historian's 'interest'.

The ghost of Baconian realism haunted neo-Kantianism, as it haunted writers such as von Kries, who were sensitive to the dependence of their claims on the selection of conceptual categories that could not be assumed to correspond to 'reality'. Weber spoke to this problem in two ways, one of which makes him sound like some sort of 'soft determinist', the other of which makes him sound like a simple relativist, for whom deterministic laws, if there are any, would be merely another frame. In the 'Logic' paper, he spoke of the von Kriesian causal explanations (i.e., those that use the vocabulary of the historian or the common culture) as having a 'conceptual character' and resting

on the abstraction of certain constituents of *the real causal chain*, on the generalisation in thought of the remainder in the form of judgments of objective possibility and on the use of the latter to form the course of events into a causal complex having a certain structure (1978b, p. 130; 1949, p. 188; 1922, p. 290, emphasis supplied).

Perhaps by 'the real causal chain' Weber meant no more than the causal relation of events in their infinite particularity. But the statement suggests something more: that there is a real causal structure, and the 'forming' into causal complexes pertains only to the von Kriesian technique of causal analysis, which one relies on in the social sciences as a consequence of the fact that the social scientist, and particularly the historian, is limited in his choice of concepts by an 'interest' which includes the aim of giving explanations in terms that are intelligible to those with whom one shares a culture.

In 'Objectivity', however, there is no such apparent capitulation to the idea of a real causal structure beneath the level of von Kriesian explanations. Weber's main concern seems to be to reject essentialism. In the course of his attack on the idea of a presuppositionless science he said such things as, "A chaos of 'existential judgments' about countless individual events would be the only result of a serious attempt to analyze reality 'without presuppositions'" as Mommsen had recommended (1949, p. 78; 1922, p. 177). These strictures seem to apply to natural science as well as social. When he said that "an *exhaustive* causal investigation of any concrete phenomena in its full reality is not only practically impossible – it is simply nonsense" (1949, p. 78; 1922, p. 178), he ruled out Baconian realism and Millian atomism (which presumably denies that it is nonsense, at least at the level of ontology).

As Weber's critics in the twenties recognized, anti-atomistic or anti-essentialist arguments get into difficulties if one supposes that there is an ontological basis for such arguments. The problem is quite simple. Weber said, for example, that "'Culture' is a finite segment of the meaningless infinity of the world process" (1949, p. 81; 1922, p. 180) and that human beings confer meaning on this segment. Weber's critics seized on this and similar phrases to suggest that there was a conflict between Weber's attempt on the one hand to base his methodology on a view of reality as a chaos on which we selectively confer meaning and on the other hand to deny that there are any essences. If 'meaning' gets 'conferred', there must be something it is conferred on, even if this thing is a 'chaos'. So the image of infinitude or chaos itself seems to serve as a kind of metaphysics or claim about the essential character of reality. It will suffice to note here that Weber's assertion of the conceptual irrelevance of descriptions based on historians' interests to descriptions based on psychologists' or physicists' interests did not compel him to embrace such a metaphysics. The assertion is consistent with atomism as a metaphysical doctrine, and indeed, is congenial to it, if one considers the ease with which, in the 'Logic' essay, he slipped into a naturalistic or atomistic way of speaking about 'real causal structure'.

Weber's positive account of historical explanation goes beyond the claim that the descriptive vocabulary, and therefore the causal relations of interest to the historian, are irreducible to the descriptive vocabularies of the physical sciences. But this is a starting point which he did not abandon. There is also perhaps some reason for considering it to be more basic than his commitments to neo-Kantian epistemology. Although Weber took epistemology seriously, he was not trained as a philosopher, but as a lawyer. Biography often tells: the earliest forms of intellectual discipline which a person acquires usually have a deeper hold than the doctrines, however persuasive, of contemporaries. It is thus plausible to read Weber's appeals to the terminology of contemporary philosophers like Heinrich Rickert, which do not always fit the sorts of points he wished to make, as a matter of convenience rather than commitment and read his commitments on the subject of description as fundamental. Weber's tactical uses of convenient borrowings makes for a methodological oeuvre that is a great deal more confusing and difficult than Durkheim's, but to the extent that these borrowings bring him into contact with a more diverse set of influences, it is also potentially more fertile.

CHAPTER TEN

RATIONALITY AND ACTION

Mill's writings on cause and economic rationality presumed that a nomic psychology that did not radically conflict with commonsense interpretations of action was possible – indeed, that it was readily achievable. Durkheim wrote after this moment of innocence had passed, and chose to discard both psychology, understood as a foundation for the social sciences, and commonsense interpretation. Reasoning from the broad binary opposition between 'events in their full particularity' and 'the world known and described through general concepts which abstract from this full particularity', Weber found a place for each set of considerations, and was faced with the problem of sorting out their relations – a problem he never satisfactorily resolved, and on which the emphasis of his writing changed over the years. The writings are not, as in the case of Durkheim, directly concerned with constructing a methodology – they are polemics against the methodological doctrines of his contemporaries.

THE ATTRIBUTION OF INTENTIONS

Weber took relatively little notice of the practical problematics of the logic of interpretation in the early writings. His most extensive methodological discussion of an example of interpretation in the early writings focused on the questions of the presuppositions of interpretation and the epistemology of the ideal-type. In the early writings, the targets of his criticisms are various philosophical accounts of interpretation, especially doctrines that emphasize intuition and empathy. His basic thought was this: the problem of the explanation of action is a causal problem, and *causal* questions demand factual answers or answers with factual warrants such as the technique of 'adequate cause' provides.

The notion that once one has true descriptions of an action (description enabled by the construction of ideal-types, if need be), one needs only to apply the technique of the adequate cause theory is not, of course, sufficient. Different true descriptions lead to different results, and this led Weber to warn that "not only can there be no question, obviously, of any transfer of principles from the 'calculus of probability' strictly so called to the work of causal analysis in history, but great caution is required even in attempting to make an analogous use of its points of view" (1978b, p. 113n; 1949, p. 167n; 1922, p. 269n). Another difficulty is that although many of the relevant descriptions, even in Weber's own examples, involve motives and intentions, we are nowhere told how such descriptions are to be warranted, or what would resolve issues between alternative descriptions involving intentions. The historiographic conflict to which the essay 'The Logic of the Cultural Sciences' is largely addressed, the conflict between intentionality and cause, was sustained by this, and by the belief

that it is the historian's 'hunches' or 'intuition', rather than generalisations and reflection on 'rules', which disclose causal connexions; that the difference from work in natural science is precisely that the historian is concerned to explain events and personalities which can be 'interpreted' and 'understood' by direct analogy with our own mental lives; and that, finally, in the historian's account, it is again a question of the 'hunch', of the suggestive vividness of his narrative which allows the reader to 're-live' the events described, just as the historian himself has experienced and beheld them intuitively, rather than puzzled them out by reasoning (1978b, p. 120; 1949, p. 175; 1922, pp. 277–78).

Weber gave one example that directly relates the adequacy theory and the attribution of intentions. "Let us assume a temperamental young mother who is tired of certain misdeeds of her little child, and ... gives it a solid cuff" (1949, p. 177; 1922, p. 279). He described the following colloquy between the *paterfamilias* and the young *Hausfrau*: he will "remonstrate with 'her'," and she might give the excuse that

if at that moment she *had* not been, let us assume, 'agitated' by a quarrel with the cook, that the aforementioned disciplinary procedure *would* not have been used at all or would not have been applied 'in that way'; she will be inclined to admit to him: 'he really knows that she is not ordinarily in that state'. She refers him thereby to his 'empirical knowledge' regarding her 'usual motives', which in the vast majority of all the generally *possible* constellations would have led to another, less irrational effect. She claims, in other words, that the blow which she delivered was an 'accidental' and not an 'adequately' caused reaction to the behavior of her child (1949, pp. 177–78; 1922, pp. 279–80).

This is precisely how the historian or lawyer reasons.

Even though, exactly like Molière's philistine who learned to his pleasant surprise that he had been speaking 'prose' all his life, the young woman would certainly be astounded if a logician showed her that she had made a causal 'imputation' just like an historian, that, to this end, she had made 'judgments of objective possibility' and had 'operated' with the category of 'adequate causation' ... yet such is precisely and inevitably the case from the point of view of logic (1949, p. 178; 1922, p. 280).

The reasoning corrects an imputation of intention. The young *Hausfrau* says that the misdeeds of the child would not ordinarily have caused her to cuff him; the 'cause' was the 'accidental' additional condition of the quarrel with the cook.

The point of the *Hausfrau* example, as another example given by Weber (not involving intentional language) shows, is the familiar point of the necessity for abstraction. "Our need for causal explanation would be satis- factorily met only when the conditions of this frequency of occurrence were formulated in rules and the concrete case could be 'explained' as a particu- lar constellation arising from the 'joint action' of such rules under concrete 'conditions'" (1949, p. 179n; 1922, p. 281n). The source of this second example is Karl Vossler, a critic of nomic historiography, who is informed that "the repulsive search for laws, isolation, generalization" and the like could be found "in the very intimacy of his home" (1949, p. 179n; 1922, p. 281n).

'Empirical knowledge' enters into the *Hausfrau*'s reasoning in a peculiar way. She says that, in combination with various other condition complexes, the misbehavior of the child would not have led to the cuffing. The know- ledge is empirical knowledge of the probable course of various 'typical' courses of events, to which the actual course of events is compared. The constellation containing the quarrel with the cook combined with the other circumstances is a typification that is an adequate cause, while the other typifications are not. Some typifications are causal, and treating them as causal is warranted by past experience; for other typifications of condition complexes, the probability of the given outcome is not sufficiently high to call it an 'adequate cause'. The role of 'empirical knowledge' is thus to sort *typifications*, sort them into those that are causal in the sense of the adequacy theory and those that are not. This prefigures his final position.

The imputation of intentions, then, is solely a matter of the application of typifications. But the question of the relation between publically observable events and intentions is not answered by this line of argument, and Weber nowhere answered it directly. Indeed, he said, at various times, two kinds of things on the interpretation of intentional action which appear to conflict. One is that "the 'publicly' observable event is certainly not 'the entire event'" (1977, p. 110; 1922, p. 332). The other, consistent with the *Hausfrau* example, is that "the hypothetical 'interpretations' supplied by empathetic 'understanding' are ... verified by the use of 'observational experience'" (1975, p. 197; 1922, p. 136). The underlying thought that makes these consistent is that certain observable things are, so to say, part of the *res gestae* of the possession of a motive or reason. When we typify some explanation of an action, these observable things – the red face of the angry man, yon Cassius's hungry look, and so forth – are *part* of the typification, and if they are missing we must suspect the truth of the description, just as we would suspect the truth of a description of a 'horse' if we were also told, 'Of course it was a curious horse – no tail or neck to speak of'.

The difficulty with this thought is brought out by the claim made by the 'positivist theory of *Verstehen*', that the *truth value* of the description consists solely in 'observable' elements and that *Verstehen* adds, and can add, nothing to the *explanatory* import of the description (Abel, 1948). Weber, of course, did not think in terms of the positivist notion of 'observables'. For him, the issue took the neo-Kantian form of identifying the 'presuppositions' of various vocabularies, and consequently his argument is largely subordinated to, and merged with, a concern with the fact-value distinction, and in particular the claim that valuative or normative concepts are 'presupposed' by descriptions, the fact that the descriptive vocabulary of the social sciences often is either akin to or identical with normative vocabularies, and the consequence that this 'value-relatedness' might be held to render these descriptions 'valuative' in contradistinction to 'factual'.

In 'Critique of Stammler', he dealt with description in the context of this broader issue. The example Weber considered was the explanation of actions in the game of skat. The 'rules of the game' have a normative character, yet are the source of some of our descriptive vocabulary. They are also an 'ideal-type', in the sense of an 'abstraction', as when they are used in distinguishing "the game itself" from "the fortuitous 'milieu' of a given game of skat: cigar smoke, beer drinking, beating on the table," and so on (1977, p. 120; 1922, p. 340).

Weber responded to the claim that 'normative' rules are presuppositions of 'empirical' knowledge by conceding that the rules of skat are such a 'presupposition'. The issue, he suggested, was whether we are treating the rules as 'normative' or as 'empirical' (i.e., as a means of defining the object of investigation).[1] If the rules are simply means of defining the object, "only the *beginning* point of the investigation" (1977, p. 121; 1922, p. 341, emphasis in original), they have a hypothetical character. The hypotheses in which they figure may of course fail, like other empirical hypotheses.

In empirical study, he argued, the rules of skat are treated *solely* in a non-normative manner (1977, p. 115; 1922, p. 336). They may be used to define the object; they may figure as ideas of actors as to how to act, which then cause them to act in particular ways (or as ideas which they attribute to other actors and which then guide expectations of the actions of others, thus influencing the actor); or they may be used as a heuristic technique, as when the 'empirical maxims' of skat (under which heading Weber included the rules as well as the maxims of strategy) are used as a method for identifying those 'intentions' of the agent "which are germane to a causal explanation" of his action (1977, pp. 122–23; 1922, p. 342). Weber said little about this last use, and assimilated it to the concept of an ideal-type. His example was the case where one derives expectations concerning the probabilities of various outcomes of plays from the use of the rules of skat together with an assumption that play is strictly rational. Particular games of skat, he suggested, approximate this ideal-type to varying degrees.

The term ideal-type, here as elsewhere, covered a multitude of potential problems. One problem that later bedeviled him, the question of the status of the notion of 'strictly rational', is ignored here. In a note, he described the assumption of rational play in skat as analogous to the laws of economic theory. But the characterization of the notion as an 'ideal-type' deflected him from the question of whether 'strict rationality' is an *a priori* or an empirical notion. Used heuristically, it seems in some sense indispensable. But Weber also spoke of indispensability when he suggested that the historian of art "in quite the same way, employs *his own* (normative) aesthetic 'judgment' as an heuristic technique. He employs it as a – *de facto* – indispensable method for identifying the actual 'intentions' of the artist" (1977, p. 122; 1922, p. 342, emphasis in original). Indispensability thus does not mean objectivity. One's aesthetic judgment Weber would have called a 'private' starting point, while the notion of 'strictly rational' and the laws of economic theory presumably are not. These problems over the status of the concept of rationality were taken up at length only later, in the 1913 essay 'On Some Categories of Interpretive Sociology', known as the '*Logos* essay'.

PROBABILITY AND EXPECTATION

The von Kriesian 'adequate cause' theory was ill-starred, and by the teens was taking heavy criticism in the legal contexts from which Weber had originally taken it (Fletcher, 1978). Gradually – but only gradually – it slips from Weber's own writing. In the *Logos* essay, the terms 'objective possibility' and 'adequate cause' survive, but 'isolation' and 'generalization' do not. In the older material an adequate cause was a kind of ersatz law, a warrant for causal claims in situations in which the concepts cannot be replaced by the more refined but 'unintelligible' concepts envisioned by Mill or Durkheim. In the *Logos* essay Weber exploited a different side of the concept, the distinction between objective possibility and subjective probability or expectation. In von Kries's writing on probability the distinction between 'objective possibility' and expectation enters largely as an invidious epistemological distinction between an objective thing to be known and an entirely subjective possession of an individual. The contrast fit certain legal purposes in connection with guilt, since guilt depends both and separately on what was expected as a consequence and what actually was the consequence of a given action. If, for example, I scare you with a joy buzzer and objectively this was likely to give you a heart attack, but I did not know about your heart condition and expected that you would merely have a good laugh over it, my expectation is part of the cause of my using the joy buzzer and also is noncriminal, for it does not involve 'the bad will.'

In 'Critique of Stammler', in the cryptic discussion of the heuristic uses of rules and maxims, Weber used the notion of expectations as causes. He spoke of the "empirical fact" that the maxims of skat known to the players "exercise a causal influence upon their conduct" (1977, p. 122; 1922, p. 342); he also spoke of the teleological-rational character of the play as a basis for attributing intentions. It is a short step from these two notions to the argument of the *Logos* essay, which attempts to both contrast and systematically relate the concepts of cause and expectation.

The causal relations may be seen in some simple examples. 'Objective possibilities' (i.e., the factual likelihoods in a situation) can themselves be the causes of expectations. If the telephone works half the time in my experience, as a causal consequence of this experience I have expectations about how often it will work. More interesting, expectations can cause objective possibilities. If you expect to be mugged on a particular street, the objective possibility of your taking a walk on that street will be lowered.

In the *Logos* essay, Weber noticed that this reciprocal causal relation between objective possibilities and expectations can be used to enable the construction of sociological concepts of certain social relations on an 'individual' basis. Shared expectations of certain kinds, for example, are necessary causal conditions for certain kinds of social relationships, such as marriage; and the objective possibilities of the partners in the marriage acting in certain ways are the cause of the expectations. The concept of the state also seems to fit this. The sociological meaning, as Weber is at great pains in this essay to demonstrate, can be constructed entirely in terms of the concepts of expectation and mutual expectation, together with the consideration of the ideas held by the individuals with the expectations, which define some expectations, e.g. those involving obedience to authorities, as 'legitimate'.[2]

The Triad of Reasons, Causes, and Expectations

Weber's treatment of the problems of interpretation in the *Logos* essay is incidental to his aim of avoiding a 'collective' concept of the state. So here, as in the earlier essays, we do not get an argument aimed directly at the problem of action. Nevertheless, the discussion is unusually extensive. From the point of view of the problems of action explanation, the significant innovation is that Weber noticed that true expectations (i.e., those that accord with actual likelihoods, the von Kriesian 'objective possibilities') are not only 'adequate causes' of action, they are also reasons for action and as such are potentially intelligible to the sociological or historical interpreter. In the *Logos* essay the problematic character of the triadic relation between intellegible reasons, causes, and expectations is recognized. In 'Critique of Stammler' the difficulties were not: the heuristic, presuppositional, and explanatory uses of the three types of concept seemed to be related as though they were three aspects of the same enterprise. Here Weber recognized that they can conflict, and considered the contrast between the cases where they do not conflict and the cases where they do.

To explicate the situation where there is no conflict, he gave an example, which is in some respects not very different from the case of a game of skat, of a case in the history of logic where the logician comes up with an idea that is the objectively correct solution to the problem. The logician's *reason* for the idea and the *cause* of the idea are the same – the problem situation – *and* the idea is *itself* "objectively correct" (Weber, 1981, p. 155; 1922, p. 410). The cases that are 'most understandable' to the historian studying the action are those where these three elements – objective correctness, his reason, and the cause – coincide. The triad also can be used in a 'heuristic' way. Notice that if we 'assume rationality' in such cases we are assuming that the 'actual probabilities' coincide with their 'true expectations', so we can use our knowledge of the actual probabilities as a basis for thinking that a person whose actions we are interpreting has particular expectations.

Rarely, however, is the problem of interpretation so simple, for, as Weber pointed out, these conditions are not often met. Some actions, such as the agricultural practices of primitive societies or the health precautions of a neurotic person, may be factually correct, but done for 'reasons' that are not 'rational' (1981, p. 155; 1922, p. 410) or even understandable. Some things that are understandable as reasons, e.g., beliefs about salvation, need not have any correspondence to 'objective correctness'.

One of the most significant leitmotifs of this discussion is that Weber routinely tried to avoid giving 'objective correctness' any special status in relation to explanation. As he pointed out, the determination of 'objective correctness' of an action is properly not a matter for sociology but for the special disciplines in whose provinces they fall. The criteria of correctness are nothing more than the criteria and established results of these disciplines. These may be 'normative', as in the case of ideas about law, or 'factual', as in the case of agricultural methods. In neither case do we need to make metaphysical claims about 'objective correctness': "Logically, with no difference in principle, an expediently chosen 'incorrect type' can also serve the purposes of the investigation" (1981, p. 158; 1922, p. 414). This is a claim that, as we shall see, is the source of several troubles.

One trouble may be seen if we compare Weber's argument to the later decision-theoretic literature on rationality and the later literature on action explanation. Compared to later writers on decision theory, Weber made do with a rather simple account of rationality. This was noticed early, by such critics as Hermann Grab, who suggested that if one took Weber seriously, one would say that a person whose goal was to go from the third floor of a building to the street would have to throw himself out the window to achieve the goal 'most rationally'. The claim is not entirely fair, for Weber did speak of having "the secondary results ... all rationally taken into account and weighed" as a criterion of rationality (1978a, p. 26; 1976, p. 13). However, it is difficult to see what this might mean, for in this passage ends are taken to be themselves irrational, on the grounds that ultimately they are either affectually determined or oriented to absolute values (which he took to be irrational). Weber conceded that, given these premises, "the orientation of action wholly to the rational achievement of ends without relation to fundamental values is ... only a limiting case" (1978a, p. 26; 1976, p. 13). So the problems raised by Grab's example and similar puzzle-cases are avoided by making all action irrational de facto, and 'rational' only in degree of correspondence to an unattainable ideal-type. The question of the potentially self-contradictory character of this notion of the unattainability of rationality need not detain us here. To compare Weber's views to the later literature it will suffice to notice how 'secondary results' are taken into account in decision theory. The usual device for doing this does not readily graft onto Weber's conception. It involves the notion of the total utility of an action: the total utility of flinging oneself from a window is obviously less than the total utility of the saving of the three minutes it takes to walk down the stairs, since we would never trade three minutes of walking for three weeks in the hospital, or death.

Some of the trouble over explanation proper may be seen in Grab's example. One could imagine someone in such a frenzy to get from the third floor to the street that he would leap from the window. We would not call such a person 'rational', unless we could make circumstances plus the total utility dictate the choice (e.g., by saying the building was on fire). But what is the *explanatory* force of calling an action rational? It seems wrong to say that the mere rationality of an action suffices to explain it, and Weber was particularly sensitive to this – it is one motivation for his concern to characterize rationality as an ideal-type. Yet 'rational' is not just a classificatory term either. If it were, the question 'Why?', the explanatory question, would still need an answer – and it is puzzling to think of there being an alternative answer. Thus the usual strategy is to turn the reasons into explanations, and there are various devices for doing this.

One way of making an answer out of the 'rationality' of the action is to make 'decision theory' into an empirical psychological account of behavior, which would serve as the causal law underwriting rationalizations of action. Another approach is to turn the category of 'the rational agent' into an empirical account of people's dispositions to act, on analogy to the ideal gas laws (Hempel, 1962, p. 19), by constructing a psychology that tells us that people have a disposition to be rational. These suggestions are motivated by the thought that in order to make a reason explanatorily relevant to action explanation one must supply a causal or explanatory component that takes the form of a general law. Weber's appeal to the concept of adequate cause replaces this. He was not faced with precisely the same problem: he did not need a 'theory of rationality' underwritten by a law that *generally* warrants the use of the type 'rational'. But, to the extent that he appealed to a model of rational action, he was forced to settle the question of its status and bearing on explanation and attribution of meaning.

Weber waffled on this subject. He wished to avoid any claim to the effect that 'rationality' has any privileged status, because he thought that 'rational' was an ideal-type. So he stressed that

the specific self-evident nature of instrumentally rational behavior does not ... entail viewing interpretation in rational terms as the special goal of sociological explanation. One could as well claim the opposite, given the role that 'irrational' (*zweckirrationale*) emotions and 'feelings' play in the actions of men (1981, p. 152, cf.156; 1922, p. 405, cf.411).

Yet shortly he said that

in every explanation of 'irrational' processes ... it is necessary, above all, to determine how the rational ideal-typical limiting case of pure instrumental and correct rationality *would have* proceeded. Only when this is determined, as the most superficial deliberation indicates, can the course of action be causally attributed to both objectively as well as subjectively 'irrational' components (1981, p. 154; 1922, p. 408).

Phrases like 'necessity' make this particular 'ideal-type' into something much more like an *a priori* framework after all, and not just a starting point which we could replace by its 'opposite'.

One of his motivations for speaking of 'rational' as just another ideal-type was that 'rational' is also an evaluative concept; he was afraid that a claim that it is 'necessary' is tantamount to saying that a particular value choice is necessary. The same difficulty, as we have seen, arises with objective possibility and expectation: some expectations are right, or correspond to the 'objective possibilities', and others do not. Weber's strategy here was to avoid the metaphysical or epistemological implications of 'objective' by saying that objective here just means 'whatever the relevant scientific discipline says the probabilities are' and that we could just as easily use false expectations as a standard of comparison.

In connection with 'rationality' this seems quite peculiar. We often decline to count as 'rational' persons whose expectations deviate drastically from objective likelihoods, and we may do this simply on the grounds of those deviations. Consider phobics or paranoids. Their behavior is not 'subjectively meaningful' to us, in many cases, *because* of their strange expectations. Also, when we attribute a 'subjective meaning' to someone else, the attribution entails certain expectations on the person's part. If a person thinks he is flipping a fair coin, he has certain expectations about results. If his behavior betrayed other expectations (e.g., insistence on having heads, or on dealing in a card game), we would suspect our attribution of his 'subjective meaning'.

The difficulty here is neatly captured by comparing Weber's argument to Carl Hempel's: Weber attempted to separate the epistemological, the evaluative, rational, and causal parts of the problem; Hempel notices interdependencies, especially between belief attributions and goal attributions. "It seems," Hempel says,

that generally a hypothesis about an agent's objectives can be taken to imply the occurrence of a specific overt action only when conjoined with appropriate hypotheses about his beliefs; and *vice versa*. Hence, strictly speaking, an examination of an agent's behavior cannot serve to test assumptions about his beliefs or about his objectives separately, but only in suitable pairs as it were (1962, p. 16).

Hempel goes on to speak about the empirical assumption of rationality in such a way that the pair becomes a triple: the denial of an agent's rationality usually undercuts our initial attribution of goals and beliefs to the agent –

though sometimes we hang onto the attributions and drop the assumption of rationality instead.

Hempel's account saves ordinary 'reasons' explanations by providing a particular sort of foundation for them. Ordinary ideas about rationality become, in Hempel's terms, "quasi-theoretical conceptions" containing a "dispositional protopsychology," in which, as he says, the conception of the rational agent is akin to the ideal gas law. This account solves the problem by making what Weber took to be a mere ideal-type into an explanation. The evaluative uses of the concept, Hempel says, are not inconsistent with the explanation, but they are in no way necessary to it.

Hempel's account also helps with individual attributions of beliefs, goals, and 'rationality', i.e., in what Weber called the 'heuristic' uses of the concept, by warranting the use of the assumptions about beliefs that one needs in order to attribute goals and the use of the assumptions about goals one needs in order to attribute beliefs. Similarly, the actions of the agent plus some general ideas about people's dispositions or goals (including a disposition to be rational) warrant particular hypotheses attributing beliefs to that agent; and these hypotheses can in turn be used in revising particular hypotheses about goals, which can in turn be used to revise hypotheses about beliefs. Thus the 'dispositional' conception of rationality underwrites a process of interpretation.

Weber's approach forces him to think of these elements as separate. 'Constituting the object' is one step, the 'understanding' of intentions is a separate step, akin to observation, and causal explanation is yet another step, dependent on 'constituting' but with an obscure relation to the step of understanding. His thought seems to be that *Verstehen* is, as observation is for certain positivists, a primordial act. To make *Verstehen* dependent on a prior 'assumption of rationality' or some analogous psychology or philosophical anthropology would make sociology dependent either on the 'assumption of rationality', much criticized in the German economics of Weber's time, or on these other disciplines. So Weber argued that the 'assumption of rationality' is just another ideal-type. His approach to the general problem of dependence on psychology was to argue against particular versions of the claim of dependence, such as the notion that marginal utility theory could be underwritten by psychophysical principles, on the grounds of the problem of many descriptions – and here he resembles Donald Davidson.

The consequence of the separation of these elements is that Weber is without an account of the rational warrants for attributing beliefs or reasons for actions. With Hempel, it may be recalled, the presumptively 'empirical' notion of a psychological disposition to rationality was part of the ground for attributing belief. Without some such device – some grounds for triangulating beliefs or reasons on the basis of overt action plus 'assumed rationality', for example – attributing beliefs or reasons becomes a mysterious process. This is what makes people think of Weber as an 'intuition' thinker of some sort. By cutting out empirical psychological assumptions about rationality and goals (or, more generally, by making rationality an optional starting point) he cut out a primary means of attributing beliefs. And if there can be a means of attributing beliefs or goals that does not 'assume rationality', it is difficult to see what it might be, apart from 'intuition'.

What Weber did instead (which makes him, in many contexts, sound unlike an intuition theorist) was to covertly rely on, as quasi-empirical or *a priori*, the rationality assumptions he labeled as nonempirical 'ideal-types'. Thus he said that

in the construction of general concepts ... sociology credits actors with an average measure of the capacities required to evaluate ... probabilities. That is, sociology typically assumes that objectively existing average probabilities are, on the average, subjectively taken into account by instrumentally rational actors (1981, p. 161; 1922, p. 420).

If this formulation sounds innocuous, it is only because, where 'sociology assumes rationality' appears to be radically *a priori*, the idea of an agent who is 'average' sounds empirical. However, 'average' is a concept that is extraordinarily demanding on the theorist. A psychological theory of 'average capacities to evaluate probabilities' would be an extremely complex affair.

Weber, of course, had no such theory, and this suggests that interpretive sociology, in constructing ideal-types, and in interpretation generally, implicitly relies on the rich store of commonsense ideas about motivation and reasons for action which the sociologist shares with the rest of the culture. To the extent that these ideas can be said to constitute a 'theory' they are perhaps not far removed from the 'reasonable and prudent man' theory found in common-law jurisdictions. If something like this were not in some sense assumed, Weber would have had to supply us with a whole set of things he went out of his way not to supply us with, namely *grounds* for attributing beliefs, goals, or rationality.

So why did Weber explicitly characterize 'rationality' as an ideal-type, and why did he believe that he did not need an empirical theory or an *a priori* doctrine of rationality? The reason seems to be this. *Part* of the work that such a theory does for a theorist like Hempel is to turn reasons into causes, to make the evaluative notion of 'rationality' an explanatory one. Weber thought he could get this done *directly* by the adequate cause theory, which says that a reason is a cause if it increases the probability of the outcome. He did not notice that the doctrine of rational man plays a role not just in making reasons explanatory, but also in warranting the attribution of the reason or goal to the agent.

The curious thing about the *Logos* essay is that here he comes closest to getting a grip on this problem. At the point where he looked at the example of the card players we see that an attribution of 'subjective meaning' to an agent implies certain expectations which, if they are not met, suggest that the attribution must be revised. This is the only place where Weber gave us any picture of the process of *revising* subjective attributions in which there is a criterion of improvement in interpretation (i.e., that the interpretation generates better expectations). But this is the road not taken.

What we would get down this road is a Bayesian theory of interpretation as rational reconstruction. But to take this road, at least if he had stayed with the idea that rationality was a model or 'type', Weber would have had to come to grips with various problems: choosing between the different kinds of rationality assumptions one might make to generate expectations, dealing with the undecidability between various interpretations that generate different expectations, answering the question of how to choose between probable and improbable interpretations when the 'improbable' interpretation – the card shark coming by the royal flush by an honest deal – may be the true one.

Rationality and Interpretation: Weber's Final Position

The road Weber did take, in his 'Introduction' to *Economy and Society*, written after the *Logos* essay, comes to a quite different, and ambiguous, end. Weber's intentions in this text, his last discussion of action explanation, are obscure. There are several possibly significant changes in language. 'Objective possibility' and 'adequate cause', the last of the von Kries–Radbruch technical terms, drop out, just as the other technical terms of this theory, 'isolation' and 'generalization' had vanished in the *Logos* essay. The concept of expectation, which figured so heavily in the *Logos* essay, both in the discussion of action and in the discussion of various social relations, also drops out. In defining a 'social relationship', for example, he now says that the relationship "consists entirely and exclusively in the existence of a *probability* that there will be a meaningful course of social action" (1978a, pp. 26–27; 1976, p. 13). In the *Logos* essay the existence of an 'objective' probability would not have sufficed – a 'subjective' expectation would have also been required. Similarly for his definition of legitimate authority: he dropped the requirement of an expectation of obedience, and made do with the paired criteria of the agent's possession of the idea that the command is legitimate and the existence of an actual probability of obedience (1978a, p. 212; 1976, p. 122). Yet Weber cited his own earlier essays, taking no notice of a change in his views (1978a, pp. 3, 4; 1976, pp. 1, 4).

This suggests that the 'Introduction' is a simplification of his earlier views, and not a new position, and indeed Weber described the text as such. Yet here we find for the first time his most famous formulation on the subject, that sociological explanation must be adequate on the level of cause and adequate on the level of meaning (1978a, p. 12; 1922, p. 512), and this seems to be a departure from his earlier views.[3] The criterion of 'adequacy on the level of cause' is similar to the criteria of causality in the adequate cause theory, though it is perhaps slightly weaker. In juristic contexts, the thought was that some minimum degree of probability must be met to call a relation causal. All Weber now required for adequacy on the level of cause was '*some*' degree of dependent probability of the outcome event on the cause. Adequacy on the level of meaning comes down to 'fit' with an ideal-type that is itself intelligible. This too contrasts to the early writings, for now the requirements of 'adequacy' are treated as independent but complementary. In the early writings, the logical relation between description in terms of ideal-types and causal analysis was sequential: first one describes (1978b, p. 121; 1922, p. 179), then and only then can one apply the machinery of the adequate cause theory.

Weber's eye in this section seems to have been on the problem of Why do we think an ideal-type explains anything? and he used the criterion of adequacy on the level of cause to answer the question in this way: 'Because the "ideal-type" may in empirical applications possess a degree of dependent probability'. The type is made good as an explanation or as a causal factor by the empirical fact of the probability. But the consideration of the existence of a degree of probability has no other role. It does not play a role in the revision and improvement of interpretation, other than perhaps by excluding some interpretations: it is a criterion solely. Moreover, it is difficult to see what it excludes. The requirement for counting an explanation as causally adequate, 'some' degree of probability, means literally that only statistically irrelevant events and events that cannot be conceived of as 'conditions' are excluded. If one considers the class of all interpretations of a given action or sequence of events that are at all plausible 'on the level of meaning', it will be evident that few, if any, of these interpretations would be excluded. Thus Weber has come a long way from the methodological optimism of the early essays, to the point where causal criteria and methods of analysis apparently play no real role in assessing alternative explanations.

In practice, then, the sole criterion available to decide between various interpretive hypotheses turns out to be 'adequacy on the level of meaning'. Yet it is strange to think of this sort of consideration as a criterion or decision procedure at all, and Weber said little to show how the consideration of 'adequacy on the level of meaning' can be used as a part of a hypothesis-selection procedure. He proceeded in quite a different way. His examples of interpretation in the 'Introduction' are almost exclusively cases of applying the ideal-type of 'rationality'. Although he was careful to stress that, in principle, 'irrational' ideal-types are equally valid and necessary in sociological explanation, he seems to have thought that in practice rationality is almost invariably the most useful ideal-type in the explanation of action. The criterion of adequacy on the level of meaning itself, as Weber used it in the discussion, seems to favor 'rationality' as a type – 'rationality' explanations happen to be the most intelligible, and therefore have 'the highest possible degree of adequacy on the level of meaning'. In short, he did not concern himself with the details of the process of deciding between alternative interpretive hypotheses based on alternative ideal-types because he thought that the 'rational' ideal-type, where it is applicable, invariably wins these competitions, since, where it can be made to fit, the 'rational' type is invariably the most adequate.

Thus the position Weber arrived at in the 'Introduction' is quite complex. It depends on the separation of two levels, the practical level of description and attribution of motives, which is done largely by the application of the 'rational' ideal-type, and the level of explanation and epistemology, at which virtually every interpretation is credentialled as 'causally adequate' and every descriptive terminology is presumed equally valid, because each is equally 'ideal-typical'. The argument compares to Davidson's argument on Hempel's discussion of rational action, though there are some differences.

Like Weber, Davidson accepts the causal character both of intentional and 'physical' language. But Davidson deals with the question of what makes intentional language 'causal' differently. Davidson argues that the use of 'cause' in accounting for action is underwritten by the existence of laws that apply under another description. For Weber, the same sort of underwriting of causes of action by laws is not necessary, for the under-writing is done by the empirical fact of dependent probabilities. Thus, what both Davidson and Weber have done, in contrast to Hempel, is to reduce the problem of making a reason into a cause to a minimal issue, largely separate from the problem of interpretation.

In discussing Hempel, Davidson points out the hopelessness of the task of transforming reasons explanations into genuine laws by way of some sort of dispositional psychology. The frequency with which people perform actions for which they have reasons must be quite small. "What is the ratio," he asks, "of actual adulteries to the adulteries which the Bible says are commited in the heart?" (1982, p. 264). So reasons explanations are very low-grade statistical explanations, a point Weber would have been fond of. If we try to make these statistical explanations into full-blown nomological explanations, we need to add a great deal in the way of dispositional claims. Hempel treats rationality as a kind of character trait, and thinks this will do the trick of making reasons empirical. Davidson points out that it will not.

People who don't have the trait are still agents, have reasons and motives, and act on them. Their reasons are no doubt *bad* ones. But until we can say what their reasons are – that is, explain or characterize their actions in terms of their motives – we are in no position to say the reasons are bad (1982, pp. 266–67).

We need to be able to identify their reasons, which is to say give reasons explanations, prior to applying the assumption of rationality as a dispo-sitional law to *explain* what they do. The law, in short, comes around after the reasons are determined.

Davidson points out that, because of the *post hoc* position in which formal theories of rationality (such as decision theory) are found in relation to the attribution of reasons, what we are doing when we employ them is translating our already established attributions of reasons into decision-theoretic terms. This does not add much, if any, empirical content to the explanation, simply because there cannot be any conflict between the reasons explanations and the decision theory: any conflict between the reasons explanations and theory gets resolved, not by throwing out the theory, but by restating the agent's preferences so they satisfy the theory, no matter how 'bad' the reasons. If my frenzy to get down the stairs results in my leaping out the window, to choose Grab's example, it might be concluded that I have an overwhelming preference for speed, but the reason is not in 'conflict' with decision theory.

This sounds like Davidson is saying, as Weber almost did in some moods, that "the rationality assumption" is a necessary truth "or that it states part of what we mean by saying someone prefers one alternative to another" (1982, pp. 272–73). But Davidson denies this. He compares decision theory to theories like the theory of measurement for length and mass. We would have no idea what to make of an attempt to measure length for which 'longer than' failed to meet the axiom of transitivity. "Similarly for 'preferred to'," Davidson says (1982, p. 273). The axioms are not, incidentally, 'assumptions' if we are not in a position to pick an alternative.

Weber seems to have been saying something different, at least in some moods, when he labeled rationality as a 'type' we can somehow decline to 'assume'. In other moods, however, he conceded both its indispensability and the lack of any alternative. Because Weber thought of both particular ordinary reasons explanations *and* the 'model of rationality' as 'ideal-types', he thought that the fact that we can choose various different reasons explanations (some of which sound 'irrational', meaning 'still reasons, but bad ones') means we are in the same sort of choice situation for 'rationality' itself – that we can somehow choose not to 'assume rationality'. He could not tell us what this would be like, but the label 'ideal-type' trapped him: he could not see any reason why the same principle of choice would not apply to all ideal-types, or why one should be special.

The position Weber took in the 'Introduction', then, amounts to this. He spoke of relying on 'the usual methods of causal attribution', but the fact that he demanded only 'some probability' in the causal connection means that little indeed is demanded to accredit an explanation as 'adequate on the level of cause' (and much less than is demanded in legal contexts). The problem of subjective meaning is also minimized. All that seems to be required to have an explanation is an intelligible reason, good or bad. In good neo-Kantian fashion, he supposed that if something is intelligible it is so by virtue of being an instance of a presupposed general type.

These 'in principle' considerations kept Weber out of many of the standard difficulties over the application of 'law' models of explanation. However, they tell us little about the practice of explanation and attribution. They justify, or appear to justify, too much.

The practical explanatory strategies Weber contemplated may be seen in two examples from the 'Introduction'.

In attempting to explain the campaign of 1866, it is indispensable both in the case of Moltke and of Benedek to attempt to construct imaginatively how each, given fully adequate knowledge both of his own situation and of that of his opponent, would have acted. Then it is possible to compare with this the actual course of action and to arrive at a causal explanation of the observed deviations, which will be attributed to such factors as misinformation, strategical errors, logical fallacies, personal temperament, or considerations outside the realm of strategy. Here, too, an ideal-typical construction of rational action is actually employed even though it is not made explicit (1978a, p. 21; 1922, p. 522).

This example, reminiscent of Karl Popper's discussion of the 'Zero method' (Popper, 1964, pp. 141–42), is the most elaborate in the 'Introduction'. There are much simpler patterns as well: "we understand the motive of a person aiming a gun if we know that he has been commanded to shoot as a member of a firing squad, that he is fighting against an enemy, or that he is doing it for revenge" (Weber, 1978a, p. 9; 1922, p. 508).

Both types of cases were treated by Weber as instances of the use of the 'ideal-type'. In considering the Moltke case, it should be evident why Weber spoke of "the unavoidable tendency of sociological concepts to assume a rationalistic character" (1978a, p. 18; 1922, p. 519). No headway in the practical task of interpreting Moltke's conduct, and particularly in attributing his beliefs, could be made using any other starting point. Even a psychoanalytic account would only modify a 'rationalistic' attribution of beliefs, rather than provide a fullfledged alternative. In the case of the example of the motivational explanation of the shooting, the issues seem different. No elaborate set of ideas about information, strategy, temperament, and so on seem to have much to do with the interpretation: it is, Weber said, 'direct'. Thus, treating both types of cases as instances of the application of ideal-type, Weber avoided the suggestion that 'rationality' is, in the sense suggested by Davidson, a *general* starting point for which there is no alternative. Rather, Weber would say, there are many ideal-types that are starting points – it just happens that where there is any possibility of the elaborate application of the 'rational' ideal-type, as in the case of Moltke's actions in command in 1866, the rational type happens to be overwhelmingly preferable, because it is overwhelmingly superior on grounds of 'intelligibility' or 'adequacy of meaning'. In simpler cases, such as the shooting example, both 'rational' (because he was ordered to shoot) and 'irrational' (out of revenge) interpretations stand on a more nearly equal footing.[4]

CHAPTER ELEVEN

LARGE-SCALE EXPLANATIONS: AGGREGATION AND INTERPRETATION

The relation between Durkheim's *Suicide* and his *Rules of Sociological Method* is this: *Suicide* is, at least in part, an attempt to exemplify the doctrine expounded in the *Rules*. The relation between Weber's methodological works and his writings on capitalism, both of which develop and change, is less straightforward. Weber referred to 'Objectivity' in 'The Protestant Ethic' (1958, p. 200), but he did not make explicit appeals to von Kriesian language or considerations in the body of the essay 'The Protestant Ethic'. The primary evidence in Weber's own writ for connections between the thesis of the protestant ethic essay and the methodological essays comes from the contemporary methodological essays themselves. In 'Objectivity', when he discussed the methodological problems of explaining capitalism, he seems to have been telling us how he regarded the explanation in 'The Protestant Ethic' (1949, pp. 89–98; 1922, pp. 189–99; 1958, p. 200).[1]

The strongest common strand in 'Objectivity' and 'The Protestant Ethic' is the theme of the 'one-sidedness' of explanation. This theme involves both the von Kriesian notion of causality and the concept of ideal-types.

IDEAL-TYPES AND ADEQUATE CAUSES

Weber is vague on the precise relation between the concept of ideal-type and the adequate cause theory (1949, p. 103; 1922, p. 205). Perhaps this vagueness should be put down to the vagueness of the concept of ideal-type in Weber's writing, a vagueness that results from his use of the concept in a variety of unconnected or incommensurable ways. There is an analogy in this respect with the history of the reception of Kuhn's use of 'paradigm': what first appeared to be a unitary concept turned out on analysis to be equivocal. The usual interpretation, helped by Weber's own allusions, is that the concept derives from Rickert (Burger, 1976). But the term was more widely used (it appears in Durkheim as well), and the way Weber formulated the concept reflects a broader slice of the heritage of scheme-content distinctions of which all of these writers were legatees. Many usages are 'neo-Kantian' in origin: the notion that "all of our knowledge relates to a categorically interpreted reality" (Weber, 1978b, p. 130; 1949, p. 188; 1922, p. 290), of concepts as alternative frames for the meaningless chaos of the world, the idea of a *hiatus irrationalis* between concept and reality, the idea of reification and the related notion that one can mistake concept for reality (Anglicized as 'the fallacy of misplaced concreteness').

Beyond this, his skepticism over natural kinds, atomism, and essentialism had other sources, including a dim sense of what we would now call the underdetermination of theory by data, the recognition that a variety of theories may fit the facts. Mixed with these ideas were a number of methodological intuitions: the recognition of the pragmatic necessity of simplifying historical complexity to produce any sort of historical narrative, causal or otherwise; the recognition that natural science simplifies by eliminating features from its scope of concern (e.g., the color of an object in an acceleration experiment). Some of the sources of skepticism were outside of neo-Kantianism entirely: the notions of abstraction, 'ideal', and precision suggest a realm of mental objects, like those of mathematics, to which the world does not fully correspond. Weber nowhere sorted these arguments out, and his usages are often at odds with the systematic account found in Rickert.[2]

When he spoke of the contrast between an ideal-type and the world process, he used the notions of "infinity" and "inexhaustibility" (1949, p. 78; 1922, pp. 177–78) to indicate the necessity of the presupposition of categories that confer order and significance upon some finite portion of this process, a necessity that suggests a preference for presuppositions that are self-conscious, or understood as 'heuristic', and a preference for 'precise' heuristic concepts, i.e., ideal-types. This 'epistemological' doctrine is paralleled by the doctrine that holds that real causality occurs at the level of full particularity, i.e., that

where the *individuality* of a phenomenon is concerned, the question of causality is not a question of *laws* but of concrete causal *relationships*; it is not a question of the subsumption of the event under some general rubric as a representative case but of its imputation as a consequence of some constellation. It is in brief a *question of imputation* (1949, pp. 78–9; 1922, p. 178, emphasis in original).[3]

In assessing causes, "We select only those causes to which are to be imputed in the individual case, the 'essential' feature of an event" (1949, p. 78; 1922, p. 178).

There are at least two kinds of selectivity or one-sidedness at stake in Weber's account. The first is epistemological and relates to the ideal-type. The second is explanatory, and relates to the procedures of causal impli-

cation in the adequate cause-objective possibility theory, in particular to
its two processes of abstraction: 'isolation', the selection of a limited set of
possible causes, which is dictated by the fact of the infinity of causes
influencing a given event; and 'generalization', which is epistemologically
equivalent to the selectivity that any construct has in relation to concrete
individuals or to the infinitude of the world process. For Weber,
epistemological and ontological considerations were prior to, and took
precedence over, considerations of causality and methodology. In part this
was neo-Kantianism; in part it was simply a matter of polemical tactics
dictated by the fact that many of his methodological opponents denied a
place to causality in history. In a highly general methodological essay such
as 'Objectivity', he was concerned to make points that applied to these
opponents as well. Moreover, he wished to suggest that the deficiencies he
was forced to concede with respect to his kind of causal account are
deficiencies shared, at least on the epistemological level, with the historical
methods of his opponents who rejected his causal aims.

THE GENETIC IDEAL-TYPE

The two kinds of issues bear on all adequate cause explanations of
'historical individuals': each causal explanation necessarily selects from the
infinity of conditions; beyond this, the concepts in terms of which the causal
explanations are constructed are themselves imperfectly related to the full
reality. In the case of explicitly 'causal' concepts, the relations between the
two types of consideration are obviously close. Genetic ideal-types, which
are idealizations of complex causal processes, are "constructs in terms of
which we formulate relationships by the application of the category of
objective possibility. By means of this category, the adequacy of our
imagination, oriented and disciplined by reality, is *judged*" (1949, p. 93;
1922, p. 194, emphasis in original). Genetic ideal-types have the logical
form of objective possibility-adequate cause accounts, and can be assessed
for their intelligibility and factual adequacy accordingly. 'Objective possibility' provides the logical framework within which the causal relations are
conceived. The task of putting it into the framework itself constitutes a kind
of test of the adequacy of our conceptualization. Genetic ideal-types are
also ideal-types *stricto sensu* – consciously constructed idealizations to
which nothing may actually correspond (as distinct from 'historical
individuals' which can be given proper names, such as 'the Long Parlia-
ment').

Although he did not explicitly say so, presumably the ideal-type presented in 'The Protestant Ethic' is of the 'genetic' variety, and hence to be understood as an 'objective possibility' construction. Presumably, Weber believed that the cause he identified increases the probability of the outcome sufficiently to be considered an 'adequate' cause. The notion of degree is signaled in 'The Protestant Ethic' by his remarks on the problem of showing "the quantitative cultural significance of ascetic Protestantism" (1958, p. 183).

To characterize without subtlety an argument whose subtleties have mystified generations, the explanation consists in the following sequence: the Protestant reformers had divergent, but related, theological views on salvation. The doctrine of worldly callings, found particularly in Luther, fit together with the doctrine of predestination for salvation and damnation, produced a particular kind of psychological type, persons anxious over salvation – over membership in the predestined 'elect' – who assuaged this anxiety with evidence of their diligence in and devotion to their vocations, their frugality with the Lord's bounty, and the like. As the theological fires of the reformers cooled into more conventional religious feeling, the patterns (of guilt, joylessness, and the economic attitudes captured in the maxims of Benjamin Franklin) set, and the processes of capital accumulation made for the expansion of the market into areas of life hitherto governed by traditional economic forms and practices. The demands of market rationality kept the patterns and attitudes in place. The sequence does not precisely fit any given Protestant experience, so it is an ideal-type in the 'imperfect correspondence' sense. It is 'genetic' and formed into objective possibilities in that one stage follows another and the succession of stages from the beliefs and practices of Calvin to those of Franklin is probabilistic, not mechanical.

Weber also considered the materialist explanation of history to be a genetic ideal-type, and this seems to suggest the possibility of an assessment of the relative adequacy of the two accounts. The point, after all, of the adequate cause-objective possibility doctrine in law is that it provides a means of dealing with the question of degree of contribution. But Weber shied away from this question. The crucial passages on Weber's view of his own text, in the conclusion of the essay, purposely characterize the argument in a way which distances it from any debate with Marxism. He placed the sequence alongside a series of other sequences, each of which overlaps with his own, but at the points of *cultural* rather than economic facts. He then proposed a series of analogous studies. As 'The Protestant Ethic' was a study of certain cultural effects of ascetic religion, these parallel studies would show the significance of other, independent cultural influences, such as "humanistic rationalism,... philosophical and scientific" development, and "technical development" (1958, p. 183). He also suggested other studies that would show noneconomic consequences of ascetic Protestantism, such as its influence on forms of social organization "from the conventicle to the State" (1958, p. 182), and place Protestantism in the larger process of the development of ascetic religiosity from its medieval origin to its current diminished form. These suggestions put the essay in a particular frame: they support the idea that the Protestant Ethic essay is a piece of 'cultural history', and not a contribution to universal history or philosophy of history, a point that we should keep in mind.

These passages also suggest a picture: that the subject of historical inquiry is a vast mosaic of overlapping sequences. The list of studies points to the huge variety of causal factors which a full explanation would involve. The concluding sentence of the essay says that if a materialistic or a spiritualistic interpretation of culture "does not serve as the preparation, but as the conclusion of an investigation, [it] accomplishes equally little in the interest of historical truth" (1958, p. 183). This formulates a standard of historical argument. The length of Weber's list of factors itself shows the extensive historical research that would be needed to seriously examine the issues, and this bears against 'materialism', for materialist explanations of religious phenomena available at the time were schematic, and not up to this historiographical standard.

Other clues to the purport of the essay, which give a sense to the list, are more explicit. In the final paragraph he cautioned that "it is, of course, not my aim to substitute for a one-sided materialistic an equally one-sided spiritualistic causal interpretation of culture and history," and explained that he has "only attempted to trace the fact and the direction" of the influence of Protestant ascetic religious "motives in one, though a very important point" (1958, p. 183). Constructing an ideal-type and showing its applicability is not the same as showing the quantitative significance of a factor: he had done the former without doing the latter. He suggested that it would "be necessary to investigate how Protestant Asceticism was in turn influenced in its development and its character by the totality of social conditions, especially economic" (1958, p. 183) in order to approach a full understanding of its causal role.

The one-sidedness in question in these passages is the 'causal' kind, rather than the epistemological kind generic to all 'ideal-typical' constructions. Weber's point was not that he was, himself, giving anything other than a one-sided explanation, but rather that his account and the 'materialist' account are both equally one-sided. His materialist opponents

– Marx is not mentioned by name – make the separate error of turning a causal interpretation into a philosophy of history. Weber warned his readers *not* to do this with the interpretation he provided in 'The Protestant Ethic'.

The *reason* Weber did not attempt to replace these intentionally 'one-sided' explanations (Weber, 1949, p. 67; 1922, p. 165) of capitalism with a comprehensive explanation of capitalism was that such an explanation was precluded by the logic of causation in the von Kries-Radbruch theory. The theory precludes any general confrontation between 'culturalist' and 'materialist' explanations as well. As we have seen, the technical reasons for this are straightforward. As long as a putative causal factor has some degree of adequacy (i.e., a sufficient difference in the probability of an outcome results from 'subtracting' a factor from a given constellation of factors), it must be accredited as an adequate cause of the outcome. The weight of the cause, the *degree* of adequacy, however, depends on the selection of the constellation, and there are no general grounds for the selection of the set of background factors: in present jargon, selections are 'interest-relative'.

The interest of the courts serves, more or less, as a *de facto* device for selection, and there are some loose analogues to the 'interest of the court' in scholarly contexts. Thus in 'Objectivity', Weber suggested that comparing the causal influence of a given economic factor only to other economic factors is warranted by considerations of convenience: "training in the observation of the effects of qualitatively similar categories of causes [e.g., economic causes] ... offers all the advantages of the division of labor" (1949, p. 71; 1922, p. 170). At the close of 'The Protestant Ethic', the list of suggestions of other influences to be investigated is a list of *cultural* influences (1958, pp. 182–83). But this is a choice dictated *only* by convenience.

The inevitable selectivity or 'one-sidedness' that is implicit in the process of causal abstraction precludes any general interpretation of history. We may recall the complaints of Bernard and Mill on statisticians who come to premature stopping places. A similar complaint applies to any attempt to turn causal analysis into a philosophy of history. In the conclusion to 'The Protestant Ethic', Weber remarked that one might "proceed beyond" his deliberately restricted account "to a regular construction which logically deduced everything characteristic of modern culture from Protestant rationalism." He then said that this "may be left to the type of dilettante who believes in the unity of the group mind and its reducibility to a single formula" (1958, p. 284).

An analogous comment on those who follow the views of the *Manifesto* is made in 'Objectivity'. They are compared to single-minded racialist theorists who believe that "'in the last analysis' all historical events are results of the interplay of innate 'racial qualities'" (1949, p. 69; 1922, p. 167). The "dogmatic need to believe that the economic 'factor' is the 'real' one, the only 'true' one, and the one which 'in the last instance is everywhere decisive'" (1949, p. 69; 1922, p. 167) results from the "eager dilettantes'" erroneous "thought that they could contribute something different and better to our knowledge of culture than the broadening of the possibility" of imputing concrete historical causes to concrete cultural events "through the study of precise empirical data which have been selected from specific points of view" (1949, p. 69; 1922, p. 168). The error, in short, is the wish to go beyond self-critical historical knowledge which concedes its cognitive limitations, to a *Weltanschauung* or a 'formula'.

THE LATER SUBSTANTIVE WRITINGS

The program of future research sketched out, however diffidently, at the end of 'The Protestant Ethic' was never followed up by Weber. He pursued a quite different program of research, in which the 'religious factor' retained a significant role. But this research program was completed only in part, and its nature and aims have been a matter of continuous dispute. Neither the early methodological essays nor the suggestions for research found in 'The Protestant Ethic' do much to illuminate the projects Weber ultimately undertook. This raises the question of whether Weber significantly altered the account of capitalism found in 'The Protestant Ethic' in later work. As we have seen, the later methodological essays appear to revise some of the central notions of the early methodological essays. Tenbruck goes so far as to speak of 'methodological shocks' in the later substantive writings (1980, p. 333). This doubtless overstates the degree of the departure from the past. Weber was curiously defensive about changes in his views. The later edition of 'The Protestant Ethic' is filled with parenthetical remarks to the effect that a passage is unchanged, or that something had been elaborated only to deal with unforeseen (and what to Weber were astonishing) misinterpretations. Yet there was a definite shift in emphasis.

In the *General Economic History* (1961), based on notes for the series of academic lectures delivered shortly before his death, Weber reiterated what can be found scattered throughout his later writings. "Drawing together once more the distinguishing characteristics of western capitalism and its causes," Weber said, "we find the following factors. First, this institution alone produced a rational organization of labor.... Everywhere and always there has been trade; it can be traced back into the stone age." He went on to point out that elaborate forms of finance and profit seeking had also existed elsewhere, thus stressing the distinction between Western capitalism and capitalism in general (1961, p. 232). The lists of 'distinguishing characteristics' and 'causes' vary, even within this text. One includes "rational capital accounting," "the absence of irrational restrictions on trading in the market," "rational technology," "calculable law," "free labor," and "the general use of commercial instruments to represent share rights in enterprise" (1961, pp. 208–09). At another point he said that

> In the last resort the factor which produced capitalism is the rational permanent enterprise, rational accounting, rational technology and rational law, but again not these alone. Necessary complementary factors were the rational spirit, the rationalization of the conduct of life in general, and a rationalistic economic ethic (1961, p. 260).

The lists are clearly important. But their status is left vague: 'distinguishing characteristics' and 'causes' are never distinguished. The rational organization of labor is at one moment 'produced by' Western capitalism, at another its primary cause, at another its distinctive feature. This ambiguity makes it difficult to treat the lists as explanations at all, and it creates a puzzle about Weber's intent in producing them.

Contemporary critics such as Brentano had made the point that the thesis of 'The Protestant Ethic' was circular, because the distinctive features of the spirit of capitalism were logically or conceptually entailed by the Protestant ethic as Weber characterized it. The issue comes down to this: Weber wanted to explain a very narrow thing in 'The Protestant Ethic,' namely a particular methodical form of personal economic practice, and not to 'explain capitalism'. The form of life, or 'spirit', which he explained 'causally' is the form of life that a Protestant ascetic, as Weber *conceived* him, would live: to live any other kind of life would be to fail to fit the type 'Protestant ascetic'. Thus the explanation is not falsifiable by attacking the causal link: if one produces counter instances of 'Protestant rational ascetics' who are at the same time speculators, profligates, or unself-conscious economic traditionalists, this does not suffice, for by definition such people are not rational ascetics in Weber's special sense. This means that Weber's account is falsifiable only by showing that there were rational ascetics with a different causal history.

The usual strategy for doing this was to produce pre-Reformation capitalists with an acquisitive, calculating, self-disciplined style, and pre-

Reformation theologians who justified this form of life in 'ethical' terms. Weber responded to these cases by saying that these persons did not bear on his argument because their conduct lacked the relevant *psychological* religious sanction, i.e. anxiety over salvation, and the theological rationalizations of their conduct did not produce this sanction. But neither the examples nor the response quite settled the issue of whether Weber had defined the 'spirit of capitalism' in such a way that the distinctive feature of ascetic Protestantism, namely the 'psychological sanction', was built into the definition, or whether the definition was constructed in a way that made it fit the *explanans* so closely that the question of 'cause' was empty.

Weber bristled at Brentano's suggestion that the argument of 'The Protestant Ethic' was tautologous, but the criticism would have been very much to the point if these lists were intended as explanations. The lists are not so much an answer to what Weber called the question of "the emergence of *homo economicus*" (1978a, p. 1125) as a restatement of it at the institutional level, a restatement which broadens it, radically, into the question of the origin of *homo rationalis modernus*. The new question is the historical question of the cause of the break between what Weber thought of as the traditional and the rational, a question that comes close to the Marxist problem of the transition between feudalism and capitalism (cf. Macfarlane, 1979, pp. 34–52). This broadening suggests some different modes of interpretating the entire Weberian corpus.

TELEOLOGICAL READINGS OF THE LATER TEXTS

In the original version of 'The Protestant Ethic' essay Weber spoke of a "'rationalization' process" (Weber, 1905, p. 29; cf. Mommsen, 1977, p. 378). This and his formulation of traditional and rational as ideal-types, suggest an interpretation of his later work that treats capitalism as incidental to, and a by-product of, a larger process of rationalization. Weber was never explicit about this. Yet he said some things, especially in the *General Economic History*, that are highly congenial to this kind of interpretation, as when he remarked that the reason that various distinguishing features of modern capitalism, such as the rational organization of work, appeared *only* in the West must be found in the special features of its general cultural evolution (1961, p. 232). Some writers think that the substitution of the notion of evolutionary rationalization for the problem-set of the earlier essays was wholly intentional on Weber's part, and that his premature death prevented his articulation of a fully developed universal history with rationalization as its theme. Two such revisionist interpretations, one 'causal' and one 'teleological', may by briefly considered here.

The first is the view of Tenbruck, Schluchter, Lüthy and others, that the thematic center of Weber's work is the historical process of rationalization, a problem which, as I have suggested, displaces Sombart's problem of explaining capitalism. One merit of this account as an interpretation is that it enables one to make sense of the lists of the distinguishing features of modern capitalism: the lists, of 'rational this' and 'rational that', become the explanatory *object* of Weber's universal history, and economic development is treated as incidental to the achievement of rationality in these realms. The market, it may be conceded, hastens the process of rationalization by coercing laggards to rationalize to survive, and bureaucratic structures serve the cause of rational discipline. But the framework of 'rational' institutions is a precondition for these processes, which are thus secondary to the primary historical process, rationalization. The primary difficulty with this line of interpretation is that there is a generic conflict between Weber's methodological writings, which are causalist, antiessentialist and antiteleological, and any construal that makes Weber into a teleological historicist.

If we are to regard Weber as saying that he has found what might be called the meaning of history in the rise of rationality, we raise the question of whether he has fallen into precisely the traps he wished, throughout his career, to avoid: the traps of taking an 'arbitrary' ideal-type for reality, and of concluding that one's own historical moment or values constitute the teleological *terminus ad quem* of the historical development of consciousness (cf. Schluchter, 1981, pp. 19–24). This would be to attribute a radical inconsistency to Weber. Yet an interpretation of rationalization that is not in conflict with the methodological texts can be readily constructed. Rationalization is a kind of quasi-autonomous process, an unraveling which, once started, seems to emerge in new forms and take on a life of its own. One can take such processes in this way: each step in the unravelling is contingent, and interpretable in terms of human choices and beliefs that are plausible under the particular historical circumstances; the 'process' itself is an aggregate description without any causal or explanatory power of its own. This interpretation would fit Weber's account of the character of historical ideal-types, and would commit him to no historical metaphysic of rationality. Thus the problem for an interpretation of Weber that treats 'rationalization' as a teleological force is to state Weber's account of rationalization in a way that reveals his teleological commitments.

Tenbruck comes to terms with the issue of inconsistency by locating the inconsistency in what he calls the 'methodological shock' of Weber's use of a 'real' type instead of an 'ideal' type in dealing with the influence of religious ideas. He locates this 'shock' in the early pages of a short paper written to integrate parts of what was to become the *Religionssoziologie*.[4] Here Weber said that "the rationality, in the sense of logical or teleological 'consistency', of an intellectual-theoretical or practical-ethical attitude has and always has had power over man" (1946, p. 324). Thus 'rationality' is not merely in the eye of the ideal-type-constructing beholder: it is also a 'force', real apart from the ideal-typical constructions one places on it. Since this is the conceptual sin Weber attributed to dilletantish Marxists in 'Objectivity', this is indeed an interesting departure.

Weber remarked that "religious interpretations of the world and ethics of religions created by intellectuals and meant to be rational have been strongly exposed to the imperative of consistency" (Christianity is a case of this). Weber went on to say that "the effect of the *ratio*, especially of a teleological deduction of practical postulates, is in some way, and often very strongly, noticeable among all religious ethics" (1946, p. 324). This is universality enough for Tenbruck to treat it as a candidate for the role of key universal historical force. Perhaps it is too much universality, for 'consistency' in this broad sense is such a general notion – like 'meaning' – that to say that everyone seeks it once in a while is not to say much at all. Tenbruck is aware of this; he stresses the distinctiveness of the mechanism of rationalization in the religious sphere, namely the process of disenchantment through rendering theodicies consistent, a process he treats as immanent. "Religion advances according to its own laws," he says. "A rational development of religious images of the world proceeds apace with the rational logic specific to religion" (1980, p. 334).

Historical circumstance provides openings in which this universal, but ordinarily weak, force may have dramatic effects, and this was the case with Protestantism. This accounts for *one* of the kinds of rationality on the lists found in the lectures. Tenbruck treats the others as more or less fortuitous. "The world, for Weber, is made of partial rationalizations which are called into being according to the interests of the moment – economic, technical, military and administrative" (1980, p. 341). He distinguishes these rationalizations from the religious one, and singles one out as key: "The modern economy originated from the pressure of discipline and not from the gratification of interests" (1980, p. 341), and the source of discipline was Protestantism. As Weber said in the lectures, "Such a

powerful, unconsciously refined organization for the production of capi-
talistic individuals" as the Protestant sects has never existed in history
(1961, p. 270). One difficulty in this line of interpretation is that Weber did
not make the sort of sharp distinctions between varieties of rationalization
produced by the interests of the moment and rationalization that proceeds
according to an inner logic which Tenbruck's account relies on. Weber's
attitude toward 'immanence' arguments is, to be sure, peculiarly offhand.
In the passage Tenbruck relies on so heavily, Weber did allow, in a limited
way, for a universal tendency toward rationalization, *ratio* as a 'real' type
or force. But he did not abandon his scruples about the use of these types.
Indeed, the passage begins with a restatement of his skepticism on
ideal-types. His concession to them as a 'real' force amounts, he said, to
an interest in finding out "how far certain rational conclusions, which can
be established theoretically, have been drawn in reality," i.e., to discussing
the 'conditions' under which "a construction might mean more" than an
ideal-type (1946, p. 324). The logical function of 'immanence' is to enable
the substitution of an asymmetric causal question, i.e., what conditions
permit or prevent the continuation of a process, for the symmetric question
of what conditions cause an outcome. This is a departure, but its significance depends on what one makes of the 'process' of deriving implications
from theological tenets. A similar substitution of asymmetric causal forms
is found in *Economy and Society*, where Weber discussed the immanence
of market forces. Again, he made nothing of this departure. Weber also
made a number of remarks of a 'philosophical anthropological' character
which resemble his remark on seeking consistency. These also have an
asymmetric form: the desire for meaning, charisma, and so on are given in
one place or another as part of human nature. But Weber never attempted
to put these together into any sort of coherent whole. They are left as asides,
and are perhaps meant to be taken as inessential to the strict meaning of
his argument. The strict meaning is, perhaps, that which the 'Introduction'
to *Economy and Society* would suggest: that the 'logical' process, which is
meaning-adequate, is paralleled by a causally adequate process, an 'empirical' probabilistic sequence, such that the causal process is the source of its
explanatory force. In any event, the particular immanence argument that
Tenbruck stresses so heavily was not stressed by Weber. In one of the lists
of 'rational' factors quoted earlier, he calls discipline 'complementary' to the
permanent rational enterprise, which Weber said was the factor which "in
the last resort" produced capitalism (1961, p. 260).

CAUSAL READINGS OF THE LATER TEXTS

The language of 'factors', 'produces', and so on suggests a causal rather than teleological interpretation of Weber's account of the origins of capitalism. Yet attempts to overcome, by a causalist interpretation, the ambiguity and obscure purport of such things as the lists of factors in the lectures have faced difficulties as well. These are well illustrated by Benjamin Nelson's argument that the later work, especially the *Religionssoziologie*, was an attempt to interpret the "sociological experiment" left us by history (Nelson, 1974, p. 275). Weber, he says,

> tells us plainly that he is applying Mill's 'Method of Difference' and, therefore, looking for the factor or chain of circumstances which helped to explain some unique outcome of a given experiment. The unique outcome, as he saw it, in the Protestant ethic was the spread of a rationalized sociocultural order based on the assumption of vocational asceticism. In his later work, his comparative work, he sought to show that all other components which were involved in the Western fusion could be found separately and in combination in other places, but these had not undergone the spur which was supplied by Luther, Calvin, the Protestant ethic, and the spirit of capitalism in the West. His successive writings on the social psychology of the world religions ... were all devoted to further testing of this hypothesis (1973, pp. 111–12).

The "master clue to his aims," Nelson suggests, is the 'Introduction' to the *Religionssoziologie*, in which the break between the noncomparativist 'Protestant Ethic' and the comparativist, 'universal historical', later work is most fully articulated. Nelson agrees with Tenbruck that the 'Introduction' shows that rationalization had become Weber's central concern, and that the change alters 'The Protestant Ethic' by placing it in a different explanatory structure. But Nelson's notion is that the new explanatory structure is Mill's Method of Difference.

Contrary to Nelson's claim (1973, p. 111), which he fails to support by any specific citation, there is no place in which Weber "tells us plainly" that he was using the Method of Difference, and it would be a 'shock' if he had. As we have seen, Weber had embraced an anti-Millian doctrine of cause in the 1903–1907 essays and subsequently wrote on methodology without explicitly embracing a doctrine congenial to large-scale civilizational causal comparisons of a distinctively Millian variety. The shock might be overlooked if one could use Millian terms to construe Weber's texts into an explanation that was significantly coherent or lent coherence to the *Religionssoziologie*. But the explanation, construed in Millian terms, turns out to be a disappointment.

We again face the problem of distinguishing 'distinguishing features', the *explanandum*, from differentiating causes, the *explanans*. Nelson's solution is to treat Protestantism as a differentiating element *not* found elsewhere, the 'spur' which, together with the spirit of capitalism, promotes rationalization. This is the logical core of the quoted paragraph:

In his later work, his comparative work, he sought to show that all other components which were involved in the Western fusion could be found separately and in combination in other places (1973, pp. 111–12).

If the other components could *not* be found elsewhere, the Method of Difference would fail to distinguish the 'cause' from the mere 'conditions' on the list. But this line of interpretation is belied by the 'Introduction' itself, which stressed the uniqueness to the occident not *only* of the 'spur' of Protestantism but of rational art and architecture, rational science, bureaucratic state organization, constitutionalism, the rational enterprise, the rational organization of formally free labor, rational bookkeeping, and the separation of enterprise and *oikos* (Weber, 1958, pp. 13–24). It is also belied by Weber's discussions in *Economy and Society*, where, in speaking of the transformation to capitalism, he said explicitly, "It is not possible to enunciate any general formula that will summarize the comparative substantive powers of the various factors involved in such a transformation or will summarize the manner of their accomodation" (1978a, p. 577).

Randall Collins has presented an account that presents Weber as concerned, especially in the General Economic History lectures, with producing a comparative explanation of Western capitalism in terms of causal conditions. Collins's focus is on the lists, which he makes into 'conditions' by locating them temporally and spatially, and concluding that they in fact *preceded* the original appearance of capitalism (1980). This approach is superficially appealing, not least because it appears to avoid entangling the interpretation in philosophical or methodological subtleties; conditionality is treated by Collins as a generic and uncontroversial notion, and the causal explanation is converted into a familiar type, the type favored by historians of the 'for want of a nail' school. But there are evident obstacles to such an interpretation, and these obstacles point to another approach.

One obstacle is that Weber clearly rejected the kind of simple application of these concepts demanded by this interpretation. When he discussed the concepts in *Economy and Society*, he was always careful to stress the extent to which the relevant distinctions, especially those involving the definition of 'capitalism', are not the sort that can be applied in a precise spatio-temporal way. Thus, in distinguishing the *oikos* from the capitalist enterprise, he remarked that the range of historically realized possibilities includes "all imaginable transitions" (1978a, p. 383). A similar point may be made with respect to such concepts as 'rational law'. To identify the spatio-temporal moment at which law becomes 'rational' would have been absurd, and Weber himself made no effort to do so. On the contrary, he was more concerned, in both *Economy and Society* and the 'Introduction' to the *Religionssoziologie*, to show the *deeprootedness* of these forms of rationality in the Western tradition (in this case in Roman law, in the case of science in Greek science), and to stress their *uniqueness* to the West.

Another obstacle is the problem of the implicit doctrine of historical causality Collins attributes to Weber. Collins makes no attempt, as Nelson does, to construe Weber's account in terms of any particular method of causal reasoning. As Collins reformulates the argument, the substantive causal issue is reduced to the matter of temporal precedence. Weber was never satisfied with *post hoc ergo propter hoc* arguments of this sort, and his sensitivity to the difficulties, conceptual and substantive, of causal analysis in these contexts is evident in many remarks in his later writings, particularly in *Economy and Society*. He treated the relation of "a rational religious ethic" and the modern type of commercial rationalism itself with great caution (1978a, p. 480), a caution induced primarily by the question of mechanism. More generally, he was suspicious of general formulae, such as Collins and Nelson profess to find and which would be necessary to make causal attributions of the Millian sort, as we have already noticed. Their desire to read Weber as an exponent of some sort of 'comparative civilizational' perspective is of course not baseless. After all, the 'uniqueness' argument is itself implicitly 'comparative' and 'civilizational' – the question is whether and in what sense it is causal.

Weber was fond of the imagery of causal chains, so it is useful to apply this imagery to his own explanations. If we treat the lists *as* the explanation, we may ask, 'Where does this leave us on the causal chain'? The reiteration of the term 'rational' on the lists suggests the possibility that the rationalities of the various spheres of Western social life are related or have a common origin, a possibility that is enhanced by Weber's discussion of them as "special features of its general cultural evolution [*Entwicklung*] which are peculiar to" the occident (1961, p. 232). The same thought seems to be behind many of Weber's broader remarks comparing Asia and the West. In describing the economic consequences of religion in Asia, he suggested that

For the various popular religions of Asia, ... the world itself remained a great enchanted garden, in which the practical way to orient oneself, or to find security in this world or the next, was to revere or coerce the spirits and seek salvation through ritualistic, idolatrous, or sacramental procedures. No path led from the magical religiosity of the non-intellectual strata of Asia to a rational, methodical control of life (1978a, p. 630).

This is a 'mentalities' or 'mental affinities' argument, of which a surprising number may be found in *Economy and Society* and the *Religionssoziologie* (e.g., Weber, 1978a, pp. 480, 556–72, 630, 853, 1186).

One might take Weber's appeal to the 'special features' of Western cultural development as a whole to be a large 'mental affinities' argument – an attempt to show that the rationality of distinct institutional spheres may "be explained by their rootedness in the same beliefs and attitudes," by showing "that they rest upon similar normative and epistemological premises" (Kronman, 1983, p. 119). Kronman, who suggests this interpretation, carefully avoids construing the common cultural 'premises' of the West as a cause. His instinct here is quite right. If Weber had intended general culture as the causal explanation of the sphere-specific rationalities on the lists, he simply intensified the problems over vagueness, causal mechanism, and logic which bedevil the lists construed as causal explanations.

CAUSAL INTERACTIONS

The lists thus remain an enigma. In themselves they are uncharacteristically schematic and mechanical, vague as to the causal mechanisms by which the effects are produced, and lacking a framework of logic that would give sense to a notion of them as causes. As explanations, they appear to conflict with Weber's opinions on method: to the extent that they weigh factors, they conflict with the discussions of 'objective possibility' in the early writings. Because they are explicitly *culturalist* schema, they conflict with his caution about culturalism, as well as with the disdain for historical formulae expressed in *Economy and Society*. Methodological considerations aside, the sheer opacity of these lists as explanations in itself leads one to believe that Weber never intended them as causal explanations in any strict sense.

But what did he intend? The clues in the 'Introduction' to the *Religionssoziologie* are sparse, but there are clues, and there are clues in the 'Introduction' to *Economy and Society* as well. A contemporary described Weber's views as follows:

Max Weber sets himself the task of understanding the nature of a society in terms of the psychological motivation of individual actions. He allows organic explanations derived from the nature and function of sociological structures to serve only as preliminary orientations and aids to analysis (Hintze, 1975, p. 380).

This is the explicit theme of the methodological 'Introduction' to *Economy and Society*.

In historical explanation, this commitment to individual explanation implies that such *explanans* and *explananda* as the Protestant ethic and the spirit of capitalism, rational law, rational accounting, the rational organization of labor, and so on must be treated in a particular way: they cannot be treated as 'effective forces'; their causal and explanatory adequacy depends on the possibility of our 'cashing them in' for individual explanations. To disaggregate historical explanations appealing to these concepts into individual patterns of motivation and conduct one must normally appeal to ideal-type concepts. In disaggregating 'the state' one appeals to ideal-typical concepts of beliefs in legitimacy and patterns of conduct in response to command. In disaggregating large-scale historical explanations, the same principles apply, but where the explanations are genetic, the focus changes from conduct and belief to 'motive' (1978a, p. 10; 1922, p. 509). The articulated reason for this is that if one explains belief by the immediate circumstantial plausibility of a belief, and conduct by the immediate circumstances of belief and interest, the long-term transformation of belief and interest must be explained by some element of individual meaningful action that is deeper and more permanent.

Genetic historical explanations characteristically make these appeals. Thus in theology a pattern of conduct motivated by a desire to make doctrines consistent will produce one and then another pattern of belief, as the creation of new doctrines makes possible their systematization, refinement, and supplanting by more new doctrines which overcome the flaws of the old. Similarly in law, where such long-term underlying motivations as internal considerations of legal technique in a particular legal tradition or the professional interests of lawyers produce successive changes in conduct which in turn change the circumstances under which successors choose and act (e.g., Weber, 1978a, pp. 688, 709, 853, 855, 874, 884, 886).

The most interesting historical 'genetic' processes are those which interact and transform the conditions under which they and others develop. The Protestant ethic, as a *genetic* ideal-type, is an account of motivation with respect to the ethical conduct of life, from the original reformers to the succeeding generations of preachers, to Franklin, to "victorious capitalism," which today "rests on mechanical foundations" and "needs its support no longer" so that the original "idea of duty in one's calling prowls about in our lives like the ghost of dead religious beliefs" (Weber, 1958, pp. 181–82). Two points need to be noticed about this genetic ideal-type.

First, the fact that Weber can trace out this genetic process in terms of intelligible individual motivations – necessarily, for pragmatic historiographic reasons, 'typified' – warrants his use of Protestantism as a historical variable. Second, any list of the 'distinctive features' of a phenomenon for which genetic types of this sort may be provided is *itself* a causal explanation of the features, simply because the genetic types are themselves 'causal'. Taken by themselves, the lists are not meaningful as causal explanations. They *are* meaningful as preliminaries, aids to analysis, and summaries of arguments. But the genuine explanatory work is done on the level of the individual acts that make up the genetic ideal-type patterns, not on the level of 'factors'.

In the 'Introduction' to the *Religionssoziologie*, a 'late' work, Weber characterized the problem of explaining various forms of rationalization as 'genetic' (1958, p. 26). In 'Objectivity', the Marxist account was so characterized. Weber's account of the rise of a centralized administrative bureaucracy out of the struggles between monarchs and their enfeoffed vassals is presumably a 'genetic' ideal-type as well. *Economy and Society* is a compilation of ideal-types, which makes frequent reference to their 'genetic' aspects and to the interactions between developmental processes. The primary theme in each of these genetic explanations is the interaction between various processes and economic interests (which are, of course, also developing and changing), but there are other important kinds of interaction as well, in particular the kind captured by the 'mental affinities' arguments mentioned earlier.

The interaction between distinct 'genetic' processes of rationalization suggests a different approach to the question raised by Kronman as to the relation between the various forms of rationality. The origins and internal development of various forms of rationality, e.g., accounting, law, administrations, the disenchantment of the world, science, theodicy, asceticism, and canon law, are proper subjects for genetic typifications. Changes in belief and conduct in these various spheres are successive. Weber stressed with respect to science, for example, that it is always in the business of surpassing itself. Similarly for theodicy, law, and the like: the pursuit of the activity itself changes the subject of the activity and the conditions under which successors pursue the activity. Weber pointed out that one consequence of asceticism was worldly success, a consequence with evident implications for the practices and beliefs of successors in this tradition.

Asceticism had other implications as well, particularly for the possibility of certain forms of work discipline, which altered the conditions under which other activities developed. In the case of modern rationalism, there arose a dynamic of interactions between various 'genetic' processes, in which intelligible changes in one reinforced, hastened, and encouraged changes in others. The relation between business practice and dis-enchanted religion is a simple instance of this: hard-bitten businessmen had little interest in religions with 'magical' elements; ascetic religionists proved to be successful in business and to be assiduous, disciplined workers, asceticism encouraged business, the rise of a business class served to expand the base of ascetic religion.

If one traces out the interactions between changes in law, ethics, administration, religion, and so on, one finds a powerful dynamic of interactions of this sort. The *dynamic* is the 'explanation' of modern rationality, and incidentally of modern capitalism, which is part of the dynamic. But there is no more to the explanatory force of this dynamic than that which comes from explaining the intelligible actions of individuals and their consequences. So the explanation must be a work of tesselation, the composition of a pattern of actions. Ideal-types were a shorthand means of describing the patterns in this mosaic, but no more – not Millian causes made up of institutional facts, and not the immanent universal historical forces of rationalization. Each act in the mosaic was to be itself intelligible, and each step in these genetic processes was to be construed as contingent in the way human action is contingent. This at least was Weber's methodol-ogical ideal at the time he wrote the 'Introduction', and he never repudiated it.

STATISTICAL PATTERNS

We have now strayed very far from the practical problems of cause and probability. But in straying, we have returned to some familiar territory. The reappearance of the theme of rationality is a humbling denoument to a century which began with Comte, Mill, Quetelet, and Buckle – not to mention Lecky, and a host of others – who had believed the triumph of intellectual forces to be the key to historical development. Weber, as he is now seen, represents a curious reversion to this central preoccupation. His means of approaching it, and particularly the basic strategy of breaking large-scale historical processes into meaningful individual components, also brings us back to a familiar problem.

Weber was no statistician, in the sense of collecting and commenting on statistical material. But he used statistical material, particularly in the opening chapter of 'The Protestant Ethic', which showed the numerical predominance of Protestants in urban business, the technical professions, and the skilled trades (1958, p. 35), and was aware of, and approved, efforts to collect statistical material. In the 'Introduction' to *Economy and Society*, he took up the problem of the significance of uniformities by making a distinction between interpretable and noninterpretable uniformities. "Certain psychic or psychophysical phenomena such as fatigue, habituation, memory, etc." and correlates of racial properties are noninterpretable facts (1978a, pp. 7, 8; 1922, p. 507). Similarly for statistical relationships.

There are statistics of processes devoid of subjective meaning, such as death rates, phenomena of fatigue, the production rate of machines, the amount of rainfall, in exactly the same sense as there are statistics of meaningful phenomena. But only when the phenomena are meaningful do we speak of sociological statistics. Examples are such cases as crime rates, occupational distributions, price statistics, and statistics of crop acreage. Naturally there are many cases where both components are involved, as in crop statistics (1978a, p. 12; 1922, p. 512).

The reasoning that applies to large-scale historical processes, particularly the insistence on disaggregating patterns into intelligible, motivated, individual actions, applies to statistical uniformities. "If adequacy in respect to meaning is lacking, then no matter how high the degree of uniformity and how precisely its probability can be numerically determined, it is still an incomprehensible statistical probability, whether we deal with overt or subjective processes" (1978a, p. 12; 1922, p. 512). This insistence Weber justified in terms of the "cognitive purposes" of sociology and history (1978a p. 13; 1922, p. 513).[5]

An incidental consequence of this strategy is that it provides a solution of sorts to the puzzle of distinguishing 'accidental' statistical relationships from 'causal' relationships. As we have seen, von Kries avoided the problem in a questionable fashion. Uninterpretable statistical relations are one form in which the problem intrudes again. Weber's approach has implications beyond the immediate problem, as well. It serves to explain why, in the subsequent history of statistical sociology, the problem has not been as overwhelming as one might have expected. One traditional approach treats it in terms of the problem of 'accidental' generalizations, holding that a correlation, like a generalization, may become explanatory by virtue of derivation from a theory.

'Theories' in sociology have rarely, if ever, had a form that is appropriate for such 'derivations'. It is common to use semantically imprecise propositions with a great many exceptions as resources for giving verbal interpretations to statistical relationships, in the course of what I have called here 'statistical commentary'. These are not 'derivations', and characteristically there is little in the way of formal structure to these interpretations. Yet empirical sociologists are usually satisfied with these formulations, and, when they are not writing under the influence of ideals of explanation imported from the natural sciences, do little to improve them in the direction of deductive precision and semantic clarity. Why should this be so?

Disaggregating the statistical pattern into a (hypothetical) set of (typified) reasons and motives, as Weber suggested doing, is a way of 'linking' variables: such hypotheses about reasons play a role analogous to the role played by laws in physical science, i.e., of making a fact, such as a correlation, into an explanation, by filling in the sequence which intervenes between the statistically described categories with 'links' that may themselves be taken to be explanatory. Thus the technique of giving an interpretation of a statistical relationship in terms of reasons and motives is an 'interpretational' surrogate for the 'infilling' explanations suggested by Venn.[6]

As a philosophical matter, 'infilling' with rational reconstructions is sharply distinguished from 'infilling' with nomic causal links. In sociological practice, however, the distinctions are not so sharp. Typically, the concepts employed by the sociologist in fact possess a degree of 'intelligibility' beyond and apart from whatever nomic or psuedo-nomic relations may be claimed to hold between variables that have been 'operationally defined'. Consider the concept of role conflict: it is intelligible to us in terms of our ordinary experience with the reasons and motives of persons in situations of role conflict. When the concept is explained and applied to a given set of cases, it is explained by giving examples of persons, or typical situations, where motives and reasons having to do with a given role lead to conflicts with the requirements of living up to other roles. The explanatory force of the explanation derives largely from this informal kind of 'sense making'. 'Role conflict' is not exceptional as a concept. Indeed, perhaps most interpretation of statistical relations in sociology, in the course of distinguishing explanatory correlation from 'mere' correlation, covertly appeals to the intelligibility of the connections, rather than to the lawlikeness of the hypotheses in which the concepts figure.

THE END OF THE ASCENT

Karl Pearson's *Grammar of Science*, was published with new chapters on statistics in the edition of 1911. With this text, we arrive at the moment of the origins of American statistical sociology before the First World War. The early 'inductive sociologists' at Columbia University read the statisticians of the nineteenth century. Both Durkheim and Quetelet were subjects of prewar Columbia dissertations. The FHG Club, – the initials are those of its mentor, Franklin H. Giddings – included the young sociologists who were to become leaders in statistical sociology. One member of this club, F. Stuart Chapin, an early Columbia Ph.D. in sociology, recalled in a memoir of these years that "H. T. Buckle and Karl Pearson were a great inspiration." [1]

PEARSON ON CAUSE AND CORRELATION

Pearson's book is a peculiar document, with one hand in the past, the other in a future that was visible to few of his contemporaries. Part of the book is devoted to such pastimes as quibbling with Comte and Spencer over the classification of the sciences. Part is devoted to such problems as multiple correlation, which proved to be central to the disciplines of population genetics, econometrics, and quantitative history, as well, of course, as sociology. Pearson gave what is perhaps the most extreme accounts of the problem of the relation between cause and probability ever given, and it is useful to follow it through, both because of its undoubted historical influence and because of the paradoxical ending to which it comes.

Pearson echoed and extended the critique of cause developed by Venn, Jevons, and others, by arguing that the term 'cause' as employed by such writers as Herschel was "animistic" (1911, p. 121), and

that law in the scientific sense only describes in mental shorthand the sequences of our perceptions. It does not explain *why* those perceptions have a certain order, nor *why* that order repeats itself; the law discovered by science introduces no element of necessity into the sequence of our sense-impressions; it merely gives a concise statement of *how* changes are taking place (1911, p. 113).

The basis of Pearson's attack was a rejection of various attempts to find features that distinguish causal sequences from other sequences. "For science, cause, as originating or enforcing a particular sequence of perceptions, is meaningless" (Pearson, 1911, p. 128). 'Necessity' cannot be demonstrated by science; it is a property of conceptual constructions solely (1911, pp. 134–36). The 'explanatory' character of these descriptions is entirely subjective.

The corpuscular, the elastic-solid, and the electro-magnetic theories of light all involve a series of conclusions of logical necessity, and we may use these conclusions as a means of testing our perceptions. So far as they are confirmed, the theory remains valid as a description; if, on the other hand, our sense-impressions differ from these conclusions, the conclusions have just as much mental necessity, but the theory while valid for the mind is not valid as a description of the routine of perceptions (1911, pp. 135–36).

The validation of such hypotheses has no implications for the validity of the 'explanatory' element of the hypothesis. "We can but describe experience, we never reach an 'explanation', connoting necessity" (1911, p. 152). The binary opposition between necessity and probability finds a place here. What science does is reduce sequences of perception to a formula: "we give expression in the concept *probability*" to the belief "that … [a sequence] will continue to recur in the future" (1911, p. 113, emphasis in original).

Issues arising in connection with the ascent from common sense get equally short shrift. For Pearson, "the 'freedom of the will' lies in the descriptive fact that exertion is conditioned by our own individuality, that the routine of mental processes which intervenes between sense-impression and exertion is perceived physically neither by us nor by any one else, and psychically by us alone" (1911, p. 125). But this is purely a matter of epistemology: "will" is "only a limit at which very often our power of describing a sequence abruptly terminates" (1911, p. 125). The causal problems of common sense are those of science. "The sameness of the 'routine' which the man in the street is familiar with may be far looser than the routine of experiment which the physicist or chemist idealises as absolute sameness; but the sameness is in both cases one of degree" (1911, p. 154).

The difference that is key to Weber and von Kries, between the concepts of the world of action, in which the occupants of a given category are not precisely the same, and the physical sciences, in which they are, is also treated as a matter of degree.

The conclusions of the physicist and the chemist are based on *average* experiences, no two of which exactly agree; at best they are routines of perception which have a certain variability. This variability they may attribute to errors of observations, to impurities in their specimens, to the physical factors of the environment, but it none the less exists and, when it is removed by a process of averaging, we pass at once from the perceptual to the conceptual, and construct a model universe, not the real universe (1911, p. 154, emphasis in original).

If we keep in mind that the relations hitherto called causal are in actuality themselves only 'ideals', it follows that the relationships found in a contingency table (which is the lineal descendant of the actuarial tables invented by Halley and found in Farr and Quetelet) or a scattergram are merely looser forms of what we are accustomed to call causal relationships.

Take any two measurable classes of things in the universe of perceptions, physical, organic, social or economic, and it is such a dot or scatter diagram, which we reach with extended observations. In some cases the dots are scattered all over the paper, there is no association of A and B; in other cases there is a broad belt, there is only moderate relationship; then the dots narrow down to a 'comet's tail', and we have close association. Yet the whole series of diagrams is continuous; nowhere can you draw a distinction and say here correlation ceases and causation begins. Causation is solely the conceptual limit to correlation when the band gets so attenuated, that it looks like a curve. Under the one category, correlation, all our experience whatever of the links between phenomena can be classified; under the other category no actual experience whatever can be ranked; it is a purely descriptive conceptual limit reached by statistical processes from observed phenomena: invaluable as an economy of thought, roughly corresponding to likeness of routines, but in itself providing no measure of the deviations or want of sameness that will actually be experienced in routines – to determine that requires us to know the actual variation in the arrays, the correlation, or degree of contingency (1911, p. 170).

With this loosening of the concept of causation we enter into a new world. The aim of science itself changes. It "ceases to be the discovery of 'cause' and 'effect'; in order to predict future experience it seeks out the phenomena which are most highly correlated" (1911, p. 173). The change also erases the distinctions between the social and physical sciences that were as obsessive concern of Mill, Comte, and for that matter Quetelet, with his call for a new Newton. "From this standpoint it finds no distinction in kind but only in degree between the data, method of treatment, or the resulting 'laws' of chemical, physical, biological, or sociological investigations" (1911, p. 173).

THE NOMIC WORLD AND THE CORRELATIONAL WORLD

The consequences of this new vision are puzzling. One set of puzzles arises from the fact that the concept of correlation does not serve as a sieve that eliminates, as does the concept of law, large numbers of putative causes. The concept of the infinity of causes, which appears in a confusing way in von Kries, is embraced by Pearson. "Everything which has previously occurred or is simultaneously occurring in the universe is to a greater or

less extent a cause of everything else" (1911, p. 154). The idea of a cause
as the combination of conditions that absolutely determines an effect is
abandoned: "the search for one cause, or a combination of causes, which
will absolutely define one or the other is hopeless, but the determination
of correlations between these and other phenomena is easy and is of
first-class practical importance" (1911, p. 171n). The ideal of complete
explanation by identifying all the causes is also dismissed:

the idea that multiplying causes will reduce variation ultimately to zero is similar to that of
most such ideas; it is due to the thrusting of a mental conception out into phenomena, and
not realising that it is actually a limit, not a reality of experience (1911, p. 172).

As a practical matter,

in the universe as we know it, all these factors are themselves to a greater or less extent
associated or correlated, and in actual experience, but little effect is produced in lessening the
variability of B, by introducing additional factors after we have taken the first few most highly
associated phenomena (1911, p. 172).

In itself, this serves as a sieve, for "actual experience of correlation shows
it is only a few highly correlated variables that matter" (1911, p. 173). But
it is a peculiar sieve, as a consequence of something we noticed in
connection with the problem of conceptual revision in the case of Farr's
concepts of 'healthy counties' and 'polluted water', with the case of Weber's
discussions of the reliance of the historical sciences on pregiven categories
that are not revised (because to revise them would render the subject
matter of the historical sciences unintelligible, as an atomic description
would be, and because von Kriesian probabilistic causality does not
provide a test of concepts which serves as an effective sieve), and with
Bernard's problem of premature stopping points for investigation.

Pearson grasped the indeterminacy of choices between alternative selections of concepts within a given set of intercorrelated variables. Rather than
serving to describe more and more of the variation, with the aim of
ultimately reducing all the variation to strict functional relations, adding
new variables with some correlation to the original set quickly reaches a
point of diminishing returns. Little new variation is accounted for, and no
limit of full explanation – Quetelet's ideal – is approached. If one selects
a different set of variables or differently defined 'variables' which cover the
same knot of intercorrelations, the values of the correlation coefficients,
and the degree of tightness of fit between variables, will perhaps change,
but the total amount of variation captured by the concepts will not increase
substantially.

The *de facto* consequence of this feature of correlational analysis is that the pressure for conceptual refinement produced by the correlational method is slight. Discovering all of the most relevant variables, the variables that describe the knot of related variations, is key. But refining one's concept of them is not – to substitute an 'improved' concept for another has little effect other than to change the other values in a correlation matrix containing the set of variables – the total variation described by the combined correlation remains much the same. So theory-choice in a correlational social science is *de facto* a very different matter than theory-choice in physics. *Mutatis mutandis*, this point may be applied to other statistical methods which became popular among social scientists in the twentieth century, such as the methods of inferential statistics borrowed from R. A. Fisher and agricultural experimentation.[2]

Although Pearson rejected the concept of explanation, and rejected 'why' questions as theological and cause as animistic, the problems of accidental laws and spuriousness do not disappear so much as disappear from view. In practice, social scientists have not found it possible to dispense with these concepts. The concept of spuriousness and the term 'explained variance' are both central to the practicing social scientists' use of the methods of correlational analysis. Yet both concepts are inadmissible on Pearsonian terms, and it is doubtful whether any defensible account of either concept exists. To borrow a saying of Weber's, they 'prowl like the ghost of dead religious beliefs'. The ghost has proved to be a lively one. Pearson himself provided a dramatic object lesson of this in the course of the debate over Mendelism in the first decade of the century. The biometricians, of whom Pearson was a leading figure, initially dismissed the gene hypothesis, and Pearson continued to his death to dismiss it, long after the others were won over. In the 1911 edition of the *Grammar*, he asked,

What if the attempt of some biologists to replace vital variation by 'unit' characters be really a retrogressive change, and the persistency and absence of individuality to which they appeal as comparable with chemical changes be ultimately a false analogy, because the sameness of chemical theory is a *statistical* experience which may ultimately admit differentiation within the class? (1911, p. 156, emphasis in original).

Of course, it was not a 'retrogression', so the interesting point about Pearson's skepticism is that the conceptual change represented by the gene hypothesis is not only in conflict with the Pearsonian acceptance of variation as the rule of nature, it shows that the acceptance of variation, and the readiness to stop at the point of identifying a knot of variation (defined by the redundancy or statistical irrelevance of added variables) *can* be an 'acceptance of ignorance' and a 'premature stopping point' of precisely the sort that troubled Mill, Comte, and Bernard. In the case of genetics, at least, the demand to push on to the identification of mechanisms proved fruitful as a regulative ideal. This casts a shadow on the social sciences – the search for underlying mechanisms has not proven to be a particularly fruitful ideal in the social sciences, though it has not disappeared. The ideal is one shard of the Durkheimian program. It was kept alive, by Marcel Mauss, and was turned in a new direction by Levi–Strauss in the form of structuralism. The *instantiae luciferae* which have seemed to reveal an underlying law-governed order of mechanisms or rules, such as Durkheim's *Suicide* and Levi–Strauss's *Elementary Structures of Kinship*, have not been successfully followed up, as the *instantiae luciferae* of Mendel's garden was – the 'light' these instances shed proved to be false light. Reductionisms, psychological, biological, and the like have had a long and largely fruitless career. The form of 'reductionism' that had been most successful, translations into economic or decision-theoretic models, share with Weber's ideal-type 'rationality' an ambiguity between the causal, the normative, and the constitutive.

THEORY, STATISTICS, AND INTERPRETATION

The failure of social science to score the sort of decisive successes that would grant special validity to a new conceptual vocabulary, together with the limited discriminative force of statistical considerations alone, leaves social science 'theory' in an odd position. Without being successful in the sense of playing the role that Mill or Quetelet envisioned, it has proven more persistent in the empirical social sciences than Pearson might have expected.

For Pearson, the paradigm of knowledge acquisition was drawing black and white balls from a bag and recording their proportions. Mill had remarked that a "very slight ground of surmise that the white balls were really more numerous than either of the other colours, would suffice to vitiate the whole of the calculations made in our previous state of indifference" (1973, p. 537). Keep in mind what Pearson observed to be the case with correlations, that "little effect is produced in lessening the variability of B by introducing additional factors after we have taken the first few most highly associated phenomena" into account (1911, p. 172), and the fact that alternative descriptions of the variables that are associated in this way do not strongly 'lessen the variability'. In the face of this choosing a statistical model, or choosing a set of 'variables', becomes a highly problematic task. In the first place, there is the profusion of models (that is, the sets of descriptive categories or 'variables' whose mutual variation is measured by the correlation coefficient) which more or less fit. Pearson's key pragmatic argument, that while determinate cause is hopeless the determination of correlations is "of first-class practical importance" (1911, p. 171), is itself undermined by this profusion, for practical conclusions and predictions, as any reader of the soothsaying econometricians on the financial pages is aware, vary substantially between models which are not substantially dissimilar as to the body of variability and association they cover. Indeed, the range of models that more or less fit is often so broad that one can scarcely consider them knowledge at all.

Here Mill's point has bearing. Mill grasped something of cardinal importance when he observed that even a little extra-statistical knowledge of the right kind transforms our expectations about the continued proportions of colors of balls drawn from bags. Mill was vacillating about what this transformation consisted in, and the adequate cause theory was a product of his vacillation. We may alter his point: to decide between the abundance of possible models of a knot of associated phenomena, some extra-statistical means or procedure beyond the consideration of lessening the total variability is necessary. In practice, the means is to use 'causal assumptions' to decide between alternative structures of relations between variables, and to select the *predictive* models out of the profusion of models on the basis of these assumptions (Simon, 1954, Simon and Rescher, 1966, but see Meehl, 1970, Turner, 1982). Usually these assumptions are matters of common sense. In a sociologist's model of status attainment, father's status is taken to predict son's status, and not *vice versa*. But often the assumptions involve the more fully articulate logical structures of economic theory (e.g. rational expectations theory used in a model of inflationary pricing), or such extensions of common sense as the concept of role conflict.

The selection on nonstatistical grounds of some set of causal models out of the many models which (although they will have different statistical properties) all more or less cover the same body of variation is something not countenanced by Pearson – to concede the *necessity* of doing this would for him have been to concede the insufficiency of the concept of correlation (conjoined with temporal succession) as a substitute for the concept of cause. In practice, of course, Pearson's austerity has not prevailed. The actual work of statistical analysis in the social science more closely resembles the statistical commentary of Farr than the nomic science envisioned by Mill. The sense making performed by commentary thus has a specific logical role: it increases our confidence in the expectations we have on the basis of a given model by increasing our confidence in the selection of this model out of the profusion of possibilities that are more or less statistically equivalent with respect to total variation. The office of statistical commentary is thus to provide the 'very slight ground of surmise' by which our indifference between alternatives can be overcome.

With this we come back to Weber – to the interpretation of subjective meaning, rationalizations, and the stylized forms of commonsense explanations he called ideal-typical. If one considers complex examples, such as econometric cases, the role of rationalizations – that is, interpretations that supply reasons for actions – becomes clear. Deciding between the enormous set of conceivable descriptive concepts and combinations of these concepts that would cover the variation in a given econometric model is impossible on statistical grounds. A rational interpretation that identifies those considerations that bear on action, and that supply a concept that corresponds to these considerations, e.g. the price of credit, supplies a starting point that enables one to simply ignore the profusion of possible models, except where an alternative model enables significantly more variation to be encompassed.

Our reason for supposing that the motives and reasons we include in the model are the motives and considerations governing action in the case at hand is that these interpretations have worked – that is, did not break down – in similar circumstances in the past. The character of these grounds, whether they are to be analyzed as empirical, experimental, quasi-nomic, correlational in Pearson's sense of including the mental successions we experience in our own minds, or however else it is to be regarded, is of course open to question. What is evident, however, is that the grounds are external to the particular choice between statistical models we are faced with, and carry some cognitive weight which is independent of the statistical evidence for the model.[3] These are modest grounds, and the other kinds of interpretive grounds used by social scientists to connect 'variables' are often more modest. In this context, however, all that is called for is a 'very slight ground of surmise'. The role of 'theory' in connection with this kind of statistical commentary and model selection is therefore important but very unlike the roles Mill, Quetelet, and Durkheim cast it for, and the theories that have developed in the social sciences to serve the purposes of statistical commentary are not very impressive affairs. But they would serve these purposes no better if they were.

The character of these theories raises the question of whether there is a path of 'ascent' from common sense and statistical results to a more precise and higher level of theory. The two-tiered model shared by Quetelet and Durkheim depended on the argument for the stability of rates. Stability served to make the rates into stable 'facts' which could, once observed, be subject to higher-level laws. The indeterminacy between models that Pearson described destroys this stability: the precise numbers in the rates are not autonomous, rock-like facts, but are determined by the selection of descriptive concepts that admit a great deal of irreducible variability and an indeterminacy between alternative descriptions that renders the realist ideal of conceptual precision pointless. The two-tier model, which depends on treating stability as a mark of realist fact, loses the 'facts' in the first-tier: rather than one set of quantitative facts to which to fit a curve, we are faced with alternative possible sets of quantitative facts. If there are other paths of ascent, not subject to these difficulties or to analogous difficulties, they have not yet been marked out. The ideal is as distant today as it has ever been.

NOTES

CHAPTER TWO

[1] Comte was regularly denounced by the French philosophical and cultural establishment, Buckle by the English ecclesiastical and literary establishment.

[2] 'Verification' is used in this period in a sense broader than the sense in which it was used later (Laudan, 1981, p. 144).

[3] The details of the question of just how far Comte went in his acceptance of the hypothesis is discussed by Laudan, who shows how difficult it is to be very precise about Comte's views on the subject (1981, pp. 154–56).

[4] Warren Schmaus correctly stresses the extent to which the transitions from one stage to another do not take the form of discontinuities (1982).

[5] Virtanen recounts the history of Bernard's criticisms of Comte in a way that is revealing of the temper of the times, and charitable to both of them. Bernard, he says, "is certainly unfair, but we can perhaps understand the feelings of the experimenter when he emerges from the laboratory and reads the pennings of a closet philosopher laying claim to jurisdiction over the sciences. One may also suspect in Bernard a lack of awareness of how much the intellectual climate in which he lived actually owed to the *Cours de philosophie positive*" (Virtanen, 1960, pp. 50–51).

[6] In the later stages of the dispute, e.g., in Taine, the term 'medium' became 'milieu'.

[7] Pathology perhaps remains something of a puzzle. The study of pathology itself is not, Comte said, part of "abstract science," and can become an *application* of biology only at some later date, when our nomological understanding is more advanced (Comte, 1858, pp. 315–16). Presumably more complete nomological knowledge would disclose causal relations that explain 'pathological' conditions, and perhaps dispense with the concept entirely.

[8] Adam Smith, whose *Theory of Moral Sentiments* fits with Comte's notions of reciprocal actions as the basis of society, is excepted from this dismissal of Political Economy.

CHAPTER FOUR

[1] 'Better', in this context, does not mean 'statistically stronger', but rather 'stated in terms of known biological mechanisms' which can be established by nonstatistical means, such as experiments.

CHAPTER FIVE

[1] Renouvier's synthetic contribution to the problem of free will is described in Hacking (1983, pp. 466–67).

[2] The new generation did a great deal in the way of elaborating the mathematics of dispersion,

which had the consequence of turning the empirical properties of distributions into formally describable properties (cf. Hacking, 1983, pp. 473–74).

CHAPTER SIX

[1] The concepts of constraint and generality seem quite different. But 'generality' is explained, a few pages earlier, by the remark that "a phenomenon is ... general because it is collective (that is, more or less obligatory), and certainly not collective because general. It is a group condition repeated in the individual because imposed on him. It is to be found in each part because it exists in the whole, rather than in the whole because it exists in the parts" (1964, p. 9; 1982, p. 56; 1937, p. 10).

[2] The fate of the term 'morphology' is usefully discussed by Strikwerda (1982, pp. 155–79).

[3] The astonishing regularity is not Queteletian; the use of the argument suggests an affinity to Whewell, a similarity that points in a direction other than that described in Schmaus (1985).

[4] Cf. Pierre Janet's *Principles of Psychotherapy* (1924). This book summarizes the thinking of this contemporary of Durkheim's (and nephew of Paul Janet) over the course of a long career in psychology. See especially his chapter on 'Forms of Mental Economy', which discusses the "budget of our mental activity," "the problem of exhaustion," and "lack in psychic forces," especially in connection with the "rest treatment" as a means of psychotherapy (Janet, 1924, pp. 149–206).

[5] It should be noted that '*cette harmonie*' in the original text refers to a previously mentioned harmony between the internal and external milieu, itself a concept originating in French antiteleological biology. Durkheim himself noted that his critics might "point to these words, 'external conditions' and 'milieu', as an accusation that our method seeks the sources of life outside the living being" (1964, p. 121; 1982, p. 141; 1937, p. 119).

[6] The presence of such principles is perhaps a better-defining criterion of teleology. In contrast to Durkheim, functionalist writers such as Luhmann and Parsons have appealed to such principles.

CHAPTER SEVEN

[1] The set of binary oppositions Durkheim employed here, between the apparent but misleading and the hidden but real is repeated throughout his writings, and is found as early as his 'Latin Dissertation' on Rousseau and Montesquieu, where Montesquieu is paraphrased as claiming that "the determinate relations we call laws are closer to the nature of things and consequently hidden within it. They are covered by a veil that we must first remove if we are to get at them and bring them to light" (Durkheim, 1965, p. 62).

[2] "l'unité extérieure de l'effet ne recouvre par une réelle pluralité" (Durkheim, 1937, p. 127).

[3] Cf. Ellis, 1968, pp. 160–82.

[4] Fatalism, or overregulation, can be treated as a fourth (Durkheim 1951, p. 276n; 1930, p. 311n).

CHAPTER EIGHT

[1] "The 'Carnot engine' consisted simply of a cylinder and piston, a working substance that he assumed to be a perfect gas, and two heat reservoirs maintained at different temperatures. The new cycle incorporated the isothermal and adiabatic expansions and the isothermal compression of the steam engine, but Carnot added a final adiabatic compression in which motive power was consumed to heat the gas to its original, boiler temperature. In describing the engine's properties, Carnot introduced two fundamental thermodynamic concepts, completeness and reversibility. At the end of each cycle the engine and the working substance returned to their original conditions" (Challey, 1970, p. 81).

[2] Presumably some, if not most, of this resistance is ultimately social in origin (cf. his discussion of inhibition). Some resistance is a matter of individual "mental constitution" (1951, p. 323; 1930, p. 366).

[3] When Durkheim argued that society breeds persons predisposed to particular collective wishes, it was on the basis of considerations like these. The mechanisms of the 'breeding' are obscure. What he seems to have had in mind is that what are called personality types or psychological types are misnamed – they are better conceived of as persons with a particular mix of more or less stable social impulses together with some rudimentary and highly general human predispositions. The latter he considered "vague and rudimentary" facts "far removed from the facts that need explanation" (1964, p. 107; 1982, p. 132; 1937, p. 106. Cf. 1964, p. 106; 1982, p. 131; 1937, p. 105).

[4] 'Completeness' has this sense. It is true, Durkheim said,

that society has no other active forces than individuals; but individuals by combining form a psychical existence of a new species, which consequently has its own manner of thinking and feeling. Of course the elementary qualities of which the social fact consists are present in germ in individual minds. But the social fact emerges from them only when they have been transformed by association since it is only then that it appears. Association itself is also an active factor productive of special effects. In itself it is therefore something new (1951, p. 310; 1930, p. 350).

The 'special effects' are the result of the transformation of forces, not their creation. Roscoe Hinkle, in an unpublished paper, 'Durkheim's Effervescence and the "Origins" of Society' (n.d.), shows the frequency with which Durkheim refers to the cyclical processes by which force is transformed from individual to social forms and back. The general pattern is best formulated by Durkheim in the course of arguing that in "moments of collective ferment ... are born the great ideals upon which civilizations rest" (Durkheim, 1974, p. 91). But this is only part of the cycle. "Ideals could not survive if they were not periodically revived. This revivification is the function of religious or secular feasts and ceremonies, all public addresses in churches or schools, plays and exhibitions – in a word, whatever draws men together into an intellectual and moral communion" (Durkheim, 1974, p. 92).

CHAPTER NINE

[1] The claim that the relative frequency sense was figurative leads directly to some awkward results, as von Mises pointed out, in such standard cases as the chances of winning a lottery if one holds one ticket, and there is one winning ticket out of ten thousand. Von Kries was forced to resort to the notion that we possess a natural capacity for identifying equally probable suppositions, such that we can see that there are ten thousand equal expectations of winning (von Mises, 1972, pp. 90–91).

[2] Von Kries's use of 'objective' is discussed in slightly different terms by Hart and Honoré (1959, pp. 413–15). A standard discussion of the problem of selecting a reference class may be found in W. Salmon (1971, p. 40).

[3] The subsequent history of the legal form of the doctrine consisted in part of attempts to find a nonquantitative basis for preferring a particular set of descriptive terms (Hart and Honoré, 1959, p. 418).

[4] Weber described the offending author as a *Führer der Naturwissenshaft*. Although this description does not fit Mill precisely, the views Weber attributed to this unnamed person are Mill's, and the phrase can have a sense of 'leader of the natural sciences' which has a better fit.

CHAPTER TEN

[1] A better term might be 'constitutive', but it would be misleading. Neo-Kantian epistemology has the effect, which is especially evident in Weber, of erasing the distinction between 'constitutive' and 'empirical'.

[2] It is not strange that Weber treated this issue as central, and treated problems of explaining action only incidentally, because the discussion of the state was crucial to Weber. Lukács, an informed if jaundiced critic, made this discussion of the state the centerpiece of his own treatment of Weber (1980, pp. 612–13).

[3] The idea is definitely foreshadowed in the *Logos* essay, as is a great deal of the specific language of the 'Introduction'. Yet the emphasis in the earlier essay is different, as when Weber spoke as though the 'usual methods of causal attribution' could somehow decide between alternative motive interpretations in cases where "behavior ... is identical in its external course and result" (1981, p. 151; 1922, p. 404). The claim that "methods of causal attribution" can be used in this way vanishes in the parallel passage in the later text (1978a, pp. 9–10; 1922, p. 509).

[4] Davidson would perhaps respond to this by saying that, even in these very simple examples, attributing beliefs presumes various rational connections between conduct and belief (1984; cf. Turner, 1981).

CHAPTER ELEVEN

[1] Marshall, in *In Search of the Spirit of Capitalism* (1982, p. 33), suggests that the 'Protestant ethic' was itself an intervention into the *Methodenstreit*.

[2] A better way into this tangle might be through the analysis of Weber's concept of concrete historical individual proposed by Wagner and Zipprian (1985). They suggest that the concept derives from Mill's view of proper names and can be construed in terms of Kripke's semantics:

if we treat Weber's 'concrete historical individual' as the subject of a proper name, some of these highly diverse contrasts become intelligible – a proper name is not reducible to nomic particulars, nor can it be fully captured in universals, mental constructs, and so forth.

[3] This passage might be glossed 'where we are interested in causal relations between phenomena with proper names, we are not interested in nomic explanations, because these are explanations under a different, general, description'.

[4] Translated by Gerth and Mills under its original subtitle 'Religious Rejections of the World and Their Directions' (1946, pp. 323–59).

[5] 'Methodological individualism' is not the only grounds one might have for a preference for accounts that disaggregate patterns into choices by individuals in various circumstances. One may, for example, simply say that this kind of account is *de facto* the most intelligible.

[6] This approach to statistical relations is perhaps also a plausible construal of the role of 'economic' rational reconstructions when they are used to account for relations between aggregate patterns by disaggregating them into the actions of individuals acting for various reasons in various circumstances. Similar analyses may be given of other social science examples (Turner, 1977).

EPILOG

[1] L. L. Bernard Papers, University of Chicago Library, Chicago, Illinois.

[2] The extension depends on this consideration: in an agricultural experiment, the inferences are based on experimental designs that eliminate or randomize the effects of other causes with the purpose of insuring that the variation to be measured is attributable to the experimental treatment itself. To generalize from the special conditions of the experiment to the world, in which these other causes are not random or eliminated, is to reason analogically from the experimental circumstances. The analogy may or may not be pragmatically valid. But nothing in the experiment can assure the validity of the analogy, a point often overlooked (cf. Turner, 1982, pp. 203–4). Pearson avoided this problem by ignoring experiment and giving an account of inference that is meant to apply to variation generally, of which experiment is only a special case.

[3] For some discussion of the notion of interpretive failure see Turner (1979, 1980, 1981, pp. 240–43), and Huff and Turner (1981).

BIBLIOGRAPHY

Anderson, O. N.: 1934, 'Statistical Method', *Encyclopaedia of the Social Sciences* **7**, pp. 366–371.

Bain, A.: 1882, *John Stuart Mill: A Criticism with Personal Recollections*, Longmans, London.

Bergner, J. T.: 1981, *The Origin of Formalism in Social Science*, University of Chicago Press, Chicago.

Bernard, C.: 1952, *Introduction à l'étude de la médecine expérimentale*, Flammarion, Paris.

Besnard, P.: 1983, 'Le Destin de l'anomie dans la sociologie du suicide', *Revue francaise de sociologie* **24**, 605–629.

Besnard, P.: 1984, 'La Reception du *Suicide* de Durkheim en France et aux Etats-Unis', paper presented to the meeting of the Research Committee on the History of Society, Munich, July 5–7, 1984.

Boutroux, E.: 1914, *Natural Law in Science and Philosophy*, trans. F. Rothwell, Macmillan, New York.

Boutroux, E.: 1916, *The Contingency of the Laws of Nature*, Open Court, Chicago.

Brown, R.: 1984, *The Nature of Social Laws: Machiavelli to Mill*, Cambridge University Press, Cambridge.

Buckle, H. T.: 1859, *History of Civilization in England*, vol. 1, D. Appleton, New York.

Burger, T.: 1976, *Max Weber's Theory of Concept Formation: History, Laws, and Ideal Types*, Duke University Press, Durham.

Butts, R. E.: 1976, 'Whewell, William', *Dictionary of Scientific Biography* **14**, 292–295.

Challey, J. F.: 1970, 'Carnot, Nicolas Léonard Sadi', *Dictionary of Scientific Biography* **3**, 79–84.

Collini, S., D. Winch, and J. Burrow: 1983, *That Noble Science of Politics*, Cambridge University Press, Cambridge.

Collins, R.: 1980, 'Weber's Last Theory of Capitalism: A Systematization', *American Sociological Review* **45**, 925–942.

Comte, A.: 1858, *The Positive Philosophy of Auguste Comte*, trans. H. Martineau, Calvin Blanchard, New York.

Comte, A.: 1875, *System of Positive Philosophy*, vol. 1, Burt Franklin, New York.

Comte, A.: 1974, *The Essential Comte*, ed. and with an introduction by S. Andreski, Barnes and Noble, New York.

Comte, A.: 1975a, *Cours de philosophie positive*, with an introduction by M. Serres, F. Dagognet, and A. Sinaceur, Hermann, Paris.

Comte, A.: 1975b, *Auguste Comte and Positivism: The Essential Writings*, ed. and with an introduction by G. Lenzer, Harper Torchbooks, New York.

Condorcet, Marquis de [Maie Jean Antoine Nicolas de Caritat]: 1971, 'The Future of Man', in F. Manuel and F. Manuel (eds.), *French Utopias: An Anthology of Ideal Societies*, Schocken Books, New York, pp. 191–215.

Darnton, R.: 1984, *The Great Cat Massacre and Other Episodes in French Cultural History*, Basic Books, New York.

Davidson, D.: 1982, *Essays on Actions and Events*, Clarendon Press, Oxford.

Davidson, D.: 1984, *Inquiries into Truth and Interpretation*, Clarendon Press, Oxford.

Diamond, S.: 1969, 'Introduction', in L. A. Quetelet, *A Treatise on Man and the Development of His Faculties*, Scholars' Facsimiles & Reprints, Gainesville, pp. v–xii.

Dunnington, G. W.: 1955, *Carl Friedrich Gauss: Titan of Science*, Exposition Press, New York.

Durkheim, E.: 1930, *Le Suicide*, Presses Universitaires de France, Paris.

Durkheim, E.: 1937, *Les Règles de la méthode sociologique*, Presses Universitaires de France, Paris.

Durkheim, E.: 1951, *Suicide*, trans. J. A. Spaulding and G. Simpson, The Free Press, New York.

Durkheim, E.: 1964, *The Rules of Sociological Method*, trans. S. A. Solovay and J. H. Mueller, The Free Press, New York.

Durkheim, E.: 1965, *Montesquieu and Rousseau: Forerunners of Sociology*, trans. R. Manheim, University of Michigan Press, Ann Arbor.

Durkheim, E.: 1974, *Sociology and Philosophy*, The Free Press, New York.

Durkheim, E.: 1982, *The Rules of Sociological Method and Selected Texts on Sociology and Its Method*, trans. W. D. Halls, ed. and with an introduction by S. Lukes, Free Press, New York.

Durkheim, E. and M. Mauss: 1963, *Primitive Classification*, trans., ed., and with an introduction by R. Needham, University of Chicago Press, Chicago.

Ellis, B.: 1968, *Basic Concepts of Measurement*, Cambridge University Press, Cambridge.

Farr, W.: 1885, *Vital Statistics: A Memorial Volume of Selections from the Reports and Writings of William Farr*, ed. N. A. Humphreys, Offices of the Sanitary Institute, London.

Finch, A. E.: 1872, *On the Inductive Philosophy, Including a Parallel between Lord Bacon and A. Comte as Philosophers: A Discourse Delivered before the Sunday Lecture Society Nov. 26, 1871*, Longmans, Green, London.

Fischer, K.: 1857, *Francis Bacon of Verulam: Realistic Philosophy and Its Age*, Longman, Brown, Green, Longmans, & Roberts, London.

Fletcher, G. P.: 1978, *Rethinking Criminal Law*, Little, Brown, Boston.

Giddens, A.: 1971, 'The "Individual" in the Writings of Emile Durkheim', *Archives européennes de sociologie* **12**, 210–228.

Gourevitch, V.: 1968, 'Philosophy and Politics, II', *Review of Metaphysics* **22**, 281–328.

Hacking, I.: 1983, 'Nineteenth Century Cracks in the Concept of Determinism', *Journal of the History of Ideas* **44**, 455–475.

Halbwachs, M.: 1934, 'Quetelet, Adolphe', *Encyclopaedia of the Social Sciences* **7**, 23.

Halbwachs, M.:1978, *The Causes of Suicide*, trans. H. Goldblatt, Routledge & Kegan Paul, London.

Hankins, F. H.: 1908, *Adolphe Quetelet as Statistician*, Studies in History, Economics and Public Law, vol. 31, no. 4, Longmans, Green, New York.

Hart, H. L. A. and A. M. Honoré: 1959, *Causation in the Law*, Oxford University Press, Oxford

Hempel, C. G.: 1959, 'The Function of General Laws in History', in P. Gardiner (ed.), *Theories of History*, The Free Press, New York, pp. 344–356.

Hempel, C. G.: 1962, 'Rational Action', *Proceedings and Addresses of the American Philosophical Association* **35**, 5–23.

Herschel, J. F. W.: 1830, *A Preliminary Discourse on the Study of Natural Philosophy*, reprint ed., Johnson Reprint Corp. , New York, 1966.

Herschel, J. F. W.:1850, 'Quetelet on Probabilities', *The Edinburgh Review* (American ed.) **92**, 1–30.

Hinkle, R.: n.d., 'Durkheim's Effervescence and the Origins of Society', unpublished paper, Ohio State University, Columbus.

Hintze, O.: 1975, *The Historical Essays of Otto Hintze*, ed. and with an introduction by F. Gilbert, Oxford University Press, New York.

Hirst, P. Q.: 1975, *Durkheim, Bernard and Epistemology*, Routledge & Kegan Paul, London.

Huff, D. and S. Turner: 1981, 'Rationalizations and the Application of Causal Explanations of Human Action', *American Philosophical Quarterly* **18**, 213–220.

Humphreys, N. A.: 1885, 'Biographical Sketch', in W. Farr, *Vital Statistics: A Memorial Volume of Selections from the Reports and Writings of William Farr*, ed. N. A. Humphreys, Offices of the Sanitary Institute, London, pp. vii–xxiv.

Janet, P. (Paul): 1878, *Final Causes*, T. & T. Clark, Edinburgh.

Janet, P. (Pierre): 1924, *Principles of Psychotherapy*, trans. H. M. Guthrie and E. R. Guthrie, Macmillan, New York.

Joule, J. P.: 1963, *The Scientific Papers of James Prescott Joule*, Dawsons, London.

Kallen, H. M.: 1931, 'Functionalism', *Encyclopaedia of the Social Sciences* **3**, 523–526.

Kries, J. von: 1888, 'Über den Begriff der objektiven Möglichkeit und einige Anwendungen desslben', *Vierteljahrsschrift für wissenschaftlich Philosophie* **12**, 393–428.

Kries, J. von: 1927, *Die Prinzipien der Wahrscheinlichkeitsrechnung: eine logische Untersuchung*, 2nd ed., Mohr, Tübingen.

Kronman, A.: 1983, *Max Weber*, Stanford University Press, Stanford.

Lakatos, I.: 1978, *Mathematics, Science and Epistemology*, Philosophical Papers, vol. 2, Cambridge University Press, Cambridge.

Laplace, Marquis de [Pierre Simon]: 1902, *A Philosophical Essay on Probabilities*, trans. F. W. Truscott and F. L. Emory, Wiley & Sons, New York.

Laudan, L.: 1981, *Science and Hypothesis: Historical Essays on Scientific Methodology*, Reidel, Dordrecht.

Laudan, L.: 1984, *Science and Values: The Aims of Science and Their Role in Scientific Debate*, University of California Press, Berkeley.

Lecky, W. E. H.: 1866, *History of the Rise and Influence of the Spirit of Rationalism in Europe*, 2 vols., Longmans, Green, London.

Levy-Bruhl, L.: 1903, *The Philosophy of Auguste Comte*, Swan Sonnenschein, London.

Levy-Bruhl, L.: 1924, *History of Modern Philosophy in France*, Open Court, Chicago.

Levy-Bruhl, L.:1966, *The 'Soul' of the Primitive*, trans. L. A. Clare, Frederick A. Praeger, New York.

Logue, W.: 1983, *From Philosophy to Sociology: The Evolution of French Liberalism, 1870–1974*, Northern Illinois University Press, Dekalb.

Lottin, J.: 1912, *Quetelet: statisticien et sociologue*, Félix Alcan, Paris.

Lukács, G.: 1980, *The Destruction of Reason*, Merlin, London.

Lukes, S.: 1971, 'Prolegomena to the Interpretation of Durkheim', *Archives européennes de sociologie* **12**, 183–228.

Lukes, S.: 1973, *Emile Durkheim: His Life and Work*, Harper, New York.

Macfarlane, A.: 1979, *The Origins of English Individualism: The Family, Property, and Social Transition*, Cambridge University Press, New York.

Marshall, G.: 1982, *In Search of the Spirit of Capitalism: An Essay on Max Weber's Protestant Ethic Thesis*, Hutchinson, London.

Martineau, H.: 1858, 'Preface', in A. Comte, *The Positive Philosophy of Auguste Comte*, Calvin Blanchard, New York, pp. 3–11.

Meehl, P.: 1970, 'Nuisance Variables and the Ex Facto Design', *Minnesota Studies in the Philosophy of Science* **4**, 373–402.

Mill, J. S.: 1910, *Utilitarianism, Liberty, and Representative Government*, E. P. Dutton, New York.

Mill, J. S.: 1973, *A System of Logic: Ratiocinative and Inductive*, Books I–III, ed. J. M. Robson, University of Toronto Press, Toronto.

Mill, J. S.: 1974, *A System of Logic: Ratiocinative and Inductive*, Books IV–VI and appendices, ed. J. M. Robson, University of Toronto Press, Toronto.

Mises, R. von: 1957, *Probability, Statistics and Truth*, 2nd rev. English ed., Allen & Unwin, London.

Mises, R. von: 1972, *Wahrscheinlichkeit, Statistik und Wahrkeit*, 4th ed., Springer, Vienna.

Mommsen, W. J.: 1977, 'Max Weber as a Critic of Marxism', *Canadian Journal of Sociology* **2**, 373–398.

Montesquieu, Baron de [Charles de secondat]: 1949, *The Spirit of the Laws*, trans. T. Nugent, Hafner, New York.

Nagel, E.: 1961, *The Structure of Science: Problems in the Logic of Scientific Explanation*, Harcourt, Brace & World, New York.

Nelson, B.: 1973, 'Weber's Protestant Ethic: Its Origins, Wanderings, and Foreseeable Futures', in C. Y. Glock and P. E. Hammond (eds.), *Beyond the Classics? Essays in the Scientific Study of Religion*, Harper & Row, New York, pp. 71–130.

Nelson, B.: 1974, 'Max Weber's "Author's Introduction" (1920): A Master Clue to His Main Aims', *Sociological Inquiry* **44**, 269–278.

Nisbet, R.: 1974, *The Sociology of Emile Durkheim*, Oxford University Press, New York.

Parodi, D.: 1934, 'Renouvier, Charles Bernard', *Encyclopaedia of the Social Sciences* **7**, 288–289.

Parsons, T.: 1968, *The Structure of Social Action*, 2 vols., The Free Press, New York.

Passmore, J.: 1967, *A Hundred Years of Philosophy*, rev. ed., Basic Books, New York.

Pearson, K.: 1911, *The Grammar of Science*, 3rd ed., rev. and enl., Adam & Charles Black, London.

Pearson, K.: 1937, *The Grammar of Science*, J. M. Dent & Sons (Everyman's Library Edition), London.

Peters, R. S.: 1967, *Hobbes*, Penguin Books, Harmondsworth.

Popper, K. R.: 1964, *The Poverty of Historicism*, Harper Torchbooks, New York.

Quetelet, L. A.: 1835, *Sur l'homme et le développement de ses facultés*, Bachelier, Paris.

Quetelet, L. A.: 1842, [translation of 1835 ed.], *A Treatise on Man and the Development of His Faculties*, reprint ed., Scholars' Facsimiles and Reprints, Gainesville, 1969.

Quetelet, L. A.: 1848, *Du Système social et des lois qui le règissent*, Guillaumin & Co., Paris.

Quetelet, L. A.: 1849, *Letters Addressed to H. R. H. The Grand Duke of Saxe Coburg and Gotha, on the Theory of Probability as Applied to the Moral and Political Sciences*, trans. O. G. Downes, Charles & Edwin Layton, London.

Radbruch, G.: 1902, *Die Lehre von der adäquaten Verursachung*, J. Guttentag, Berlin.

Robertson, J.: 1895, *Buckle and His Critics: A Study in Sociology*, Swan Sonnenschein, London.

Ryan, A.: 1970, *John Stuart Mill*, Pantheon Books, New York.

Salmon, W. C.: 1971, *Statistical Explanation and Statistical Relevance*, University of Pittsburgh Press, Pittsburgh.

Schluchter, W.: 1981, *The Rise of Western Rationalism: Max Weber's Developmental History*, University of California Press, Berkeley and Los Angeles.

Schmaus, W.: 1982, 'A Reappraisal of Comte's Three-State Law', *History and Theory* **21**, 248–266.

Schmaus, W.: 1985, 'Hypotheses and Historical Analysis in Durkheim's Sociological Methodology: A Comtean Tradition', *Studies in History and Philosophy of Science* 16, 1–30.

Selvin, H.: 1965, 'Durkheim's *Suicide*: Further Thoughts on a Methodological Classic', in R. Nisbet (ed.), *Emile Durkheim*, Prentice-Hall, Englewood Cliffs, pp. 113–136.

Selvin, H.: 1976, 'Durkheim, Booth and Yule: The Non-diffusion of an Intellectual Innovation', *Archives européennes de sociologie* 17, 39–51.

Serres, M.: 1982, *Hermes: Literature, Science, Philosophy*, ed. J. V. Harari and D. F. Bell, Johns Hopkins University Press, Baltimore.

Simon, H.: 1954, 'Spurious Correlation: A Causal Interpretation', *Journal of the American Statistical Association* 49, 467–479.

Simon, H. and N. Rescher: 1966, 'Cause and Contrafactual', *Philosophy of Science* 33, 323–340.

Singer, C.: 1959, *A Short History of Scientific Ideas to 1900*, Oxford University Press, Oxford.

Strikwerda, R. A.: 1982, *Emile Durkheim's Philosophy of Science: Framework for a New Social Science*, University Microfilms International, Ann Arbor.

Tenbruck. F. H.: 1980, 'The Problem of Thematic Unity in the Works of Max Weber', *British Journal of Sociology* 31, 313–351.

Turner, J. and A. Maryanski: 1979, *Functionalism*, Benjamin/Cummings, Menlo Park.

Turner, S.: 1977, 'Blau's Theory of Differentiation: Is It Explanatory?' *The Sociological Quarterly* 18, 17–32.

Turner, S.: 1979, 'Translating Ritual Beliefs', *Philosophy of the Social Sciences* 9, 401–423.

Turner, S.: 1980, *Sociological Explanation as Translation*, Cambridge University Press, Cambridge.

Turner, S.: 1981, 'Interpretive Charity, Durkheim, and the Strong Programme in the Sociology of Science', *Philosophy of the Social Sciences* 11, 231–243.

Turner, S.: 1982, 'On the Relevance of Statistical Relevance Theory', *Theory and Decision*, 14, 195–205.

Venn, J.: 1866, *The Logic of Chance: An Essay on the Foundations and Province of the Theory of Probability, with Especial Reference to Its Application to Moral and Social Science*, Macmillan, London.

Virtanen, R.: 1960, *Claude Bernard and His Place in the History of Ideas*, University of Nebraska Press, Lincoln.

Wagner, G. and H. Zipprian: 1985, 'Methodologie und Ontologie: zum Problem kausaler Erklärung bei Max Weber', *Zeitschrift für Soziologie* 14, 115–130.

Walker, H. M.: 1931, *Studies in the History of Statistical Method: with Special Reference to Certain Educational Problems*, William & Wilkins, Baltimore.

Weber, M.: 1905, 'Die protestantische Ethik und der "Geist" des Kapitalismus', *Archiv für Sozialwissenschaft und Sozialpolitik* 20, 1–54; 21, 1–110.

Weber, M.: 1922, *Gesammelte Aufsätze zur Wissenschaftslehre*, Mohr, Tübingen.

Weber, M.: 1946, *From Max Weber: Essays in Sociology*, ed. and trans. H. H. Gerth and C. W. Mills, Oxford University Press, New York.

Weber, M.: 1949, *The Methodology of the Social Sciences*, ed. and trans. E. A. Shils and H. A. Finch, The Free Press, New York.

Weber, M.: 1958, *The Protestant Ethic and the Spirit of Capitalism*, trans. T. Parsons, The Free Press, New York.

Weber, M.: 1961, *General Economic History*, trans. F. Knight, Collier Books, New York.

Weber, M.: 1975, *Roscher and Knies: The Logical Problems of Historical Economics*, trans. G. Oakes, The Free Press, New York.

Weber, M.: 1976, *Wirtschaft und Gesellschaft: Grundriss der verstehenden Soziologie*, 5th ed., rev., vol.1, Mohr, Tübingen.

Weber, M.: 1977, *Critique of Stammler*, trans. and with an introduction by G. Oakes, The Free Press, New York.

Weber, M.: 1978a, *Economy and Society: An Outline of Interpretive Sociology*, ed. G. Roth and C. Wittich, 2 vols., University of California Press, Berkeley and Los Angeles.

Weber, M.: 1978b, *Max Weber: Selections in Translation*, ed. W. G. Runciman, trans. E. Mathews, Cambridge University Press, Cambridge.

Weber, M.: 1981, 'Some Categories of Interpretive Sociology', trans. E. E. Graber, *The Sociological Quarterly* **22**, 151–180.

Whewell, W.: 1984, *Selected Writings on the History of Science*, ed. and with an introduction by Yehuda Elkana, University of Chicago Press, Chicago.

INDEX

Abel, T., 183
Abstraction, 103, 111, 169, 175, 182. *See also* Isolation; Generalization; Idealization
 – and concept of sameness, 220–1, 223
Accidental causes, law of, 69–73, 75–7, 80
 – as law of least squares, 72, 152
Action. *See also* Reasons and causes; Adequate cause theory; Rationality
 – equated to function, 21
 – human
  – as explained by general laws, 48–50, 81, 144–9
  – moral, 148
  – as ordinarily described, 43, 166–97 *passim*. *See also* Description
  – as oriented to absolute values, 187
Actuarial tables. *See* Rates, mortality; Tables, life–
Adaptive value, 111–12, 120
Adequacy on the level of cause, 193–7
Adequacy on the level of meaning, 193–7, 209, 217
Adequate cause theory, 30, 40, 164–76, 180–2, 184, 192, 198
 – 'weighing' in, 169, 194, 213
Aesthetic judgment, 184
Agents, 21, 166–7. *See also* Action
Agreement, Method of, 33–5, 37, 39, 130, 174
Agricultural experimentation, 223
Agricultural practices, 186–7
Alembert, J. d', 12, 15
Ampere, A., 158
Anatomy, 22
Anderson, O., 99, 171
A Priori elements
 – in concept of rationality, 184, 189, 191, 195–6, 224
 – 'constitutive', 183, 189–90, 195–6, 224, 231

 – in social science theory, 17, 24, 27–8, 51, 58
Archiv für Sozialwissenschaft und Sozialpolitik, 164
Aristotle, 84, 137, 148
Arts, 16, 19, 28
Ascent, image of, 227
 – in Bacon, 9–10, 14, 30, 58, 109
 – in Comte, 14, 58
 – in Durkheim, 109
 – in Mill, 30, 58–9, 64
 – in Pearson, 220
 – in Quetelet, 66
Association, statistical, 75–6, 133–6, 154, 193, 217–18. *See also* Correlation; Statistics, practical uses of, for causal reasoning; Partialling
 – accidental or spurious, 174, 217
 – causal, 219–27
Association for the Advancement of Science [British], 61
Astonishment, 68, 85–6, 88, 99, 229
Astronomy, 6–7, 15, 34, 69, 79, 81–4, 89
Atomic hypothesis, 13, 228
Atomism, 34–6, 173, 176–8, 199
Attributions of reasons, goals, beliefs, and subjective meanings, 189–92, 194–7, 231
Audience, 7
Axiomata media, 52, 54

Babbage, C., 61, 63
Bacon, F., 14–15, 36–7, 107. *See also Idola*
 – as anti–teleologist, 94, 118
 – image of ascent, 9–10, 14, 30, 58, 109
 – influence of, in nineteenth century, 6–10, 11–12
 – prerogative instances, 10, 33, 37, 85
 – as realist, 8–10, 110, 123, 177–8
Baconianism, 8, 29
Bankruptcy, 153. *See also* Mill

239

BOSTON STUDIES IN THE PHILOSOPHY OF SCIENCE

Editors:
ROBERT S. COHEN and MARX W. WARTOFSKY
(Boston University)

22. Milic Capek (ed.), *The Concepts of Space and Time. Their Structure and Their Development*. 1976.
23. Marjorie Grene, *The Understanding of Nature. Essays in the Philosophy of Biology*. 1974.
24. Don Ihde, *Technics and Praxis. A Philosophy of Technology*. 1978.
25. Jaakko Hintikka and Unto Remes. *The Method of Analysis. Its Geometrical Origin and Its General Significance*. 1974.
26. John Emery Murdoch and Edith Dudley Sylla, *The Cultural Context of Medieval Learning*. 1975.
27. Marjorie Grene and Everett Mendelsohn (eds.), *Topics in the Philosophy of Biology*. 1976.
28. Joseph Agassi, *Science in Flux*. 1975.
29. Jerzy J. Wiatr (ed.), *Polish Essays in the Methodology of the Social Sciences*. 1979.
30. Peter Janich, *Protophysics of Time*. 1985.
31. Robert S. Cohen and Marx W. Wartofsky (eds.), *Language, Logic, and Method*. 1983.
32. R. S. Cohen, C. A. Hooker, A. C. Michalos, and J. W. van Evra (eds.), *PSA 1974: Proceedings of the 1974 Biennial Meeting of the Philosophy of Science Association*. 1976.
33. Gerald Holton and William Blanpied (eds.), *Science and Its Public: The Changing Relationship*. 1976.
34. Mirko D. Grmek (ed.), *On Scientific Discovery*. 1980.
35. Stefan Amsterdamski, *Between Experience and Metaphysics. Philosophical Problems of the Evolution of Science*. 1975.
36. Mihailo Marković and Gajo Petrović, *Praxis. Yugoslav Essays in the Philosophy and Methodology of the Social Sciences*. 1979.
37. Hermann von Helmholtz, *Epistemological Writings. The Paul Hertz/Moritz Schlick Centenary Edition of 1921 with Notes and Commentary by the Editors*. (Newly translated by Malcolm F. Lowe. Edited, with an Introduction and Bibliography, by Robert S. Cohen and Yehuda Elkana.) 1977.
38. R. M. Martin, *Pragmatics, Truth, and Language*. 1979.
39. R. S. Cohen, P. K. Feyerabend, and M. W. Wartofsky (eds.), *Essays in Memory of Imre Lakatos*. 1976.
42. Humberto R. Maturana and Francisco J. Varela, *Autopoiesis and Cognition. The Realization of the Living*. 1980.
43. A. Kasher (ed.), *Language in Focus: Foundations, Methods and Systems. Essays Dedicated to Yehoshua Bar-Hillel*. 1976.
44. Trân Duc Thao, *Investigations into the Origin of Language and Consciousness*. (Translated by Daniel J. Herman and Robert L. Armstrong; edited by Carolyn R. Fawcett and Robert S. Cohen.) 1984.
46. Peter L. Kapitza, *Experiment, Theory, Practice*. 1980.
47. Maria L. Dalla Chiara (ed.), *Italian Studies in the Philosophy of Science*. 1980.
48. Marx W. Wartofsky, *Models: Representation and the Scientific Understanding*. 1979.
49. Trân Duc Thao, *Phenomenology and Dialectical Materialism*. 1985.
50. Yehuda Fried and Joseph Agassi, *Paranoia: A Study in Diagnosis*. 1976.
51. Kurt H. Wolff, *Surrender and Catch: Experience and Inquiry Today*. 1976.
52. Karel Kosík, *Dialectics of the Concrete*. 1976.
53. Nelson Goodman, *The Structure of Appearance*. (Third edition.) 1977.

508

54. Herbert A. Simon, *Models of Discovery and Other Topics in the Methods of Science*. 1977.
55. Morris Lazerowitz, *The Language of Philosophy. Freud and Wittgenstein*. 1977.
56. Thomas Nickles (ed.), *Scientific Discovery, Logic, and Rationality*. 1980.
57. Joseph Margolis, *Persons and Minds. The Prospects of Nonreductive Materialism*. 1977.
59. Gerard Radnitzky and Gunnar Andersson (eds.), *The Structure and Development of Science*. 1979.
60. Thomas Nickles (ed.), *Scientific Discovery: Case Studies*. 1980.
61. Maurice A. Finocchiaro, *Galileo and the Art of Reasoning*. 1980.
62. William A. Wallace, *Prelude to Galileo*. 1981.
63. Friedrich Rapp, *Analytical Philosophy of Technology*. 1981.
64. Robert S. Cohen and Marx W. Wartofsky (eds.), *Hegel and the Sciences*. 1984.
65. Joseph Agassi, *Science and Society*. 1981.
66. Ladislav Tondl, *Problems of Semantics*. 1981.
67. Joseph Agassi and Robert S. Cohen (eds.), *Scientific Philosophy Today*. 1982.
68. Władysław Krajewski (ed.), *Polish Essays in the Philosophy of the Natural Sciences*. 1982.
69. James H. Fetzer, *Scientific Knowledge*. 1981.
70. Stephen Grossberg, *Studies of Mind and Brain*. 1982.
71. Robert S. Cohen and Marx W. Wartofsky (eds.), *Epistemology, Methodology, and the Social Sciences*. 1983.
72. Karel Berka, *Measurement*. 1983.
73. G. L. Pandit, *The Structure and Growth of Scientific Knowledge*. 1983.
74. A. A. Zinov'ev, *Logical Physics*. 1983.
75. Gilles-Gaston Granger, *Formal Thought and the Sciences of Man*. 1983.
76. R. S. Cohen and L. Laudan (eds.), *Physics, Philosophy and Psychoanalysis*. 1983.
77. G. Böhme et al., *Finalization in Science*, ed. by W. Schäfer. 1983.
78. D. Shapere, *Reason and the Search for Knowledge*. 1983.
79. G. Andersson, *Rationality in Science and Politics*. 1984.
80. P. T. Durbin and F. Rapp, *Philosophy and Technology*. 1984.
81. M. Marković, *Dialectical Theory of Meaning*. 1984.
82. R. S. Cohen and M. W. Wartofsky, *Physical Sciences and History of Physics*. 1984.
83. E. Meyerson, *The Relativistic Deduction*. 1985.
84. R. S. Cohen and M. W. Wartofsky, *Methodology, Metaphysics and the History of Sciences*. 1984.
85. György Tamás, *The Logic of Categories*. 1985.
86. Sergio L. de C. Fernandes, *Foundations of Objective Knowledge*. 1985.
87. Robert S. Cohen and Thomas Schnelle (eds.), *Cognition and Fact*. 1985.
88. Gideon Freudenthal, *Atom and Individual in the Age of Newton*. 1985.
89. A. Donagan, A. N. Perovich, Jr., and M. V. Wedin (eds.), *Human Nature and Natural Knowledge*. 1985.
90. C. Mitcham and A. Huning (eds.), *Philosophy and Technology II*. 1986.
91. M. Grene and D. Nails (eds.), *Spinoza and the Sciences*. 1986.
92. S. P. Turner, *The Search for a Methodology of Social Science*. 1986.
93. I. C. Jarvie, *Thinking About Society: Theory and Practice*. 1986.
94. Edna Ullmann-Margalit (ed.), *The Kaleidoscope of Science*. 1986.
95. Edna Ullmann-Margalit (ed.), *The Prism of Science*. 1986.
96. G. Markus, *Language and Production*. 1986.